# Modern Irish Literature and the Primitive Sublime

*Modern Irish Literature and the Primitive Sublime* reveals the primitive sublime as an overlooked aspect of modern Irish literature as central to Ireland's artistic production and the wider global cultural production of postcolonial literature. A concern for and anxiety about the primitive persists within modern Irish culture. The "otherness" within and beyond Ireland's borders offers writers, from the Celtic Revival through independence and partition to post-9/11, a seductive call through which to negotiate Irish identity. Ultimately, the disquieting awe of the primitive sublime is not simply a momentary recognition of Ireland's primitive indigenous history but a repeated rhetorical gesture that beckons a transcendent elation brought about by the recognition of the troubled, ritualistic and sacrificial Irish past to reveal a fundamental aspect of the capacity to negotiate identity, viewed through another but intimately reflective of the self, within the long emerging twentieth-century Irish nation.

**Maria McGarrity** is a professor of English at Long Island University in Brooklyn, New York. She has been published in journals including the *James Joyce Quarterly*, *Ariel: a Review of International English Literature*, *CLA Journal*, and *The Journal of West Indian Literature*. She has published two monographs, *Washed by the Gulf Stream: the Historic and Geographic Relation of Irish and Caribbean Literature* (Delaware, 2008) and *Allusions in Omeros: Notes and a Guide for Derek Walcott's Masterpiece* (Florida, 2015) and two co-edited collections, *Irish Modernism and the Global Primitive* (Palgrave, 2009) and *Caribbean Irish Connections* (University of the West Indies Press, 2015).

# Routledge Studies in Irish Literature
Editor: Eugene O'Brien
*Mary Immaculate College, University of Limerick, Ireland*

**Seamus Heaney's American Odyssey**
*Edward J. O'Shea*

**Seamus Heaney's Mythmaking**
*Edited by Ian Hickey and Ellen Howley*

**Irish Theatre**
Interrogating Intersecting Inequalities
*Eamonn Jordan*

**Reading Paul Howard**
The Art of Ross O'Carroll-Kelly
*Eugene O'Brien*

**Wallace Stevens and the Contemporary Irish Novel**
Order, Form, and Creative Un-Doing
*Ian Tan*

**The Art of Translation in Seamus Heaney's Poetry**
Toward Heaven
*Edward T. Duffy*

**Masculinity and Identity in Irish Literature**
Heroes, Lads, and Fathers
*Cassandra S. Tully de Lope*

**Modern Irish Literature and the Primitive Sublime**
*Maria McGarrity*

For more information about this series, please visit: www.routledge.com/Routledge-Studies-in-Irish-Literature/book-series/RSIL

# Modern Irish Literature and the Primitive Sublime

Maria McGarrity

NEW YORK AND LONDON

First published 2024
by Routledge
605 Third Avenue, New York, NY 10158

and by Routledge
4 Park Square, Milton Park, Abingdon, Oxon, OX14 4RN

*Routledge is an imprint of the Taylor & Francis Group, an informa business*

© 2024 Maria McGarrity

The right of Maria McGarrity to be identified as author of this work has been asserted in accordance with sections 77 and 78 of the Copyright, Designs and Patents Act 1988.

All rights reserved. No part of this book may be reprinted or reproduced or utilised in any form or by any electronic, mechanical, or other means, now known or hereafter invented, including photocopying and recording, or in any information storage or retrieval system, without permission in writing from the publishers.

*Trademark notice*: Product or corporate names may be trademarks or registered trademarks, and are used only for identification and explanation without intent to infringe.

ISBN: 978-1-032-28556-6 (hbk)
ISBN: 978-1-032-28558-0 (pbk)
ISBN: 978-1-003-29739-0 (ebk)

DOI: 10.4324/9781003297390

Typeset in Sabon
by KnowledgeWorks Global Ltd.

for Lorenzo

# Contents

Acknowledgments — viii

1 Introduction: Modern Ireland and the Primitive Sublime — 1

2 Performing the Primitive Sublime: The Celtic Revival and Irish Indigeneity — 13

3 James Joyce and the Primitive Sublime: From *A Portrait of the Artist as a Young Man* to *Ulysses* and *Finnegans Wake* — 43

4 Mid-century Malaise and Desublimation in Samuel Beckett, Flann O'Brien, Kate O'Brien, and Edna O'Brien — 67

5 The Living Dead: The Late Century Resurgence of the Primitive Sublime in Works by Seamus Heaney, Eavan Boland, and Brian Friel — 97

6 Primitive Sublime Terror: Writing New York after 9/11 in Joseph O'Neill, Colum McCann, and Colm Tóibín — 128

Index — 153

# Acknowledgments

This book is the product of many years of research and scholarly conversation whether at conferences, archives, or seminar rooms. For all of those folks who aided along the way, please know that I continue to appreciate every opportunity for insight, discussion, and exchange. I wish first to thank my home university, Long Island University in Brooklyn, New York, for several research and travel grants. Especially important was the support I received from the LIU Office of Sponsored Research then under the direction of Anthony DePass. Provost and VPAA Gale Stevens Haynes found means of funding me for many a conference after which I always managed to find a week or two of work in an archive from the National Library of Ireland and the British Library to the *Musée du quai Branly* and the *Bibliothèque nationale de France*. The U.S/U.K Fulbright Commission was central to the completion of the book thanks to my Fulbright award in Irish Literature at the Seamus Heaney Center for Poetry, Queens University Belfast. Glenn Patterson, Rachel Brown, and indeed everyone created an atmosphere of welcome at the Center. I am indebted to Patricia Malone, the valiant collections manager at the Seamus Heaney Center, for providing access to the Heaney archive to listen to their collection of BBC Flying Fox radio interviews from the early 1970s onward. I am indebted to Christian DuPont, Burns Librarian at Boston College, and to James Murphy of Boston College's Connolly House Center for Irish Programs, for a summer research residence in the Burns Scholar House. It was through the Boston College work that I was able to crystalize a period of desublimation in mid-century for the project. Moore Fellowships and the Moore Institute at the Hardiman Library at the National University of Ireland Galway, and particularly the support of Daniel Carey, were key for providing access to the Abbey Theater Digital Archive which allowed me to look through the notes and typescripts to conceptualize the Celtic Revival chapter. I also wish to thank Muireann O'Cinneide for her scholarly cheer during these fellowships. The NEH Summer Seminar on the Irish Sea Cultural Province at Queens University Belfast, the Manx Museum, and the University of Glasgow under the direction of Joseph Falaky Nagy and Charles MacQuarrie established an important footing that informed my understanding of Irish primitivism related to the medieval period. Kevin Dettmar's leadership of and lasting scholarly munificence after a NEH Summer Seminar at Trinity College Dublin on James Joyce's *Ulysses* remains a motivating and encouraging force. This seminar was critical for the creation of fundamental insights about Irish primitivism related to the Congo and Roger Casement that are present in the Joyce chapter of this book. I appreciate the access to the Wertheim Study at the New York Public Library, and especially librarian Mary Jones, of the General Research division. Justin Furlong, the Assistant Keeper of Manuscripts, James Harte, Special Collections, at the National Library of Ireland, were both remarkably generous during and after my research visits. I wish to thank Jane Maxwell, Manuscripts Curator at the Library, as well as the Board of Trinity College, the University of Dublin. I must acknowledge the British Library for the access to the Joyce letters in their holdings. For reading the drafts of this book in whole or in part along the way, I must thank Greg Erickson, Beth Gilmartin, Catie Piwinski, Greg Winston, and Joyce Zonana. I must acknowledge the late Claire A. Culleton as a model of scholarly munificence. I thank Palgrave Macmillan for allowing me to reprint aspects of my chapter from our co-edited book on primitivism in the Joyce chapter of this new one. I thank Margaret McPeake for her friendship and her enduring scholarly insights into Irish Studies. And, finally, thanks to my husband, Larry, aka Lorenzo, who keeps me grounded, makes me laugh, and reminds me of what truly matters every day. With love always, Lorenzo.

# 1 Introduction
## Modern Ireland and the Primitive Sublime

In 1874, after scandal drove Sir William Wilde from the comforts of Dublin into a kind of internal exile in the west of Ireland, he published a series of articles on "The Early Races of Mankind in Ireland," in which he insisted that the Irish "trace the footprints of [the] man we have…the vestiges of his language, and the physical and psychological characteristics still attaching to his modern representatives" (245). Wilde's forceful command presages the concern for and anxiety about the primitive that persists within modern Irish culture. From the latter half of the nineteenth and through the twentieth century, Irish writers highlighted a striking series of encounters with the most ancient elements of Irish culture, identified these elements as primitive manifestations of the indigenous peoples, and uncovered these primitive constructs as an exceptional means of experiencing the sublime. While critics have begun to assert the import and function of Ireland's modern primitives,[1] no critic has yet examined the frisson of delight that such encounters engender within Irish modern culture as a whole. Ireland's primitive encounters provoke the sublime while relying on internal and troubling markers of cultural fear in order to create it. The experience of the sublime is uniquely related to indigenous Irish primitivisms that twentieth-century writers have endeavored to retain as a marker of cultural distinction within the British Empire. It is the proximity to the primitive, which is itself a term that is highly contingent and always in flux, that seems to mark Irish writing, and thereby serves as a means to separate this indigenous eruption of the form from other twentieth-century configurations of primitive fixations. Unlike the English, for example, who move outside of the confines of their national borders to locate the primitive, the Irish most commonly recognize and encounter the primitive at home.[2]

Examples of primitivism abound in Irish art, which ranges from experiences of global migrants in Ireland to an Irish drive toward comparative indigeneity with such peoples. Works by Colum McCann, Brian Friel, and Jim Sheridan, to name a few, explore these connections and identify and articulate primitive alterities that reside within modern Irish culture.

DOI: 10.4324/9781003297390-1

## 2  Introduction

McCann's portrait of destruction in *Let The Great World Spin*, Sheridan's portrayal of an African Caribbean man in *In America*, and Friel's use of the figure of a returned Irish priest in *Dancing at Lughnasa* manifest a seemingly relentless drive toward the primitive in Irish writing. The construct of primitivism functions variously as a fanciful imagined nostalgic past, as a peril of the alien and unfamiliar, or as a possible illustration of comparative distinction or relation. The notion of the "primitive" within Irish cultural discourse remains a mutable and conditional construct rather than one of consistency or unity (McGarrity and Culleton 1–2). Sinéad Garrigan Mattar explains simply, "Primitivism is the idealization of the primitive" (3). And, as David Brett finds, "Ireland has stood for the primitive" quite commonly in cultural discourse (30). Yet, within these straightforward assertions, there is a fundamental tension, such as when Garrigan Mattar conceptualizes Irish primitivism of the early twentieth century as a form of "proper darkness" (19). She finds that this "darkness... becomes tantalizingly paradoxical" and then asks "how can darkness be 'proper,' in the sense of the morally and socially correct, any more than it can be the 'property' of any one social grouping?" (19). She underlines a nexus of possession, identity, and darkness to suggest the unsettled perspectives that create Irish primitivisms; the identification of "primitives," then, becomes highly subjective and relative to cultural alignments and modes (McGarrity and Culleton 2–3). Garrigan Mattar distinguishes between romantic primitivism evident in well-worn tropes, including, most notoriously, the authentic and pure "Noble Savage" and the modernist primitivism evident in the shifting idealizations of the "brutal, sexual, and contrary" (4). The unique condition of Ireland's position as a British colony with the contingent independence that partition created refracts multiple visions of primitives within and beyond its borders, often as a peculiarly reflected portrait of Irish culture and art.[3] A stunning inversion of the so-called "civilized" in Ireland becomes more acutely evident within twentieth-century artistic and literary experimentation. Widely evident during the modernist literary period's pyrotechnic aesthetic modes that shift, destroy, and illuminate boundaries and hierarchies within any conventional cultural formation, Irish writing beyond this period also becomes intensely focused on exploring the notions of self and other, of culture and belonging, at home and abroad. My publication with Claire A. Culleton of *Irish Modernism and the Global Primitive* was a key first step in this endeavor. Yet, the question of the enduring appeal of the primitive remains. What I suggest in *Modern Irish Literature and the Primitive Sublime* is that the primitive rhetorics within twentieth-century Ireland prevail because of their capacity, or their cogent force, to provoke the sublime. This movement is not merely a casual recognition of Ireland's primitive indigenous history, but a repeated rhetorical gesture that beckons the primitive sublime, a momentary and transcendent elation brought about by the recognition of the troubled, ritualistic, and sacrificial Irish past that consistently emerges in the long twentieth century.

This book will not attempt to impose a stable conception of Ireland's sublime, but rather it will examine its relentlessly unsettled formation(s) and dissipation(s) as they relate to the primitive during the twentieth century. Ireland's notion of the sublime as it becomes transformed in Irish modernity is distinctively associated with the "dark, uncertain, and confused" elements that distinguish it from mere aesthetic magnificence. In fact, it is this very alienated state of bewilderment and horror in Irish cultural production that ultimately surrenders emotional pleasure in a repeated rhetorical movement that repels and seduces the Irish at once. Jerome Carroll notes that the sublime has "as many interpretations as it has appearances" (171). This notoriously elusive and mutable concept erupts, subsides, and then emerges again in twentieth-century Irish writing. These necessarily plural conceptions of the primitive sublime seem to follow the emerging nation state and its vexed cultural positioning as a former colony that achieves a kind of independence through partition, but remains situated in a challenging cultural nexus due to an enduring colonial legacy. According to Jean-François Lyotard, the sublime is "the only mode of artistic sensibility to characterize the modern" because it serves as an "expressive witness to the inexpressible.... pleasure and pain, joy and anxiety, exaltation and depression" (93). Although Lyotard asserts that this sublime facility emerged after World War II, the cultural turmoil surrounding an emerging Irish nation provoked a sense of sublime terror much earlier. Lyotard's arguments reside amid the network of theorists of the postmodern sublime which include Gilles Deleuze ("The Idea of Genesis in Kant's Aesthetics"), Julia Kristeva (*Powers of Horror: an Essay on Abjection*) and Fredric Jameson (*Postmodernism, or the Cultural Logic of Late Capitalism*). Yet, Lyotard's conceptions of the brutality of the interiority of the sublime are most prescient for this study of Ireland's modern primitive sublime. The notion of the sublime as evident in the primitive specifically in Ireland has been recently established by Luke Gibbons's *Edmund Burke and Ireland*, in which Gibbons chronicles his colonial sublime around the subaltern revolt against imperial authority. Gibbons reclaims Burke for Irish cultural discourse as an important if problematic figure given his writing against the French Revolution. Gibbons does not attempt a facile recuperation but rather engages with the nuanced complexity of Burke's aesthetic vision as it relates to Ireland's colonial position.

The long history of the sublime reaches back to Longinus and his treatise "An Essay on the Sublime," written in the first century of the Christian era. The intellectual endurance of Longinus's conception of the sublime as a rhetorical notion reaches from the ancient world through

4  *Introduction*

the Renaissance and up until the advent of modernity. Unsurprisingly, the rhetoric of Longinus's sublime becomes key during the eighteenth century's exaltation of both highly stylized expression and reason. Alexander Pope mocks and reveres him at once, Longinus "Is himself that great Sublime he draws" (qtd. In Costelloe 6). The most famed philosophers of the sublime establish dichotomies between the sublime and the beautiful (Edmund Burke) and the inherent relation of the moral sublime (Immanuel Kant). In Irish writing, the conjoining of the primitive and sublime is consequential, even if it often relies on colonial ethnographic notions of culture and meaning. Matthew Rampley finds:

> Although the sublime is a recurrent trope in accounts of the "primitive," a crucial question concerns the limits of sublimity. It therefore becomes urgent to address not simply the obvious racist overtones of Kant, Hegel, and others—this is perhaps the more obvious point of critique—but also the limits of a theory formulated to account for the experiences of the Western subject.
>
> (260)

What seems striking, then, for Irish writers is the degree to which they aestheticize the experience of the sublime through encounters with the primitive. They are both the agents as Western subjects and the objects of the primitive gaze as colonized subordinates in the British imperial endeavor.

The European Enlightenment philosophers were often captivated with consideration of the "others" in the emerging imperial systems at the same time as they endeavored to provide a rigorous intellectual framework for consideration of the human condition: social, material, cultural, and scientific. Edmund Burke is most recognized for his importance in the development of visual aesthetics. As Sara Suleri notes, "when Burke invokes the sublimity... he seeks less to contain the irrational within a rational structure than to construct inventories of obscurity.... Such [an obscure] intimacy provokes the desire to itemize and to list all the properties of the desired [or sublime] object" (28). The sublime object therefore relates to both a sense of intimacy and obscurity—of the intensely close and the densely opaque. While the visual remains paramount for Burke's work, in a discussion of the "Celto-Kitsch," one critic observes Burke's import to the development of art reaching into the twentieth century (though he does frame Burke traditionally within the visual approach of spectacle):

> The Sublime... a condition of awe and it may be terror before the spectacle of Nature at Her grandest and least humanized, and before

the spectacle of human lives attuned to such grandeur. The concept, as first defined by Burke in his *Philosophical Inquiry* should be regarded as Ireland's principle gift to the discourse of art and nature; as subsequently developed by Kant, it is the lynchpin of Romanticism and, some have argued, the founding moment of an important aspect of modernism.

(Brett 29)

What I suggest is that it is this founding moment of modernism, which as Brett argues was gestured toward by Burke centuries earlier, that becomes critical for Irish writing in the twentieth century in general and its delineations of the primitive sublime in particular.

While the philosophers of the eighteenth and nineteenth centuries examine the nuances of the sublime and its workings in visual art, the phenomenon of the sublime in literary studies has received too little critical attention. The philosophical underpinnings of the sublime and its link with the primitive provide a nexus for further analyzing the literary engagements with the phenomenon. As one critic points out, there is an enduring tension in the primitive sublime: "For Kant the capacity for sublimating terror into an aesthetic experience is both natural and a consequence of acculturation; the primitive both is and is not capable of experiencing the sublime" (Rampley 260). In Ireland, this fraught negotiation of the primitive as it becomes linked with the sublime suggests the degree to which its depictions navigate, reflect, and refract imperial authority and cultural positioning. Burke himself turns toward the poetic as a means of experiencing the sublime. While this may surprise contemporary readers today, given that Burke's theories are often associated exclusively with external markers, usually landscapes, Ellen Scheible acknowledges language as central to his theories. "In Burke," she writes, "words occupy a separate space in our comprehension of the outside world, arguably one characterized by fiction and metaphor, yet they are still able to elicit the 'ideas of beauty and of the sublime' brought about by nature and art" (235). She explains further: "Because of the curious position of language in the excitation of emotion associated with the beautiful and the sublime, Burke isolates the effect of words on the senses, which eventually leads him to an analysis of poetry" (235). In the twentieth century, scholars and critics have reasserted the continued presence of the sublime and have expanded on Burke's poetic conceptions despite his aesthetics as being somewhat out of fashion as antiquated ideas. Yet, more recent thinkers have conceptualized the sublime not merely as an external encounter of the majestic and awe-inspiring that, in Burke's most well-known form, is also associated with terror; rather, they have expanded it from the conventional external stimulus into a psychological expression of modern interiority. For example, Scheible finds that for Burke the mind "feels," rather than "thinks," the sublime (228). Thus, the eighteenth-century "feeling" mind gives way in the twentieth and twenty-first centuries' fractured interiority and consciousness.

It is the sublime of psychological interiority to which twentieth-century Irish writers seem particularly drawn. The experience of and psychological response to external geographies, however, do afford the catalyst for this movement within Modern Ireland toward the primitive sublime. According to Homi Bhabha, "being in the 'beyond,' then, is to inhabit an intervening space, as any dictionary will tell you. But to dwell 'in the beyond' is also... to be a part of revisionary time, a return to the present to reinscribe our cultural contemporaneity; to reinscribe our human, historic commonality" (7). A sense of temporal and geographic duality emerges within the primitive sublime. A particularly critical formation for Irish cultural discourse linking the primitive with the sublime can be traced to the Aran Islands, which is a location that is central for the Revivalists. Heather Clark explains the 1896 journey undertaken by Arthur Symons and W.B. Yeats to Inishmore, the largest geographically of the Aran Islands:

> The two spent three days wandering among the cliffs and villages, taking stock of both archaeological ruins and island folk alike in their search for the last vestiges of Irish Ireland. Symons published his observations four months later in an article entitled "The Isles of Aran," in which he described the islands as primeval, *primitive* and *sublime*. ...He grasped that the island's allure would always be shadowed by a sense of alienation, "we seemed also to be venturing among an unknown people, who, even if they spoke our own language, were further away from us, or foreign than people who spoke an unknown language and lived beyond other seas" (306).
>
> (30, emphasis added)

The primitive sublime that Symons describes in his essay has enduring consequences for Irish writing through the twentieth century. This notion of belonging amid alienation, of extremes within contained spaces, reverberates from the shores of the Aran Islands and Galway Bay throughout Ireland and even, ultimately as we will see, onto New York harbor. Much like primitivism writ large, the primitive sublime is not a singular, but a plural manifestation. It is not easily reducible to a single framework, but rather transforms within the development of temporal, geographic, political, and psychological networks and perspectives.

The sublime in Irish writing rests upon historical intersections of colonial encounters. This manifestation of the sublime often rests upon language and rhetorics of politics rather than exclusively space or location. In his work "The Irish Sublime," Terry Eagleton finds:

> If the Irish are the greatest talkers since the Greeks, as Oscar Wilde once remarked with himself well in mind, it is partly because language in a society where print arrived fairly late remains cast in an oral, oratorical mold, partly because discourse is a form of displacement from a harsh social reality, and partly because language in colonial conditions becomes a terrain of political conflict.
>
> (28)[4]

The centrality of language, as Eagleton describes it, for the Irish sublime is profoundly linked with Ireland's colonial condition. Elsewhere, Eagleton asserts that the Irish Famine was "in Burkean parlance, a sublime event, for the mind-buckling power of the sublime is by no means simply pleasant rhetoric, and if it stirred some to rancorous rhetoric, it stunned others into an appalled muteness" (31).[5] While the Famine as a sublime event in Irish cultural history and its enduring memory seems a shocking suggestion even today, Eagleton's assertion of nationally traumatic events in the nineteenth century as sublime prefigures Ireland's twentieth- and twenty-first-century cultural horrors that provoke the primitive sublime.

There are two dominant and related courses that characterize the primitive sublime and that manifest, subside, and then remerge throughout the twentieth century. In the following chapters, these progressions initially emphasize a sense of Irish indigeneity and the desire for connection amid the colonial world as it becomes increasingly fractured, after the Second World War, into postcolonial and neocolonial frameworks. The turn of the twentieth century saw a profoundly influential movement toward native Irish folklore, literary arts, and cultural performance. While the Rising of 1916 becomes immortalized in Yeats's encapsulation of the primitive sublime with his refrain of "terrible beauty," Irish writers begin to question the immortalization and nostalgia so present in the Revival fairly quickly thereafter, especially evident in the Revivalist mockeries of James Joyce in his *Ulysses* (1922) and *Finnegans Wake* (1939). During the mid-century period after the establishment of the Free State and the Second World War, Irish writing evidences a pronounced desublimation away from primitive alterities and toward the quotidian difficulties of economic conditions and social repression. With the advent of "the Troubles" in the late 1960s, the primitive sublime reemerges with a powerful surge through the fraught cultural dynamics of the period that ended with the hope of the imperfect, yet enduring Good Friday/Belfast Agreement, which established a difficult peace in the North.[6] Finally, what I assert stands as the end of the primitive

## 8  Introduction

sublime manifests in three post-9/11 novels. From then on, the desire for a return to a lost past and the transcendent elation it potentially holds is revealed to be illusory.

The opening chapter of this book, "Performing the Primitive Sublime: the Celtic Revival and Irish Indigeneity," examines the primitive sublime as it emerges during the literary enactment(s) of Irish indigeneity during the period of the Celtic Revival. Due to the dominance of the stage in the creation of a national identity for the Irish, the essential markers of this predominantly dramatic movement become foregrounded in the analysis. W.B. Yeats, Augusta Lady Gregory, and John Millington Synge are the central and most famed practitioners during this period who set their works either within or as refractions of Irish indigeneity that served as a catalyst for the primitive sublime. These writers foreground the avian in their movements toward transcendence that reflect the unique aspects of their engagement with the markers of the primitive sublime. Surprisingly, these writers gesture toward the work of George Bernard Shaw and his commentary on animal vivisection in his stage play, *The Doctor's Dilemma*. Yeats, Gregory, and Synge seek out ways to negotiate between the modern and the primitive as they collapse the boundaries between the two realms. This reliable penetrability seeks to underscore the ways in which these writers make the contemporary and the historical intersect habitually. They venerate the peasantry in their symbolic recuperation of the primitive as they suggest that these figures offer a unique capacity to provoke and reflect upon the experience of sublime rapture. The horror at the root of so many of the dramatic works during this time suggests the appeal of sacrifice and violence that seem to repeatedly emerge. This violence and even terror become a seductive mode of cultural engagement that continually attracts the writerly and the public imagination(s).

The following chapter, titled "James Joyce and the Primitive Sublime: *A Portrait of the Artist as a Young Man*, *Ulysses* and *Finnegans Wake*," charts the development of Joyce's primitive sublime using the intersecting tropes of the desire for/of the feminine and the African other. Joyce's depiction of his primitive sublime emerges clearly with the transcendence of the final scene of *Portrait* when Stephen escapes his labyrinth and grows to incorporate Joyce's increasingly sophisticated and nuanced depictions of both the Irish and African figures in *Ulysses* and *Finnegans Wake*. For Joyce, the primitive sublime is a reflection of the troubling desire for distinction between and fear of communion with other globalized colonial figures and societies. Joyce is aware of the primitive movement within European literature and cultures from the time of his undergraduate days at University College Dublin. He stakes out bold movements against cultural censorship and finds that confrontations with the primitive at home and abroad help to create a sublime vision of Irish identity. Joyce uses the Irish in Africa and especially the work of Roger Casement in both *Ulysses* and *Finnegans Wake* to suggest both the Irish identification with and desire for distinction from fellow colonized peoples. The depiction of the Paris Colonial Exposition of 1931 in *Finnegans Wake* provides a lens into the commonality with and desire for African figures that capture a desecration of and longing for them at once. This tension between the two conflicting sentiments creates Joyce's primitive sublime.

This book's next chapter, "Mid-century Malaise and Desublimation in Samuel Beckett, Flann O'Brien, Kate O'Brien, and Edna O'Brien," identifies and analyzes the representations of desublimation in Irish writing of the period. These disappointments are related to the realities of independence and its associated conservative political movements that insisted on placing Irish women in the domestic sphere and squashing progressive social ideas. The reaction to independence within becomes complicated due to the peculiar position of the Republic as officially neutral and the North/Northern Ireland being subject to repeated German bombing campaigns due to its position as a part of the United Kingdom. The period after the Second World War was one of large scale decolonizing movements across the globe. In Irish writing the newly bipolar world amid the collapse of European empires is reflected in an increasing outward migration, often to London, a sense of entrapment at home especially acute for women and artists, and the emergence of an anxiety related to the intersection of globalized "others" and the Irish "self." Ireland's tenuous cultural position of a newly independent nation that is also a former colony, a part of which remains part of the United Kingdom, creates a sense of profound malaise and disappointment. What seems most salient, however, within this dynamic bricolage of global change and increasing intersection is the virtually complete disappearance of the primitive sublime in Irish writing. The Celtic Revival's privileging of indigenous Irish expressions of primitivism and its capacity, indeed relentless drive, to provoke the sublime, all but evaporates. The Revival became a subject of ridicule in the midcentury. The concerns that manifest in Irish writing from the late 1930s to the early 1960s relate to social suppression and the troubling immanence of cultural provincialism. In Samuel Beckett's *Murphy*, the hero is caught in an urban labyrinth and wishes after his death to have his ashes flushed down the toilet of Dublin's Abbey Theater during a performance. In Flann O'Brien's often overlooked drama, *Faustus Kelley*, the hero sells his soul not for starving peasants as in Yeats's *Countess Cathleen* but rather for his own political advancement and seat in the Dáil, the Irish Parliament. In O'Brien's novel, *At Swim-Two-Birds*, the hero seems caught in webs of narrative circuitousness and self-regard that mock the Celtic Revival and Irish history. In *Pray for the Wanderer*, Kate O'Brien's novel of suppression and censorship, she shows the dangers for an artist in attempting to live freely while in Ireland. While Kate O'Brien makes her protagonist figure male, Edna O'Brien's *Country Girls Trilogy*, foregrounds the feminine perspective overtly and shows the dangers inherent in Ireland for women as subjects of an oppressive state. In the final novel of O'Brien's trilogy, the enduring anxiety of others reemerges profoundly as a threat to cultural exclusivity and an opportunity for cultural exchange. The peculiar form of Irish independence creates a state reliant on censorship and suppression that is unable to stop cultural exchange and increasing intersection.

"The Living Dead: the Resurgence of the Primitive Sublime in the late Twentieth Century," the penultimate chapter, analyzes the reemergence of the primitive sublime from the late 1960s through the late 1990s. This chapter examines the rapture of Ireland's primitive sublime related to the reanimation of the Irish corpus from bog and isle to negotiate the specter of political and familial violence within the primitive affiliations manifest in Ireland's broad Viking and Atlantic world histories. Three writers, Seamus Heaney, Eavan Boland, and Brian Friel foreground the troubling connections that rely on primitive alterities drawn from within but profoundly engaging others abroad as they manifest in Irish culture. Heaney's bog poems offer up victims of Iron Age human sacrifice to comment upon his contemporary victims as reanimations of the Troubles in The North/Northern Ireland. Eavan Boland uses frameworks from across the Atlantic world to foreground the very notion of a colony and to examine how the dead necessarily rise again in a postcolonial nexus of cultural interchange. Brian Friel's *Dancing at Lughnasa* suggests the complexity of the Irish position with his characterization of a priest, "gone native," who returns to the rural Donegal of 1936 to suggest a moving affinity with colonized peoples and their practice of sacrifice and possession. These writers use the trope of the undead and the practice of reanimation amid the postcolonial world to provide a scathing critique of the enduring costs of colonial violence and to revel in the productive cultural intersections of the globalized world. The avatars of the undead serve as manifestations of the primitive sublime as the resurgence becomes linked with the Irish self even as it confronts unremitting violence and recognizes another period of lamentable and uncomfortably familiar sacrifice.

The final chapter, titled "Primitive Sublime Terror: Writing New York after 9/11 in O'Neill, McCann, and Tóibín," examines Irish artistic production set in New York City and published in the aftermath of September 11, 2001. These works reflect on the Irish position in New York City during the period both before and after the events of 9/11. Jim Sheridan's 2002 film, *In America*, serves as a starting point to suggest how the Irish in New York rely upon depictions of the other to reflect the Irish self in the wounded cityscape. The novels, Colm Tóibín's *Brooklyn*, Colum McCann's *Let the Great World Spin*, and Joseph O'Neill's *Netherland*, express the horrors of the twenty-first century through the examination of the Irish in New York beginning in the mid-twentieth century. *Brooklyn* uses the immediate aftermath of the Holocaust to comment upon the intersection of the Irish in New York in a subtle movement of cultural occlusion and unknowing. McCann's novel, *Let the Great World Spin*, goes back and forth between the early 1970s, the American experience in Vietnam and the aftermath of the Towers' collapse, and even to New Orleans after Hurricane Katrina, to suggest the ways in which the primitive sublime erupts during a tense moment of cultural change. *Netherland*, Joseph O'Neill's novel, diagrams New York after 9/11 using both a Dutch banker and a Trinidadian entrepreneur as exemplars of cultural intersection that reveal the tense awe of the primitive sublime encountered through another but reflective of the self in the early twenty-first century. Finally, *A Ghost in the Throat*, Doireann Ni Ghriofa's translation of and reimaged response to the eighteenth-century Irish language poet Eibhlín Dubh Ní Chonaill's *"Caoineadh Airt Uí Laoghaire"* or "Lament for Art O'Leary" suggests a pivot away from the primitive sublime in a moving examination of personal and cultural loss.

## Notes

1 See both Marianna Torgovnick's *Gone Primitive* and Sinéad Garrigan Mattar's *Primitivism, Science and the Irish Revival* for further reading.
2 For further reading, see Maria McGarrity and Claire A. Culleton's introduction to *Irish Modernism and the Global Primitive*.
3 For a discussion of primitivism as an "inversion of the self," see Michael Bell's *Primitivism* (80).
4 Eagleton continues, "The term "blarney" is a political one: it derives from the sixteenth-century Earl of Blarney who when called upon to make his submission to Elizabeth I is said to have responded with such a torrent of rococo rhetoric that nobody could work out whether he was submitting or not. If language is important in the colonies, it is among other things a remarkably convenient way of hiding one's thoughts from one's masters" (28).
5 Eagleton further explains, "Christopher Morash has suggested that the great silence which followed in the wake of the Famine has been somewhat overplayed; but the historian Brendan Bradshaw maintains that only one academic study of the event occurred in Ireland between the 1930s and 1980s" (31).
6 This Agreement is known both as the Good Friday Agreement and the Belfast Agreement in the North/Northern Ireland. I am choosing to note both terms to acknowledge and include the perspectives of all communities in Belfast.

## References

Bell, Michael. *Primitivism*. Methuen, 1972.
Bhabha, Homi K. *The Location of Culture*. Routledge, 1994.
Brett, David. "Heritage: Celto-Kitsch & the Sublime." *Circa*, no. 70, 1994, pp. 26–31, https://doi.org/10.2307/25562734

Carroll, Jerome. "The Limits of the Sublime, the Sublime of Limits: Hermeneutics as a Critique of the Postmodern Sublime." *The Journal of Aesthetics and Art Criticism*, vol. 66, no. 2, 2008, pp. 171–81, https://doi.org/10.1111/j.1540-6245.2008.00297.x

Clark, Heather. "Leaving Barra, Leaving Inishmore: Islands in the Irish Protestant Imagination." *The Canadian Journal of Irish Studies*, vol. 35, no. 2, 2009, pp. 30–35, www.jstor.org/stable/41414998

Costelloe, Timothy M., editor. *The Sublime: From Antiquity to the Present.* Cambridge UP, 2012.

Eagleton, Terry. "The Irish Sublime." *Religion & Literature*, vol. 28, no. 2/3, 1996, pp. 25–32, www.jstor.org/stable/40059661

Garrigan Mattar, Sinéad. *Primitivism, Science, and the Irish Revival.* Oxford UP, 2004.

Lyotard, Jean-François. "The Sublime and the Avant Garde." *Paragraph*, vol. 6, 1985, pp. 1–18, jstor.org/stable/43151610

McGarrity, Maria, and Claire A. Culleton. *Irish Modernism and the Global Primitive.* Palgrave Macmillan, 2009.

Rampley, Matthew. "The Ethnographic Sublime." *RES: Anthropology and Aesthetics*, no. 47, 2005, pp. 251–63, https://doi.org/10.1086/RESv47n1ms20167669

Scheible, Ellen. "The Eye of the Other in Edmund Burke's *Enquiry*: Language, Confrontation, and the (Subjective) Body of the Sublime." *Criticism*, vol. 63, no. 3, 2021, pp. 223–53, https://doi.org/10.13110/criticism.63.3.0223

Suleri, Sara. *The Rhetoric of English India.* U of Chicago P, 1993.

Torgovnick, Marianna. *Gone Primitive: Savage Intellects, Modern Lives.* U of Chicago P, 1990.

Wilde, William. "The Early Races of Mankind in Ireland". *The Irish Builder*, 1874, pp. 245–6.

## 2 Performing the Primitive Sublime
### The Celtic Revival and Irish Indigeneity

The emergence of the primitive sublime in modern Ireland becomes most acutely evident on the public stage. While esteeming the peasantry often becomes a performative trope—even a cliché—during the Celtic Revival, it is imperative to highlight the enduring effect of such fundamental markers. While numerous Irish writers of the period engage with these images, three writers, W.B. Yeats, Augusta Lady Gregory, and J.M. Synge, are at the center of this endeavor. As the period's most lauded writers and those most well known for their engagement with Irish indigeneity, they often relied on native Irish characterizations to aver the primacy of an indigenous nation and ethos that was seen as less compromised or even unadulterated by British Imperialism (McGarrity and Culleton 1–4). These writers deploy the primitive not only as a form of cultural recuperation and celebration but they also revel in a fraught dynamic of a recurring tension that surfaces within Irish culture, the appeal and delight of sacrificial horror. Yeats's *Countess Cathleen*, who agrees to sell her soul to the devil for the peasantry, Yeats's and Gregory's portrait of blood sacrifice in *Cathleen Ní Houlihan*, Synge's study of reported patricide in his *Playboy* as well as his ethnographic history of *The Aran Islands* all represent cultural homecomings that engage with death and create moments of terror for the viewer and reader. The terror, however, does not horrify but engages the Irish public imagination. In fact, the notion of blood sacrifice and suffering resides at the center of Irish modernism. In these critical moments of cultural formation, the primitive eruption strikingly associated with images of the avian creates Ireland's enduring sublime rapture.

The development of an ideology and aesthetic celebrating indigeneity was as the core of the Abbey Theater's mission of cultural appreciation and promulgation. It arose in Ireland after the land dispossession of the mid and late nineteenth century: from famine, exile, and most acutely perhaps, the enduring colonial occupation. The Gaelic League had a profound influence on the cultural elites of the day, even if they were mocked by some (see, for example, James Joyce's "Cyclops" in *Ulysses*) or somehow seen as less than the hyphenated plural identities of their Anglo-Irishness. For these authors, social class and language were primary markers. Yet, these markers would not apply to the most ancient elements of Irish cultural memory, real or imagined. As Mark Williams notes of the Revival's focus on cultural recuperations through literature, "a significant dimension of this process was the tendency for writers of the time to represent Ireland as a repository of mystery and uncanniness, as strange to itself as to the outsiders [Protestant Ascendancy figures], and as a result, the search for Irish identity in the literatures of the period often quarries the unusual and the phantasmagoric" (292). Williams suggests that this process engages the close rather than far time period as a mean though which "to negotiate a contested and recently traumatic history" (292–93). The primitive relics of the past, objectified in the bodies of the dead that rise to the surface, and enter the present are suggestive of the rise of archeological evidence and interest in the immediately preceding period. According to Máirín Ní Cheallaigh: "the attention ... to the remains of the prehistoric Irish past may therefore have been an attempt to replace narratives of poverty and sudden death with accounts of past glory that were attached to places that had endured for centuries, if not millennia" (83). She posits the appeal of the apparent cultural magnificence of Celtic Ireland that had been lost and forgotten. She finds that "the success of their efforts led eventually to the incorporation of archaeology into the heart of later-nineteenth-century nationalism" (83).[1] The emergence of the prehistory of Ireland as a central nexus through which the primitive sublime would circulate and intersect during the Revival period is fundamental to the development of the burgeoning performance and understanding of national identity. Yet the source of Ireland's imagined past rests not only amid the archaeological, but the spiritual. In this movement toward the spiritual or transcendent, the tension between the land and air, ground and flight, seems to be negotiated within reoccurring images of the avian. Critics have sourced the fairy and folk lore of Celtic Ireland to its medieval literary culture that prized supernatural elements and evoked a pre-Christian mythic system full of gods and goddesses, heroes, heroines, and indigenous spiritual figures of many kinds (Williams 297). Mark Williams asserts that the new field of anthropology in the late nineteenth century contributed a key notion to the Irish understanding of its pre-Christian culture that would have critical import in the ways that people would examine the peoples of the past: essentially framing human development from the primitive "state" to a "a more developed one, with a corresponding shift on the religious level from a belief in a spirit-world to a pantheon of deities, leading eventually to monotheism." (297–298). What this movement suggests for the Revivalists becomes fundamental to understanding their view of Irish spiritual practice and myth: "folklore was debased myth, a residue of old beliefs left clinging, barnacle-like, to the flanks of a culture as it hauled itself up the shire to a higher stage of development" (297–98). The primitive sublime then derives from an interest both in archaeology (Cheallaigh 83) and growing interest in medieval texts as remnants of Ireland's pre-Christian myths and supernatural elements (Williams 297–98). These traditions that related to the mythos of early Ireland were particularly appealing to ascendancy figures who were increasingly marginalized within Ireland given the growing cultural and political movements against colonial occupation (Williams 298). For the Revivalists, the dynamic tension between their imagined mythic past, often symbolized in the grounded landscape, and their efforts to commemorate it through a supernatural spiritual element, reveals a recurring incarnation in images of flight and the avian.

The Revival's focus, particularly that promulgated by Yeats, Gregory, or Synge, would not be overt resistance to British occupation, but rather the development of cultural knowledge and pride. A discernable reconstitution effort—what Kevin Whelan terms "radical memory"—would endeavor to bring the forgotten Irish past into the contemporary moment to serve several purposes of cultural pride and encourage artistic endeavors of understanding and representing that past. Whelan explains, "the creation of an Irish radical memory that sought to escape the baneful binary of modernization and tradition—the Hegelian view that all that is lost to history is well lost" (60). While radical memory allows for the imaginative spectacle that would draw in audience(s), it also critically enables a focus on Irish pre-history, particularly the tales and myths set before the Anglo-Norman invasion of the island many centuries before the Revival. Whelan asserts plainly, "radical memory deployed the past to challenge the present, to restore into possibility historical moments that had been blocked or unfulfilled earlier" (Whelan 60).[2] The Revivalists would reveal the common British colonial binary of either/or, of tradition/modernity as facile, esthetically uninteresting, and ultimately false. The very malleability of these forces, in fact, provides a catalyst for the enchantment at the heart of the primitive sublime and the performance of Irish identity. Though, attempts to create an adoration or love of the indigenous in a National Theater, often simultaneously develop a counter modal. As Nicholas Grene notes of Irish theater, "there lurk the heroic aspirations, the sublime destructiveness supposed to be its antithesis" (57), which strikingly captures the tension between the love of the mythic/heroic and its presumed opposite: destruction. Yet, what emerges in Irish writing of the Revival is not the replacement of love or generation with hate or destruction; rather, Irish writing of the period merges these contradictory impulses into the primitive sublime commonly symbolized through the avian. Creatures of flight who can also reside on the ground seem uniquely positioned to symbolize such apparent contradictions and encapsulate a possible unity despite them.

The concept of "radical memory" supports the infrastructure necessary for the public performance of the primitive sublime. The sublime encounter that becomes ritualized on stage delights and horrifies at once. Its repetition in the public sphere transforms the structure of struggle not only on stage, but emerges ultimately as a material struggle in the streets. This struggle, of course, became actualized in the Rising of 1916, the subsequent unrest, the Anglo-Irish War, and the Civil War. In this very litany, the progressive nature of linear history becomes reinscribed to suggest the emergence of an independent Ireland as ultimately inevitable.

Yet, linearity and the time are both concepts that the Irish performance of the primitive sublime seeks to question. Several critics comment on the notion of permeability of temporal categories in Ireland, an island apart where the past and present commonly merge.[3] This notion developed out of the Victorian era's cataloging process of all matter, which attempted to order the Empire, or the Globe, through a system of knowledge management that attempted to capture, preserve, and display British global mastery. "A[n Irish] culture where temporality is disrupted, a society in which past and present are somehow coeval, or where time is understood as being other than simply linear are so prevalent as to be almost invisible," according to Conor Carville, who further explains, "Perhaps the most obvious examples are those Victorian evolutionary schemas in which Ireland is seen as primitive, occupying a position that lags behind England on some national timescale of development. In the same period the Irish body and identity were each seen as arrested: either trapped at a previous evolutionary stage, or permanently stalled in childhood" ("Keeping that wound green" 45–46). Carville's assertion highlights the relentless appeal to the past that somehow seems to emerge in the present. The call of the past for Irish writers and artists at the turn of the nineteenth into the twentieth century reflects the very practical realities of functioning in a colonial zone of domination. The politics and positions of many of these practitioners were in some ways markers of their social class, religious affiliation, and gender. Those whose identities reflected their subaltern status were drawn to question cultural norms in the present day, while those whose identities reflected the power structure in Ireland (namely, the Protestant Ascendancy whose families and fortunes would seem to call for an allegiance to the British status quo), were drawn to concepts, markers, and ideas that predated the modern Empire. What better area to celebrate indigeneity and belonging than to venture into the remote past, into an era commonly before the written word was widely available, for a celebration of a culture whose laws and norms could be deployed to question the present and suggest a powerful link to a heroic indigenous past?

The peculiar, but overt link between primitivism and terror within the Irish theater and the Revival more broadly seems momentarily, and surprisingly, highlighted in the work of George Bernard Shaw. While certainly not considered a Revivalist, his work does reveal the salient cultural currents during the Revival and evinces the primitivism so dominant during the period. *The Doctor's Dilemma*, George Bernard Shaw's drama, written in 1906, made its stage debut at the Abbey in 1917, creating a sensation when it appeared. Focusing on the enduring questions of the medical profession related to costs and treatments, the dilemma at hand is whether someone who is a bad person (i.e. a serial philanderer) deserves to be saved. It also underscores the contemporary debate regarding vivisection, the dissection of live animals.[4] In a section of Shaw's preface of the play, entitled "The Primitive Savage Motive," Shaw negotiates between civilization and savagery, between the modern and the primitive, between the native and the other, using terms of "cruelty" drawn in relief via animalistic vivisection:

> I say civilized motive advisedly; for primitive tribal motives are easy enough to find. Every savage chief who is not a Mahomet learns that if he wishes to strike the imagination of his tribe—and without doing that he cannot rule them—he must terrify or revolt them from time to time by acts of hideous cruelty or disgusting unnaturalness. We are far from being as superior to such tribes as we imagine. It is very doubtful indeed whether Peter the Great could have effected [sic] the changes he made in Russia if he had not fascinated and intimidated his people by his monstrous cruelties and grotesque escapades. Had he been a nineteenth-century king of England, he would have had to wait for some huge accidental calamity; a cholera epidemic, a war, or an insurrection, before waking us up sufficiently to get anything done. Vivisection helps the doctor to rule us as Peter ruled the Russians.
> (xliii)

Shaw initially locates modern identity in relief against a troublingly "orientalist" savagery, but ultimately finds that it is intimately partnered with the primitive aspect of humanity, not merely of the other, but of the self, again drawn in terms of the animal vivisection debates of the day. The public performance of this dance of identity posits the "Mahomet" as the "civilized" in an inversion of the "orientalist" expectation. Shaw posits the use of terror, his "huge accidental calamity," as a means through which to "advance" a people, a troubling delight in grotesquerie and of the sacrifice of animals in service of "higher" beings, both animal and human. Shaw's vivisection debate seems to gesture toward the animalistic in general if not the avian in particular as a means though which to resolve the tension and contradictions of the period.

Yeats and his fellow Revivalists counter Shaw's animalistic superiority and hierarchies even as they deploy related rhetorics that are associated with cultural memory and identity. In contrast to Shaw, whose work evinces a current debate in the language of the "primitive other," Yeats's project relies on the more typical Revivalist tension between the indigenous Irish ancient and modern that manifests as the primitive sublime.[5] Even for pacifist Yeats, the tensions of the before and the now, a creative form of radical memory, are often associated with a violent release.[6] Denis Donoghue, on Yeats's early poetry, notes that "there is no hope, only a dream song addressed to eternity, the state of heroic loss made permanent, idea, essential. History and the 'despotism of fact' are sublimed away" (32). Yeats suggests that immortality is entrapment, a mesh or net that will ensnare as surely as an awakening dream. The violence of entrapment and sacrifice seems to operate within a nexus of loss, a transcendent vision of the avian, a highly personal longing that is reaching beyond the self into a collective vision. Yeats's vision is highly attuned to both historical paradigms and mythic systems, yet he does not merely mimic events, characters, and narratives, but rather deploys and reimagines them for his works (Donoghue 86).

Yeats's gesture toward the pre-Christian and thus more singular nation allows him to avoid the divided religion and politics of his contemporary moment. The ancient gods and myths in general were of great interest to Yeats, but what seems more critical is his focus on a specific set of images of transcendence, flight, terror, and sublimity. Mark Williams, parsing an Irish god that would be deployed by Yeats, explains that "fashioned from kisses and with a mysterious song that hinted at unattainability, Aengus's birds could be taken to gesture towards the erotic… Aengus/Angus made numerous appearances in the History, and the birds were repackaged both as his permanent accessories and as metaphors for the impalpable force of romantic love which he had come to personify" (349). The transformation of an ancient Celtic myth/god to Yeats's contemporary purposes reflects both the larger cultural dynamics of Ireland, and Yeats's own individual beliefs; these personal and political shifts merge in repeated dramatic and poetic works against imperialism of the British state and the poets' independence of thought in terms of religions, notably his occult spiritualism that rejects Christianity (Williams 433). Yeats's theosophy in this context indicates not merely an independence of mind but also critically an anti-imperial endeavor. Yet, this marker of independence also has a personal link for the poet when, per Williams, "the Anglo-Irish Aengus emerges as an ambiguous product of individual and collective influences, arising from but also obscuring the Óengus of early Irish saga." He continues: "In the hermetic circles in which Yeats moved, he came with great rapidity to personify everything that was best in the native mythology… by morphing into a god of love he emphasized the delicate feeling in a mythology which was not short on bloodthirsty or sordid moments" (360). For Yeats, however, the momentary appeal of the erotic succumbs ultimately to the bloodthirsty. This blood sacrifice becomes linked to terror and the primitive sublime.

In these moments of terror and sacrifice amid the Revival, Yeats's avian images abound, suggesting a sublime transcendence that is notably in dialogue with the scientific vivisection debate regarding animals in Shaw's play. Yeats's *The Countess Cathleen* scandalized audience(s) when first staged in Dublin. The notion of an Irish woman sacrificing her soul to the devil, and thus accepting damnation, was incendiary and overtly shocking, even though this sacrifice was to facilitate Irish peasants out of famine, despair, and hunger. Despite this controversy, the play is also a key to understanding a more nuanced eruption of the primitive sublime during the Celtic Revival.[7] Harpies, devilish figures of bird-like, yet human-faced creatures, haunt the play, pursuing human souls. A character notes that "there are two birds—if you can call them birds—/I could not see them rightly for the leaves./But they've the shape and color of horned owls/And I'm half certain they've a human face" (1.1). The use of the avian to suggest a form of transcendence is inverted with the sense of damnation that erupts, as when the porter notes, "Demons were here... two owls passed me by,/Whispering with human voices" (1.3). One of these "merchants" of souls explains, "When the night fell and I had shaped myself/Into the image of a man-headed owl,/I hurried to the cliffs of Donegal,/And saw with all their canvas full of wind/And rushing though the parti-colored sea" (1.5). The owl/men demon merchants are drawn in relief against the sublime encounter with the sea and the cliffs of Donegal. The avian images are highlighted even as Cathleen's signature is enticed and performed with the "quill" of a "cock" (1.5). Cathleen's decision to sell her soul is framed within the transcendence of the heavens and the damnation of hell. Yet, what remains striking within the expected Christian dichotomy of salvation and damnation is the location of the mountain-top as a critical space for the sublime, just as the cock's feather quill is a striking avian element. The mountain top setting, almost a cliché of a nineteenth-century sublime encounter, becomes dramatically imaginative with the addition of the avian.[8] The significant geographical locus, however, is not limited to the mountaintop for the conceptualization of the primitive sublime. The author underscores the link between transcendence and terror as Cathleen describes a young man "wandering and singing like a wave of the sea—/Is so wrapped up in dreams of terrors to come" (1.1). The sublime encounter is linked with terror and the primitive, devilish threat, which is also symbolically avian, from mountain to sea and air.

The prevalence of the avian in Yeats work is significant even if it has gone relatively unnoticed by scholars. Lucy McDiarmid is a prominent exception when she analyzes Yeats's "Easter 1916" in the context of the commemorative poetry published a century later. She evinces, "the birds of 1916 are ubiquitous"("Avian Rising" 74). McDiarmud is in excellent company with her attention to this marker. No less than Yeats's fellow poet, Seamus Heaney, highlights the import of the avian for Yeats as explained in a 1989 BBC radio interview on the occasion of the 50th anniversary of the poet's passing that Yeats "as a young fella went out to listen to the cries of the seabirds in Sligo bay" with a cousin and that, if Yeats were to be reincarnated as his occult spiritual beliefs might suggest, "he's bound to come back as some kind of bird" ("Interview"). Such would be a transcending of time reminiscent of the poetic persona's transformation into a golden bird who sings of "what is past, or passing, or to come" in Yeats's "Sailing to Byzantium" (line 32). Williams suggests that Yeats's attraction toward indigenous forms of spiritualism and myth is a result of growing fears of cultural marginalization, of "political and religious precariousness" among the Ascendancy class, which he avers is "a strategy both anxious and escapist." "In fact," Williams writes, "the recovery of the indigenous divinities presented a particularly extreme example of this phenomenon: it reinforced Anglo-Irish claims to nativeness, and by appealing to pre-Christian divine powers, Catholicism could (rhetorically at least) be bypassed altogether" (306). Yeats, the "Celtic Antiquarian" and performative anthropologist, reveals the ancient Irish myths, especially symbolized through the avian, are central to his invocation of the primitive sublime as they allow him to side step the religious fractures in Irish society.

Perhaps no poem takes up as much symbolic space and currency in the Irish imaginary as Yeats's "Easter 1916."[9] If radical memory was an earlier drive during the Revival to cultivate a kind of Irish past into the contemporary moment, Yeats as a cultural agronomist sows his field with the blood of the contemporary sacrifice.[10] According to Jon Stallworthy, however, Yeats's previous works cast a profound shadow on his famous elegy. He writes,

> The romantic archaeologist of *The Countess Cathleen* and *Various Legends and Lyrics* had exhumed the heroic figures of Fergus and Cuchulain from the turf-dark depths of folk memory, and many of his later elegies elevate their subjects into statues cast in a heroic mold. Yeats' strategy is to equate his subject with some larger figure from antiquity, so that the luster of the old is transmitted to the new.... Those martyrs of earlier rising against the British stand with the shade of Cuchulain in the background of Yeats' great elegy, "Easter 1916."
> (173–74)

While seeming to relate closely to his drama, this notion of commemorative sacrifice relating to the ancient myth is nowhere more evident than in the poetic elegy of 1916. The martyrs of 1916 that are memorialized in Yeats's elegy have taken up much critical and cultural space since their tragic end. The Rising, often termed a "glorious failure," did not achieve its aims in the short term. The fallen are not significant here in themselves, but instead what their martyrdom, a kind of terror, provokes for the reader, as their deaths shocked the public in their hastened and brutal ends.[11] This viciousness of the British response to the Rising creates a terror that Yeats repeatedly features in his poem: a "terrible beauty" that would encapsulate the tension, delight, and horror of the primitive sublime. Yeats's use of "terrible" in his phrase of "terrible beauty" is commonly read as merely something awful, yet the definition of the word evokes not merely something exceedingly bad, but the possibility to excite or evoke terror and awe. Yeats's vision of terror in "Easter 1916" relates not simply to the external landscapes or seascapes of Ireland, but to the public spectacle of the performance of striving for a separate national Irish identity in the Rising itself. While the raw, bloody events of the Rising were surely not staged on the boards of the Abbey, they nonetheless became an opportunity for Yeats to create a cultural performance of a national elegy. This elegy incorporates in its third stanza a repeated gesture to the avian, "moor hens," and "moor cocks" with "the birds that range/From cloud to tumbling cloud,/ Minute by minute they change" (lines 46–48). The crux of human sacrifice is drawn in relief against the animal world in an appearance of transcendence the birds amidst the plummeting, "tumbling" of clouds, at once. In the 1989 BBC radio interview, Seamus Heaney describes Yeats's poetic vision that incorporates the natural world: "hearing curlews cry by the sides of lakes swans rising ... each one of us experiences the, in a sense, our ancestral almost previous animal being awaken in wilderness. And Yeats himself links that sensation to ethereal spirit" (Heaney). Yeats's sacrificial human subjects are framed within the potential of both achievement and a risk of abrupt descent within the images of the natural world. The "change" of the birds becomes a critical aspect which is "changed utterly" in his "terrible beauty." Lucy McDiarmid notably characterizes the avian as providing an "emotional release" for the writers of the Rising ("Avian Rising" 75). In doing so within this quest for an expressive if not material liberation, Yeats connects the natural to the spiritual, the immanent to the transcendent, the human to the avian, and the primitive to the sublime.

While the phrase "terrible beauty" is almost exclusively sourced to Yeats's 1916 poem, the phrase seems to have emerged in the late nineteenth century and is highly associated with maritime images by Joseph Conrad.[12] Conrad's *Outcast of the Islands* (1896), a novel that charts the journey of an isolated European amid the Malay Peninsula uses the striking phrase to critique the construction of the Suez Canal, a colonial geographic partition in service of maritime navigation, amid a lost, powerful, and fearsome sublime. "The sea before the time," Conrad notes as he laments, "the restless mirror of the Infinite. The hand of the engineer tore down the veil of the *terrible beauty* in order that greedy and faithless landlubbers might pocket dividends. The mystery was destroyed" (9–10, emphasis added).[13] While the Canal can now be seen an emblem of the technological sublime, Conrad instead views it as an abomination against the magnificence sublime of the sea. The location of the sublime as the sea for Conrad's "terrible beauty" is unsurprisingly for his literary work given his other profession as a sailor. For Conrad, the mystery necessary for his sublime is lost and relegated to the past alone. In contrast, Yeats's "terrible beauty" elevates not the maritime or even the vision of it but rather the political struggle and sacrifice of martyrdom against the Empire to create his sublime. In doing so, Yeats's sublime is fundamentally a departure from Conrad's not only in its manifestation but in its endurance into the present. The Revival's public performances on the stage allowed for the deliberate evocation of radical memory—the emergence of the past into the present—to depict a heroic national moment, even as the actual events of 1916 provided those moments in the contemporary public arena using violence to throw off British subjugation. Yeats no longer needed to rely on a reimagined past: the heroes and heroines of 1916 function in the present.

Yeats's elegy for the blood sacrifice achieves a kind of cultural homecoming that is catalyzed by primitive, brutal death in both the action and the aftermath that creates a rapture of sublime. Yeats continued to revise his "Easter 1916" for several years. Donoghue notes what he calls Yeats's "determination ... to run toward 'the unique,' even though the precise form of its manifestation cannot be divined. It is a commonplace in descriptions of the sublime that the perceived is struck by the blow of an event, driven beyond himself by the revelation, and it matters little whether the event is superb or horrifying. The force of the blow is what matters" (94). For Yeats in his "Easter 1916," the "force of the blow" is not solely those events of the Rising itself, but the aftermath, its executions, and the memorialization in elegiac poetry, or its encapsulation in "terrible beauty." Seamus Heaney notes that Yeats "could see in primitive ritual not something opposed and pagan but something that was correspondent and congruent" ("Interview"). This ritualized blood sacrifice is not that of the mythic, imagined Cuchulainn in Yeats's plays (notably, we see such a depiction in "The Death of Cuchulainn"), but rather the actualized bloody brutality of the Rising, with the memorialized death of John McBride, the man who Maud Gonne married and suffered with, given his alcohol abuse and domestic violence. Yeats famously elegizes him as "This other man I had dreamed/A drunken, vainglorious lout./He had done most bitter wrong/To some who are near my heart" (lines 31–34). Troubling domestic relationships and the notion of sacrifice for the nation also seem to dominate the most striking drama of the period.

If "Easter 1916" is the poetic elegy that endures most clearly from this period, perhaps no other play has captured the public imagination more than Yeats's and Gregory's *Cathleen Ni Houlihan*.[14] Imagined as a walking embodiment of the emerging nation and the long suffering of the historical past, Cathleen requires a blood sacrifice to create an enduring sublime rapture. The engagement with Celtic myths and the celebration of the Irish poetic tradition enables Yeats and Gregory to "express their indigeneity," for one critic, despite their social class and religious affiliations, which separate them from the majority of Irish; for Yeats in particular, this focus allows for the happy unification of his "aesthetic ideals" and his nationalistic feeling (Mathews 46). Together they create a sublime encounter through their reliance on a primitivist Celtic mythos to create portraits of the nation. This vision of an enraptured community relies on Irish myth for its formative precedents. Yeats and Gregory rely on the *aisling* tradition, a poetic form of a dream vision, to create Cathleen's transformation (Grene *Politics* 63). This poetic transformation is a tradition with which Irish audiences would have been intensely familiar; it is "the motif of the *puella senilis*, the old woman transformed into the young girl with the walk of a queen and used in the dramatization of the vision," Nicholas Grene explains, which "has been traced back to the Celtic ur-myth of blood sacrifice to the sovereignty goddess Eire in which the danger of death of a young man can rejuvenate the old crone to make her a fit mate for a new sovereign" (*Politics* 63). The relentless drive toward death that results in a form of transcendence or transformation for the Cathleen figure suggests the grotesque necessity of blood sacrifice. The wretched young man, whose youth, sexual expression, and marriage are eternally forestalled rests eternally in a moment of delayed climax. *Cathleen Ni Houlihan* has no "marriage consecration" but it does presage the byproducts of the coming revolution, the banality of the Free State, and the confinement of women in traditional marriage and family roles of the De Valera period (Grene *Politics* 72–75). The young man who goes forth to rejuvenate Cathleen will never experience the delight of satisfaction, instead, in the emerging Irish nation, this virgin youth will be sacrificed.

In *Cathleen Ni Houlihan*, the primitive sublime does not manifest or transcend through flight, but through a rapturous call for communal martyrdom. The single overt avian image is one from Bridget's husband meager estate upon their marriage, a "flock of hens" (4). Yet, Cathleen herself seems suggestive of an element of the primitivist Irish feminine, a Celtic goddess who is associated with the crow or raven.[15] Known as "The Morrígan," and a significant figure in the Ulster cycle, this "triple" figure operates variously "as a beautiful girl, or as a powerful woman in her prime, and other times as a hag. She may be a goddess of battle who takes the shape of a raven or carrion crow. She can foretell and bring about victory for an army or a particular hero" (Clark 223). With these associations of the Morrígan, Cathleen Ni Houlihan demands the call to sacrifice the self for Ireland as she embodies the transcendent primitive sublime encounter.

The call of the sacrifice is overt in the play. Yeats and Gregory give voice to the natural world and their vision of a correct order in the play. The repetition of the "four fields" throughout the play underscores the disputed land of the island just as the "strangers in the house" evoke the displacement of land, people, and the highly symbolic domestic architecture of the cottage. The call of the sea and the landing of the French at Killala harbor highlights the maritime potential of escape/freedom and transcendence but ultimately, as the viewer of the performance would know, portends doom. Yet, Cathleen exclaims,

> I heard one on the wind this morning. [Sings]
> Do not make a great *keening*
> When the graves have been dug to-morrow.
> Do not call the white-scarfed riders
> To the burying that shall be to-morrow.
> Do not spread food to call strangers
> To the wakes that shall be to-morrow;
> Do not give money for prayers
> For the dead that shall die to-morrow…
> (Modern and Contemporary 9,
> *emphasis added*)

Cathleen's song of sacrifice is a warning to and an imprecation upon the young man, with the insistent and repeated specter, or terror, of looming death. As Lucy McDiarmid argues, this kind of sacrifice as ritualized masculine death serves as a kind of moment of empowerment for Cathleen, highly evocative of the Fenian tradition and the rebel ballad for Gregory (223). Cathleen's call for masculine sacrifice relies upon the enduring litanies of male sacrificial figures that Gregory herself found so very appealing (McDiarmid 221).

Moments of empowerment for the female figure in the play also rely upon the tradition of keening, the ritualized performance of mourning undertaken by women in Ireland. This tradition endured through British colonization, but ultimately subsided in the mid-twentieth century under pressure from the Catholic Church which viewed it as a "pagan" ritual. At the same time, keening centers on the female experience of mourning, rather than the patriarchal church rituals of death performed by male priests alone.[16] One critic explains,

> [Cathleen] begins to sing a folk song "The Keen for Fair-haired Donough,"… The song, Yeats's rewriting of Lady Gregory's translation

of "The Keen for Fair-haired Donough," laments a young Irishman hanged by the English... a few days prior to the first production of Cathleen, Yeats wrote to the United Irishman emphasizing the importance of the song to the play: "I have put into the mouth of Kathleen ni Houlihan verses about those who have died or are about to die for her, and these verses are the key of the rest. She sings of one yellow-haired Donough."

(qtd. in Coleman 129–130)

The keening tradition is one that links death with the cultural performance of mourning in moments of sublime transcendence. Yet, for Cathleen, the death of a young man is a loss that will bring a kind of satisfaction to those who answer her call. The only satisfaction comes with the erasure of the individual body in service of the nation. *The Countess Cathleen's* self-sacrifice has become a call to agency for the peasantry to sacrifice themselves in *Cathleen Ni Houlihan*. The "white-scarfed riders" suggest those who are marked by service or perhaps masked in the funeral processions who conceal their identities. Cathleen's exit with "the walk of a Queen" beckons forth the dream vision of which she is a modern incarnation (11). However, the harsh realities of Ireland that would emerge beginning after 1916 and culminating with the conservative and anti-feminist 1937 Constitution of the new nation-state, suggest the brutal realities of governance in a messy democratic state are far from the idealized aisling, wailing keener, and transformative goddess that is Cathleen.[17]

More so than in her collaborations with Yeats, in Lady Gregory's (Isabella Augusta) solely authored plays, she prioritizes capturing the Irish peasantry in their everyday speech. Gregory is a well-known cataloguer of local folkways and folk language. She shares an intense interest in the reimagination of myth with Yeats and the culture of the peasantry with Synge. Within these efforts, however, her position as an Anglo-Irish Ascendancy woman is often complicated, not least by their subject matter and performance. Gregory took great effort to capture the language and its rhythms of those who shared neither language, class, nor custom with her social class. In doing so, she relied on the research into the indigenous peoples of the west of Ireland, as she frequently frames their experiences and positions Ireland within the broad seascape of maritime culture as well as wind and flight.[18]

In Gregory's *Aristotle's Bellows*, an uneven if intriguing play that premiered at the Abbey on St. Patrick's Day (March 17), 1921, Gregory positions Ireland as unmoored in the Atlantic. The author uses both the allure of magic linked with the transcendence of musical song to create her primitive sublime. The critical ambivalence surrounding the play is perhaps due to its nature as, per Ann Saddlemyer, "a ballad opera" (ix). Gregory ultimately positions Ireland appropriately enough, given the long tradition of linking Ireland with the ancient Mediterranean world, not merely in the Atlantic, but also in the Mediterranean Sea, two bodies of water that connect in the straits of Gibraltar but are generally understood to be discrete zones of encounter and cultural networks. Conan, the main character, is a scholar of ancient philosophy who determines that the "bellows," or a ritualized number of shouts, of the play's title are the key to relieving the primitive peasants from their witless ignorance. The deeply troubled present of Ireland is imaginatively portrayed as a contrast with the idealized ancient Greeks of the past. Yet, this past will emerge in the primitive present, because it must be confronted and somehow merged into the Irish contemporary culture. The use of the ancient world to sidestep fraught contemporary political and cultural dynamics while also suggesting a link between Ireland and the ancient Mediterranean is a means through which to assert Ireland's greatness before the advent of the modern empire and the British incursions into Ireland herself. Gregory's Conan posits that the goodness of the world has vanished overtly from but also paradoxically been incorporated into the present Irish people. It must be recovered and outwardly celebrated if there is to be hope for the contemporary world. In the play, Conan chants:

> Aristotle in the hour
> He left Ireland left a power
> In a gift Eolus gave
> Could all Ireland change and save!
>     (*The Wonder and Supernatural
>                     Plays* 269)

The Greek god of the Wind, Eolus (or Aeolus), is positioned as the source of Irish greatness and artistic inspiration. Aristotle's absence in contemporary Ireland demands an escape from the contemporary situation on the island even as the emergence of the ancient world in the contemporary one is posited as the "change" of salvation for the peasantry.[19] This "change" calls back to the ritualized blood sacrifices and terror of the "changed, changed utterly," in "Easter 1916" (lines 15; 79).

The possibility of escape for island cultures in Gregory's play becomes associated with the air and avian flight. This link between human and bird offers the image of transcendence and of a return to the primordial past, a great beyond, that offers respite from the contemporary world that is so filled with terror and blight. The return to the past as an emotional release and escape from the brutality of today emerged consistently within the twentieth century. The performance or representation of this return seems especially acute in the works of Gregory.[20] Gregory's use of the conspicuous images of flight and escape from the island into the historical past emerges from the great sea/mother that is so fundamentally at the root of the human experience, the primitive beginnings of life developing out of the sea. As Gregory's character, Mother, responds to Conan, she notes, "There are some say enchantments never went out of Ireland" (276). The phrase powerfully enacts the call to the primitive past that is so apparent in the flight, sea, and island nexus. The enchantment, the siren song, of the sea, that springs from the magician's spell remains present even as it evokes the heroic past.

Gregory's play brings the past into the present when she centers a lost treasure: the secret of the "bellows" that will be taken to the grave. As such, it is a threat not simply of the past but also of the unrelenting appearance of it in the present. Gregory writes in the voice of Conan:

> Listen now. (Sings.) (Air, "*Bells of Shandon*")
> 'Once Aristotle hid in a bottle
> Or some other vessel of security
> A spell had power bring sweet from sour
> Or bring blossoms blooming on the blasted tree'
> (267)

The lamentation underscores the threat of death and the loss of the secret of the past. Yet, it is the secret that is emerging, or is threatening to emerge, within the contemporary that seems to haunt the play. Gregory writes in the voice of Conan again:

> 'There is a rose in Ireland, I thought it would be mine
> But now that it is hid from me I must forever pine.
> Till death shall come and comfort me for to the grave I'll go
> And all for the sake of Aristotle's secret O!'
> (269)

The desire to alter the contemporary and transform it into an idealized past is underscored throughout her drama. The call of the past is a false one, however, it is not an ideal location. It only appears so because it can only be unfamiliar to us in its actuality. In what seems much akin to Whelan's notion of "radical memory," Gregory creates the past as a temporal realm in the imagination, with the aid of Aristotle to fashion their fabrics into a new contemporary social cloth. The magic of enchantment mixed with the transcendence of song is at the nexus of the primitive sublime as it terrifies and seduces at once. Gregory's notion of the sea and the escape as a means of transcendence from the quotidian might initially suggest a movement into the extraordinary. Yet, what ultimately becomes obvious through the performance of the Irish nation is that the primitive sublime comes not from the past of a distance remove but from its very persistent contemporary eruption in the twentieth century.

The depiction of the troubled brutality of Ireland's burgeoning modernity is at the root of the tension within the evocation of the primitive sublime.[21] Much like the tension between the past/present in Gregory's primitive sublime, Synge also displays a tension between the present and past. J. M. Synge's *The Aran Islands* is a classic work of early twentieth-century ethnography in the west of Ireland; crucial to this study, it also relies on a subtle trope of bird images that evoke an element of transcendence critical to the primitive sublime encounter. Synge's position in the pantheon of early twentieth-century Revivalist dramatists remains secure; the encounters that he chronicled in his travelogue, *The Aran Islands* are used as source materials for his dramas. What seems remarkable, then, in this work, is the position of Synge in Aran, his isolation amid community, and the remnants of his own interests that appear in the text that evoke the primitive sublime.

In the earliest of Synge's notebooks held in the manuscripts collection at Trinity College Dublin library, he spends a great deal of time cataloging birds with a young cousin. This early experience of bird watching, seeing the creatures soar above and then descend into the earth, provides a critical moment that Synge then captures in his later texts. The general flora and fauna of the natural world do not excite him nearly as much as do these creatures of flight. Flight then seems to capture an aspect of the sublime that Synge as a young man is yet to experience. He marvels at these animals and registers their appearances in his world, less in a spatial sense, and more through the actions they take. The two writers take a central position and note the movements of the squirrels and then, happily, the birds around them. Most striking is the notion of success in the staking out of an optimal location, as in an entry that acknowledges that the weather has an effect on their potential sightings. Synge writes: "Nov$^{\text{Day 2}}$ Come to the plantation of fir trees where we had seen the squirrels. It being a nasty day and the birds not coming down to any bread we threw so we did not stay long. But we saw some very small birds with long tails that we had never seen before that flew about the tops of the trees but we will find out and mention further on. J.S." ("Bird watcher's journal" 1–2). The mystery of the identification of these specific birds, "small... with long tails," piques an interest among the happy pair of writers. Later, Synge writes, "Nov 13th Day 6 the women gave us some beach nuts for our rabbits, and we saw a squirrel running along the ground near the mounds and we saw another up near the grove and fed the birds there too J.S" (5). The action of feeding, rather than the description of the birds, seems paramount. It is not the birds themselves that seem to interest Synge and his companion, but rather the experience of tracking, discovering, and encountering the birds either grounded or in flight. A few days later, it is the journey to a specific location from which he can encounter the birds seems acutely important to him, "[Day 8]Nov 16th We went up and fed the birds at the grove, and then crossed by beach and went up the glen, we put some sticks in hawk-hide and went home JS" (6). The hawk-hide is the place from which Synge and his companion watch the birds, and in one instance, a hawk. The landscape itself is named for their encounters and activities in a shorthand that reveals the centrality of their bird watching on this relaxing mission amid the natural world.[22] A key element amid this litany is the development of greater description, though it is broken up over several pages with other material interspersed, as well as the increasing action. Instead of mere description, Synge captures the avian movements or their promise in his prose even in this early stage of his writing. Synge locates the possibility of transcendence with flight in the natural world within his litany of avian encounters that portends his development of these ideas in his drama and prose, particularly *The Aran Islands*.[23]

Synge's position in Aran is one of both observer and participant. As Giulia Bruna explains, the Aran Islands at the "turn of the twentieth century... became a *locus amoenus* to be visited and written about .... The islands thus functioned as a kind of internal 'contact zone," a site where different encounters were taking place not only in a colonial sense but also in a nationalist and revivalist sense" (20). He cannot help but affect his surroundings and the response he received through his personal demeanor, even his actual presence is noted among the islanders, who place Synge in a series of visitors that includes Sir William Wilde. Synge writes, "the old dark man I had spoken to in the morning groped is way into the room. I brought him over to the fire, and we talked for many hours. He told me that he had known... Sir William Wilde, and many living antiquarians" (6). It seems that Synge is merely the latest traveler to seek the ancient world in his contemporary Aran islands. One critic avers,

> To reencounter the structure of feeling that gave rise to primitivism is to perceive how fervently was felt the disappearance of social worlds that were not organized according to the imperatives of commodity exchange and the production of surplus value. Across the spectrum of primitivist work this desire was profoundly caught up in the racial mediations of colonialism, mediations that took ideological vengeance when artists tried peremptorily to leap into the immediate mode as though the primitive were there for the taking. We must look to the paradoxical lyrical expressions of negritude for a primitivism that proceeds on the basis that authentic immediate experience has been damaged and so makes that condition the grounds for renewal.
> (Etherington 161)

In other words, the paradoxical aspect of a primitivist lens can be seen not only as a lamentation for what seems to be lost but also as an attempt to recuperate and make available a version of the past in the present. These "mediations" are both highly associated with and reflections of the capitalist commodification associated with colonialism. Despite the troubling aspects of a primitivist rhetoric, however, there are ways in which primitivism can operate as a celebratory and authentic form of cultural regeneration. In his narrative, Synge attempts to recuperate the "primitivist" culture of Aran as he writes of the self only as a fractured reflection of an encountered other, or what Robinson calls one of the book's "principles of exclusion" (xi). It appears that he only wishes to observe the response to him, rather than to analyze his own actions from within. This refusal to go inward appears a strange move for a writer of the modernist period. While critics note that "Synge lived during the 'technological sublime' of the Edwardian era, a time when improvements in a vast range of communication technologies... increased the speed of transmission of the word [and]... encouraged an aesthetic engagement" (Bruno 51), Synge's aesthetic engagement relate not primarily to the technologies of the day (for example, his banal depictions of the modern Steamer, as opposed to the delight of the primitive curragh), but for his avian images and their attendant capacity for transcendence that capture his imagination and provoke the primitive sublime. Synge locates the sublime within the primitive, not the modern and its contemporary technological developments.[24]

In the account of Aran itself, Synge writes constantly of the people, the landscape, the sea, and, in a highly unique manner, the birds. Synge's avian imagery often relates to competition over resources, mastery of the material abundance of the sea, and esthetic pleasure of the writer. Synge is aware of the strategic geography of the Aran Islands for both him and these creatures of flight. He writes,

> ...the Atlantic on my left, a perpendicular cliff under my ankles, and over me innumerable gulls that chase each other in a white cirrus of wings. A nest of hooded crows is somewhere near me, and one of the old birds is trying to drive me away be letting itself fall like a stone every few moments, from about forty yards above me to within reach of my hand. Gannets are passing up and down above the sound, swooping at times after a mackerel, and further off I can see the whole fleet of hookers coming out from Kilronan for a night's fishing in the deep water to the west.
> 
> (29)

The sea is not an empty expanse, but a route of navigation from the air, into the sea chasing fish, and finally on the surface of the water. The space becomes a dynamic zone of interchange. These pleasurable moments, however, are undercut or perhaps highlighted in their sense of enchantment with the power of the current and the precariousness of life, and the closeness of death in Aran. Synge explains,

> As I lie here hour after hour, I seem to enter into the wild pastimes of the cliff, and to become a companion of the cormorants and crows. Many of the birds display themselves to me with the vanity of *barbarians*. Some are wonderfully expert, and cut graceful figures for an inconceivable time without a flap of their wings, growing so absorbed in their own dexterity that they often collide with one another in their flight, an incident always followed by a wild outburst of abuse. Their language is easier than Gaelic, and I seem to understand a greater part of their cries, though I am not able to answer. There is one plaintive note which they take up in the middle of their usual babble with extraordinary effect, and pass on from one to another along the cliff with a sort of an inarticulate wail, as if they remembered for an instant the horror of the mist.
> (30, emphasis added)

Synge's avian language suggests a closeness of the cycle of life but also of the very timelessness of the experience of the birds. Their cries and calls are easier for him to interpret than the language of the human inhabitants of the islands. He celebrates the barbarism, abuse, and horror of the place that is so clearly associated with the avian. Synge views their flights and collisions in space as emblematic of their agility that is so engrossing that they lose their awareness of other creatures, dare I suggest, transcend and become transported in flight much like Synge attempts to transcend and become transported through his experiences in the Aran Islands. Yet, the encounters with birds he describes are associated with the human residents of the islands, thus commenting on the human residents and the primitive language and customs of both bird and human.

The birds are used as a relief against which other aspects of Aran and Synge's own experiences are drawn. The birds suggest transcendent flight, escape, and even, in fact, the sublime encounter. Justin Carville writes that the author "is 'troubled' by the width of the bay," which "demonstrates that Synge's experience of the sublimity of the primitive landscape" (101). Carville continues:

> All the seasons are collapsed into one another so that what exists is a kind of perpetual autumn with the entire natural world suspended in a continual appearance of decay. Indeed nothing grows on this island. All sense of progress, of change, of modernity is removed from

Synge's imaginative geography. This imaginative geography visualizes the Aran Islands as an idealized example of the primitive landscape where all of nature has been held in suspension to be observed by the sovereign eye of the ethnographer. Indeed the visualization of the landscape in this passage with all sense of temporal change having been removed from geographical space reflects the stop-time exposure of the photograph.

(101)

When Synge uses avian imagery in his account of Aran, he is participating in a centuries-long tradition of treating birds as representations of primitive culture. Given public interest during Synge's lifetime in evolutionary theory and its attendant debates, it is striking that Synge's image of the primitive posits birds as evolutionary descendants of ancient creatures. Such an interest in the evolutionary biology of certain species would certainly have piqued the mind of someone like Synge who was a voracious consumer of the theories of culture, landscape, and people.[25] He links the avian images with that of girls and women:

> As we set out I noticed among the groups of girls who smiled at our fellowship—old Mairtin says we are like the new cuckoo with its pipit—a beautiful oval face with the singularly spiritual expression that is so marked in one type of the West Ireland women. Later in the day, as the old man talked continually of the fairies and the women they have taken, it seemed that there was a possible link between the wild mythology that is accepted on the islands and the strange beauty of the women.
>
> (10)

Synge and Mairtin are likened to the cuckoo, a bird that is notorious for hiding its eggs within a pipit's nest, the cuckoo hatchling then contesting nest space with that of the pipit eggs/hatchlings. The beauty of the pipit's visage appeals to Synge as he compares its beauty to that of the Irish women of the West. That Synge is excited by women is unsurprising. Yet, it is his very link between the human and the bird, as measures of desirability that seems to promise an intersection to be examined.[26] Gilmartin explains, "the description of the women's gathering in the morning reads almost as a depiction from a naturalist's guidebook: the women are like a cluster of birds he has come across and they excite him as a birdwatcher might be by the chance encounter with a rare breed" (67). What seems remarkable is the degree to which Synge's seeming incongruity is captured in his avian imagery as a paradoxical desire for flight and an intense interest in the island and its people at once. For Synge, the avian becomes symbolic of the islands and is highly associated with women. Gregory Castle notes, "Synge was caught up in an ambivalent relationship with the dominant discourses of anthropology, and his attitude toward peasant culture—he regarded the Aran islanders as a wild and primitive, inherently noble people cut off from the modern Europe—betray an equally ambivalent investment in primitivism" (101). Yet, Synge's writing of Aran negotiates between his idealizations of the primitive and his desire to capture the transcendence associated with the sublime.

The primitivism of Synge's depiction of birds even translates to how he speaks of the human inhabitants; he notes, for example, the "primitive babble of the men" (34). The phrase suggests both a return to the past and the presence of the past in contemporary society. This tension between the temporal realms serves as an important element of the primitive sublime. Synge's phrase invokes the tower of babble, its destruction through the wrath of God, and the dispersal of peoples and languages across the globe. If Synge is attempting to suggest the endurance of the ancient world in his contemporary one, he is surely using images that suggest how troubling the endurance of the vision of a society's destruction can prove to be: "Old Pat has told me a story of the goose that lays the golden eggs, which he calls the Phoenix... heart of bird is good fortune" (47–48). Stephanie J. Pocock argues,

> *The Aran Islands* ... demonstrate[s] the ways in which "archaic" or "primitive" cultures can have a positive impact on modernity, even as modernity threatens to stamp them out. Synge's texts challenge modern understandings of temporality and history by blurring the distinction between folk tales passed down for generations, distant historical facts or memories, and occurrences in the present or immediate past. This running-together of time features prominently in the speech of the people he encounters, which often skips from myth, to history, to daily life, with little or no indication of the tense of a given tale."
> (79–80)

Synge's incorporation of the story of Old Pat evinces the way in which he relies on what Pocock terms the "running-together of time" (80). Synge continues to describe his position of isolation amid connection outside of temporal linearity:

> For the rest of my walk I saw no living thing but one flock of curlews, and a few pipits hiding among the stones. About the sunset the clouds broke and the storm turned to a hurricane. Bars of purple cloud stretched across the sound where immense waves were rolling from the west, wreathed with snowy phantasies of spray. Then there

34  *Performing the Primitive Sublime*

was the bay full of green delirium, and the Twelve Pins touched with mauve and scarlet in the east. The suggestion from this world of inarticulate power was immense…

(63)

The terror of the hurricane, a word that becomes expressive here because of its etymology, derives from the Caribbean god of the wind/storm, *Hurakán*, and the resultant terror of angering him, yields symbolic mythic recognition of the vast power of the sea and wind versus the small island-scape on which the writer stands and shelters. Synge's portrait of an "immense" and "inarticulate power" suggests a rapturous transcendent sublime framed within the winds of the hurricane and symbolized within his avian elements, the "flock of curlews" and the "pipits" who seem the relentlessly present creatures within his primitive sublime.

Synge's vision of the islands as almost disappearing amid the sea light and the stars is contrasted with his sense of the movement of the ocean waves, the noise of the birds, and the stench of weed. The avian images emerge again:

I could hear nothing but a few curlews and other wild fowl whistling and shrieking in the seaweed, and the low rustling of the waves. It was one of the dark sultry nights peculiar to September, with no light anywhere except the phosphorescence of the sea, and an occasional rift in the clouds that showed the stars behind them. The sense of solitude was immense. I could not see or realize my own body, and I seemed to exist merely in my perception of the waves and of the crying birds, and of the smell of the seaweed.

(82)

Synge's sense of isolation becomes profoundly disembodied. He has achieved a sublime state of personal erasure enabled by the birds and the waves.

Moments of transcendence in Synge's vision of the Aran Islands occur when he loses himself in the sounds of the surf, visions in the air, and the effervescent light. Yet, at other moments, the quotidian intrudes upon this perfection of place. And in certain moments, the birds go from being transcendent avatars of otherworldliness into the brutal raw material of human existence carved out on the rugged island landscape. Synge occasionally exclaims, "Sometimes when I go into a cottage I find all the women of the place down on their knees plucking the feathers from live ducks and geese. (115). He seems nonplussed by the vision, but the fact that he notes it is especially worthy for the writer and his usual avian images. These birds are creatures of the earth more than the air. In this scene, the birds seem to be placed not above the islands, but as a critical part of their terrestrial environment. They feature as Synge explains,

> This morning, when I had been lying for a long time on a rock near the sea watching some hooded crows that were dropping shellfish on the rocks to break them, I saw one bird that had a large white object which it was dropping continually without any result. I got some stones and tried to drive it off when the thing had fallen, but several times the bird was too quick for me and made off with it before I could get down to him. At last, however, I dropped a stone almost on top of him and he flew away. I clambered down hastily, and found to my amazement a worn golf ball!
>
> (126–127)

The shock and amazement of the writer upon his discovery of the object of modernity amid his primitive island zone suggests the intersection of both realms. The avian encounter facilitates a sudden and unexpected vision of the contemporary, the golf ball, into the transcendent realm of the primitive sublime. In this moment, the birds serve as a guidepost for the author to negotiate tradition and modernity, the primitive and the contemporary, the ordinary and the sublime.

The geographic location of the island, particularly as the island serves as a zone where the past emerges in the present, holds plenty of opportunity to use the imagination and prove that vision is intimately related to deception. Synge writes, "I think those black gulls and the ship were the same sort, and after that I never went out again as a pilot. It is often curaghs go out to ships and find there is no ship" (133). The loss of the certainty of encountering a phantom ship upon the sea is critical for Synge. He is lost in the world as he confronts the uncertainty and end of his piloting efforts. He is lost off the coast of the islands of Ireland. Synge evokes the sublime perhaps most explicitly after he survives an encounter on a "frantic terror of a beast," a curagh that he has been attempting to navigate between the isle and the mainland, "till the wave passed beneath it or fell with a crash beside the stern" (71). Synge reveals as he remembers this difficult yet exhilarating moment, "I enjoyed the passage. Down in this shallow trough of canvas that bent and trembled with the motion of the men, I had a far more intimate feeling of the glory and power of the waves than I have ever known" (72). The author's feelings of triumph and "power" suggest a recognition of the risks undertaken and survived. The moment passes like the water and wave, and, yet Synge finds a sense of power and sublimity amid the "trembling."

Synge takes his intense feelings and depictions in *The Aran Islands* and deploys them on stage in his dramas.[27] The breaking out and away is the primitive sublime, a transcendent elation of escape from the sacrificial horror and violence that undergird his dramas. For Synge in his brief play, *Riders to the Sea*, the sacrifice of the young man, and a greater relentless sacrifice that the island and Ireland require, are contextualized through images of the avian. These images are manifestations on the stage of the primitive sublime encounter that, for Synge, was intimately connected with the avian experience, depiction, and appreciation. The death of the sons of the family as they navigate the currents between the isle and the mainland in *Riders to the Sea* is contrasted with the false reports of the performance of patricide in *Playboy of the Western World*. While the depiction of personal sacrifice and the terror of loss in *The Aran Islands* is apparent in *Riders to the Sea*, the depiction of flight and escape in the travelogue ultimately morphs into a sense of liberation in Synge's *Playboy*.[28] In his *Inventing Ireland*, Declan Kiberd asserts that the tripartite structure of *Playboy* is based upon the organization of "Frantz Fanon's dialectic of decolonization, from occupation, through nationalism, to liberation" (184). Such is made clear when Christy Mahon's ultimate emancipation emerges after a clearly primitivist rhetoric surrounding slavery and savagery in the play. Kiberd posits that "by breaking out of binaries, through to a third point of transcendence, that freedom can be won" (184).

And when Shawn Keogh is described as "a middling kind of scarecrow with no savagery or fine words" (113), the tension between the seemingly opposite behaviors instead creates a third space for Synge to assert his primitive sublime: savagery and finery at once. This sublimity of cultural transcendence manifests as the play wraps up when Christy Mahon is described "like a gallant captain with his heathen slave" (111).[29]

Surely, for Synge the past is central to the present; the veil of distinction between the two realms is so commonly breached as to become contemporaneous. Declan Kiberd has famously suggested that Synge's project is to *"make the present past'* (173). We can see that in Synge's plays, reports of past action do not remain contained withing previous acts or actions. As Greene notes, "There is a nightmare quality also in the father who is repeatedly killed and will not stay dead" (*Synge* 96).[30] The question becomes salient not simply for Christy Mahon's father but for the ancient Irish past itself. The performance of the rhetoric of violence—violence of the past emerging into the present—creates a tension in the early twentieth century that remains central to the enduring rapture of the primitive sublime. For Synge, the primitivism of the past is not over. The primitive endures in the present and becomes critical for his vision of his contemporaneity and the experience of the sublime. In fact, Levitas notes that,

> If the *Playboy* had produced an explosion of possibility, it was an outrage displaying a panoply of revolts. Republicanism sought to

contain that diversity, directing and reducing the multivalency of its riotous discharge, and returning its singular echo in the act of insurrection. *Cathleen Ni Houlihan* may have provided the impulse... [yet] what stalked through the Post Office was the shade of Christy Mahon.

(242)

Levitas suggests that the actual violence of the Rising of 1916, a strategic location of which was Dublin's General Post Office, is most evident not in the early drama of Yeats's and Gregory's *Cathleen Ni Houlihan* that so inspired many nationalists of the period but rather in Synge's stage play dealing with a reported patricide that turns out to be a false performance of power and grandiosity.

What emerges as the primitive sublime in the Celtic Revival is the relentless drive toward indigenous Irish primitivism as a means through which to counter colonial authority while valorizing the sacrificial violence within the Irish experience as liberatory. This cultural deliverance was enabled, signified, and articulated through avian imagery. The tensions in the depictions of the Revivalists and their portraits of the primitive sublime shift throughout the revival period.[31] For Yeats, his primitive sublime relies on Irish mythic systems, both those that he reimagines to in his dramas and those he attempts to create in "Easter 1916." Yeats and Gregory in their *Cathleen Ni Houlihan* assert a vision of national sacrifice as the incarnation of Ireland herself to create sacrificial primitive sublime subtlely evoking the avian with the "Morrigan" goddess figure. Gregory's depiction of the primitive sublime in her "Aristotle's Bellows" asserts a union of human and avian, a connection between the ancient and modern worlds, and as a form of transcendence through song. For Synge, he finds his primitive sublime connects human and bird, particularly through his vision of women, in *The Aran Islands* and then uses these tropes to create dramas that show how the primitive sublime serves as a form of potential escape from the horrors of social violence and death.

The primitive sublime does not hold steady after the end of the Revival period in Ireland, so much as fracture and refract. Etherington notes that "as primitivism was neither a genre nor a school but a historically contingent aesthetic mode, its articulations do not sit within firm boundaries" (xvii). I extend this contingency to Ireland's primitive sublime as well. The harsh reality of violence destabilizes the transcendent myths of national identity that the primitive sublime evokes. The boundaries of this "historically contingent aesthetic mode" will continue to fluctuate in the realm of Joyce's works and beyond in twentieth-century Irish literature. Joyce's Ireland is in some ways a return to the time of his youth—he captures an Ireland in his novels, despite his best efforts of realistic detail, that no

## 38  Performing the Primitive Sublime

longer exists when his *Ulysses* and *Finnegans Wake* are published. After the mid-century period of desublimation reflective of the banalities and constrictions on artistic and personal freedom related to independence, later in the century, we will see figures that seem much like the father in Synge's *Playboy* who will not "stay dead." A troubling progeny of Ireland's corpus will rise again, zombie-like, in the decisive resurgence of the primitive sublime at the close of the twentieth century.

## Notes

1. For further information see Ní Cheallaigh (84).
2. As P.J. Mathews notes, "rather than seeing these 'new traditional practices' [Gaelic League, i.e.] as fraudulent or bogus, it is possible to view them as examples of an alternative modernization process that was informed by a belief in the dormant potential within pre-colonial Irish cultural forms… This stands in contrast to colonial modes of development, which invariably configured tradition as a direct antithesis to modernity" (28).
3. See for example, Luke Gibbons's *Gaelic Gothic* and Katie Mishler's "'A Phantom City, Phaked of Philim Pholk.'"
4. The nineteenth-century anti-vivisection campaign was supported by the feminist thinker of Anglo-Irish provenance, Frances Power Cobbe.
5. For general information on Yeats and the sublime, see Jahan Ramazani's "Yeats: Tragic Joyce and the Sublime."
6. *The Shadowy Waters*, an early verse play of WB Yeats, performed at the Abbey on 8 Dec 1906, evokes nostalgia for the past and laments temporality and mortality.
7. According to R. F. Foster in The Apprentice Mage, the 1900 verson of the *Countess Cathleen* relies upon a misleading vision sent by Aengus (230).
8. See for example, Casper David Friedrich's, *Wanderer above the Sea of Fog* (ca. 1818), a painting in which a man looks upon a fog shrouded mountain-scape.
9. The enduring import of Yeats's famed elegy for the martyrs of the 1916 Easter Rising within Irish culture is even reflected in popular television. The poem is recited in the 2022 Irish television drama, *Bad Sisters*, Season 1, Episode 3, during an Easter family gathering.
10. See Padraic Pearse's "Mother" for another example of the drive for blood sacrifice. Thanks to Elizabeth Gilmartin for this further textual evidence.
11. Even the trial and execution of Roger Casement, a man who is not alluded to in the elegy, becomes a cultural performance of public sacrifice for the emerging nation.
12. I am indebted to Nels Pearson for bringing this source to my attention.
13. The romantic sublime evident in Conrad's depiction of the sea has been used more recently to describe the Winslow Homer watercolor, *Inside the Bar* (1883). This painting depicts a woman in danger of being swept away by the sea, Kathleen Foster explains, "She is transformed by the terrible beauty of the time and place; her stride is magnificent" (243).
14. In *The Player Queen*, the Yeats drama performed in on March, 2 1920 at the Abbey, Yeats suggests the apocalypse of the great flood is at hand. Septimus, the representative of the poet and playwright, wants a new, regenerative era (34). Yeats's mystical turn and calling forth of a new post-Christian era

becomes clear in the use of the unicorn as a symbol to be conjured into the world. The transition between the present, past, and future appears fluid.
15 I am indebted to my seminar students in spring 2023 at Queens University Belfast for highlighting the Morrígan as a significant aspect of Cathleen's personae.
16 For further reading, see Richard Fitzpatrick's piece in the *Irish Examiner*, "Mourning the Loss of the Keening Tradition in Ireland."
17 For further information, see Denis Donoghue's discussion of the hawk figuration as it relates to the characterization of Cuchulain (101). The pared down aesthetic of Yeats's *At the Hawk's Well* highlights the primitive sublime in its intersection of language and symbolism. Cuchulian as a young man is not the portrait of futility fighting the waves in *On Baille's Strand*, but rather, he occupies a more provocative position and his potential for transcendence.
18 In Gregory's unproduced play, *The Shoelace*, (1904–20), Taig comments upon the position of Ireland and the islands. The threat lurks in the western waters off the coast, not in the Eastern incursions of the British. The contrast of the landed hero is not with the western incursion or area but with the ancient eastern heroes. The King of Mayo is thought to be preferable. In Gregory's *Meadowgate* (1910-1920), her contrast with the ancient Greek world is continued as two characters volley between the ancient and modern worlds. Finally, in her famous drama, *Spreading the News*, Lady Gregory again remarks upon the condition of enslavement for the Irish. Yet, in this play it is not with a contrast with the ancients or those abroad, but decidedly both present and local. The labor that is most alienated is not for the enslaved, or the slaving, the transformation from noun to gerund, but for those that have endeavored to help the unfortunate. Death is the true emancipation, but is nonetheless here only a threat. Thanks to the Abbey Theater Digital archive at the Hardiman Library at the National University of Ireland Galway for these versions/sources of material.
19 For a more recent example, with which Gregory was likely familiar, of the wind associated with inspiration see Samuel Taylor Coleridge's "The Eolian Harp."
20 In drafts of *Aristotle's Bellows*, in the Abbey Theater Digital archive, Gregory links release with flight. Gregory eliminates the most overt association of escape and the avian with a pencil mark, crossing out the second stanza. What remains is slightly more obscure, yet still evocative. The association between flight and air with escape is notable and the printed play underscores this link.
21 The development of fashion, of day girls, working girls, and shop girls, comes at the same time of the social revolution in shopping—of department stores stocking enticements of mass production, rather than tailors, seamstresses, and milleners making bespoke garmets and fashions for unique customers. The creation of the mass market store is the creation of desire as a commodity itself. It replaces the need of the small proprietor with the dramatic enticements that emerge with the development of shopping as an activity that marks both leisure and status. In Synge's *The Shadow of a Glen*, the author charts the reversal of an emancipatory tale: the characters become confined. The concern is not that the woman becomes civilized through her fashion, but rather that she becomes corrupted by British Victorian values.
22 A subsequent list in Synge's Notebooks can seem remarkably mundane. In his "Nature Diary," the physical markers and descriptions of the birds are intermingled with the naming of particular species. Unlike his earlier bird journal with a companion, here Synge's physical action is almost entirely absent.

23 "W.B. Yeats came in 1896 [to the Aran Islands], looking for a setting for his proposed novel, *The Speckled Bird*, which was to oscillate between mystical Paris and peasant Ireland" (Robinson, *Aran Islands* xvi). This autobiographical novel would ultimately go through several revisions, yielding up to four versions. The distinction between the city and the country, the metropolitan and the rural, figures predominantly in it. Yet, Yeats is famously the man who told Synge to go to the Aran Islands: that he should "live there as if you were one of the people themselves; express a life that has never found expression." (qtd. in Robinson xxi). Yeats instructs Synge to do what he has failed to do.

24 Synge does not view technology as sublime, much like Conrad who viewed the development of the Suez Canal as ruining his sublime sea.

25 His notes on Frazer's *The Golden Bough*, a highly respected work of cultural anthropology at the turn of the last century, take several pages in his notebooks and link death with the transcendence of bird life and a King.

26 See Garrigan Mattar's examination of the intersection of red in women as passion for Synge (144).

27 According to Elizabeth Gilmartin, "In *The Aran Islands* and his plays, Synge provides various definitions of the primitive and these complicated and shifting definitions inspire the exaggerated depictions presented in his plays" (65).

28 As Ben Levitas notes, "The Abbey staged a play; but Synge created an event" (115).

29 According to Nicholas Grene, the audience of the premiere was trapped by their own expectations of class and nation (109).

30 Kiberd writes that Synge's project on the Aran Islands participates in the modernizing changes it decries: "Synge knows that he is only an interloper on Aran, a tourist, one of the first and, perhaps one day, one of the most famous among many: and that the more successful is his book called *The Aran Islands*, the more extreme will be the consequent disruptions of tradition by day-trippers who will come in his wake. Indeed he has—though he never quite says this—a vested interest in these disruptions, because after they have had their effect, his book will be even more evocative than ever." (Pocock 79; Kiberd 173)

31 According to Nicholas Grene, "The renunciation of the sexual consummation of marriage for the higher sublimation of dying for Cathleen Ni Houlihan was edifying, admirable, magnificent. But escape from the bed of an impotent old husband – 'he was always cold, every day since I knew him, - and every night'... – to the prospect of outdoor sex with a young man – 'there'll be no old fellow wheezing the like of a sick sheep close to your ear'... – was quite another thing again. Where Yeats and Gregory move through metaphor and allegory towards a transcendental metamorphosis which the nationalist audience could ecstatically applaud, the secularizing, materializing spirit of Synge's play produced exactly the opposite effect." (76). Grene's analysis highlights the tensions within the primitive sublime. While he suggests Synge's secularization and exterior, sexual pleasure, as likely catalysts, the tension between desire and desecration occupies many Irish writers beyond Synge.

# References

Bruna, Giulia. *J. M. Synge and Travel Writing of the Irish Revival*. Syracuse UP, 2017.

Carville, Conor. "Keeping That Wound Green:' Irish Studies and Trauma Culture." *What Rough Beasts?: Irish and Scottish Studies in the New Millennium*, edited by Shane Alcobia-Murphy, Cambridge Scholars Publishing, 2008, pp. 45–71.

Carville, Justin. "Visible Others: Photography and Romantic Ethnography in Ireland." *Irish Modernism and the Global Primitive*, edited by Maria McGarrity and Claire A. Culleton, Palgrave, 2009, pp. 92–114. https://doi.org/10.1057/9780230617193_6.

Castle, Gregory. *Modernism and the Celtic Revival*. Cambridge UP, 2001.

Clark, Rosalind. "Aspects of the Morrígan in Early Irish Literature." *Irish University Review*, vol. 17, no. 2, 1987, pp. 223–36, www.jstor.org/stable/25477680.

Coleridge, Samuel Taylor. "The Eolian Harp." *The Poems of S. T. Coleridge*. William Pickering, 1844, pp. 149–51.

Coleman, Antony. "A Calendar for the Production and Reception of *Cathleen ni Houlihan*." *Modern Drama*, vol. 18, no. 2, 1975, pp. 127–40, https://doi.org/10.1353/mdr.1975.0031.

Conrad, Joseph. *An Outcast of the Islands*. Doubleday, 1925.

Donoghue, Denis. *Yeats*. Fontana/Collins, 1971.

Etherington, Ben. *Literary Primitivism*. Stanford UP, 2017.

Fitzpatrick, Richard. "Mourning the Loss of the Keening Tradition in Ireland." *Irish Examiner*, 16 Aug. 2016, https://www.irishexaminer.com/lifestyle/arid-20415997.html. Accessed 27 May 2023.

Foster, Kathleen. *American Watercolor in the Age of Homer and Sargent*. Yale UP, 2017.

Foster, R. F. *W. B. Yeats: A Life, Vol 1, The Apprentice Mage*. Oxford UP, 1997.

Garrigan Mattar, Sinéad. *Primitivism, Science, and the Irish Revival*. Oxford UP, 2004.

Gibbons, Luke. *Gaelic Gothic: Race, Colonization, and Irish Culture*. Arlen House, 2006.

Gilmartin, Elizabeth. "Magnificent Words and Gestures: Defining the Primitive in Synge's *The Aran Islands*." *Irish Modernism and the Global Primitive*, edited by Maria McGarrity and Claire A. Culleton, Palgrave, 2009, pp. 63–76. https://doi.org/10.1057/9780230617193_4

Grene, Nicholas. *The Politics of Irish Drama: Plays in Context from Boucicault to Friel*. Cambridge UP, 1999.

———. *Synge: A Critical Study of the Plays*. Macmillan, 1975.

Gregory, Lady. "Aristotle's Bellows." *The Wonder and Supernatural Plays, Collected Plays 3*, edited by Ann Saddlemyer, Colin Smythe Ltd., 1979, pp. 261–300.

———. *Collected Plays 1-4*, edited by Saddlemyer, Ann. Colin Smythe Ltd., 1979.

Heaney, Seamus. Interview. *Sunday Sequence*, BBC, 29 Jan. 1989. The Seamus Heaney Centre at Queen's Broadcast Collection, FFBBC010. Queen's University Belfast, Belfast, Northern Ireland.

Joyce, James. *Ulysses: The Corrected Text*, edited by Hans Walter Gabler with Wolfhard Steppe and Claus Melchior. Random House, 1986.

Kiberd, Declan. *Inventing Ireland: The Literature of the Modern Nation*. Harvard UP, 1995.

Levitas, Ben. *The Theater of the Nation: Irish Drama and Cultural Nationalism, 1890-1916*. Oxford UP, 2002.

Martin, Heather. "Of Flood and Fire: A Study of *The Player Queen*." *Canadian Journal of Irish Studies*, vol. 7, no. 1, 1981, pp. 49–60.

Mathews, P. J. *Revival: The Abbey Theatre, Sinn Féin, the Gaelic League, and the Co-Operative Movement.* Cork UP, 2003.

McDiarmid, Lucy. "The Avian Rising: Yeats, Muldoon, and Others." *International Yeats Studies*, vol. 1, no. 1, 2016, pp. 74–85, DOI: https://doi.org/10.34068/IYS.01.01.09.

———. "The Demotic Lady Gregory." *High and Low Moderns: Literature and Culture 1889-1939*, edited by DiBattista, Maria, and Lucy McDiarmid, Oxford UP, 1996, pp. 212–34.

Mishler, Katie. "'A Phantom City, Phaked of Philim Pholk': Spectral Topographies and Re-Awakenings in James Joyce's *Finnegans Wake* and Sheridan Le Fanu's *The House by the Churchyard*." *Joyce Studies Annual*, 2018, pp. 161–94. JSTOR, https://www.jstor.org/stable/26798631. Accessed 17 July 2023.

Ní Cheallaigh, Máirín. "Women and the Survival of Archaeological Monuments in Nineteenth-Century Ireland." *Memory Ireland*, edited by Oona Frawley, Syracuse UP, 2011, pp. 83–97. www.jstor.org/stable/j.ctt1j1w050.11

Pearse, Padraic. "The Mother." 1916.

Pocock, Stephanie J. "Artistic Liminality: Yeats's *Cathleen ni Houlihan* and *Purgatory*." *New Hibernia Review*, vol. 12, no. 3, 2008, pp. 99–117, www.jstor.org/stable/25660807.

Ramazani, Jahan. "Yeats: Tragic Joy and the Sublime." *PMLA*, vol. 104, no. 2, 1989, pp. 163–77, https://doi.org/10.2307/462502.

Robinson, Tim. Introduction. *The Aran Islands*, by J. M. Synge, Penguin Classics, 1992, pp. vii–l.

Saddlemyer, Ann. Foreword. *The Wonder and Supernatural Plays, Collected Plays 3*, by Lady Gregory, Colin Smythe Ltd., 1979, pp. v–ix.

Shaw, George Bernard. *The Doctor's Dilemma: A Tragedy.* Constable, 1927.

Stallworthy, Jon. "The Poet as Archaeologist: W. B. Yeats and Seamus Heaney." *The Review of English Studies*, vol. 33, no. 130, 1982, pp. 158–174, https://doi.org/10.1093/res/XXXIII.130.158.

Synge, J. M. "Bird watcher's journal." 1882. Papers of John Millington Synge collection. IE TCD MS 4369. Manuscripts & Archives Research Library, Trinity College Dublin, Dublin, Ireland. https://doi.org/10.48495/hx11xh48j.

———. *The Aran Islands*. Penguin Classics, 1992.

———. *The Complete Works of J. M. Synge*. Wordsworth, 2008.

Whelan, Kevin. "The Memories of 'The Dead.'" *The Yale Journal of Criticism*, vol. 15, no. 1, 2002, pp. 59–97, https://doi.org/10.1353/yale.2002.0014.

Williams, Mark. *Ireland's Immortals: A History of the Gods of Irish Myth*. Princeton UP, 2016.

Yeats, W. B. *Yeats's Poetry, Drama, and Prose: A Norton Critical Edition*, edited by James Pethica, W. W. Norton & Company, 2000.

Yeats, W. B., and Augusta Lady Gregory. "Cathleen Ni Houlihan." *Modern and Contemporary Irish Drama*, edited by John P. Harrington, Norton, 2009, pp. 3–11.

# 3 James Joyce and the Primitive Sublime

From *A Portrait of the Artist as a Young Man* to *Ulysses* and *Finnegans Wake*

Joyce commonly portrays cultural translation and displacement, identifying racial alterities and examining the role of the African figures in his works.[1] Joyce's primitive alterity is imagined and portrayed abroad, but nonetheless reveals an anxiety about primitive Ireland at home. Yet, for Joyce, the risk of such confrontations is not in illuminating a facile difference with the primitive other but in its profoundly intimate allegiance with the primitive other within Ireland. Joyce's allusions to the primitive sublime in *Ulysses* rely on Roger Casement's 1904 *Congo Report*. Joyce's engagement with the primitive sublime then becomes even more acute in his *Finnegans Wake*, where he uses Casement as a key nexus amid a series of allusions to the Paris Colonial Exposition of 1931, which finally suggests that the threat or the representation of Africa for Joyce and for Ireland are distinctly related to fears of what Christine van Boheemen-Saaf termed, "the fear of indistinction" (139). These troubling encounters in Joyce's final novel uniquely create a sublime experience surrounding figures of debased African others. I suggest that Joyce's complicated rhetorics of the primitive sublime in *Finnegans Wake* rest at the center of the Irish primitive encounter as a representation of sublime fear and enchantment, desire and desecration, that reach back to the "Cyclops" episode of *Ulysses* and revolve around Roger Casement.

James Joyce's engagement with the primitive reach back to his earliest writings, in which he was acutely aware of Irish primitivism, even if he often mocked its manifestations in the Revival. He nonetheless supported the right of Yeats to provoke controversy on the stage with his *Countess Cathleen* when he, while enrolled at University College Dublin, declined to add his name to a petition against the play. According to Richard Ellmann, Joyce also famously encountered J. M. Synge while he was living in Paris, and translated Synge's Revivalist play, *Riders to the Sea*, into Italian (though Joyce's translation remains lost to scholars). He positions Ireland amid the ancient Mediterranean cultures in his "Ireland, Island of Saints and Sages" essay that appears in *Il Piccolo della Sera*, a Triestine newspaper, in 1907.[2]

DOI: 10.4324/9781003297390-3

At the close of *A Portrait of the Artist as a Young Man*, Joyce invokes a striking image. He writes of the "old father, old artificer" as young Dedalus resolves to depart from Ireland with only his "silence, exile, and cunning" (212). The final gesture in this *bildungsroman* is one of transcendent flight, referencing the Icarus/Dedalus tale of escaping the labyrinth, but flying too close to the sun, melting the waxwings. The hero, Icarus, falls to earth, returning home to disappointment and entrapment. This famous end is a sublime gesture provoked with the portraits of the romantic primitive encounters earlier in the novel. Joyce deploys rhetorics of the primitive associate it with "savagery" and the Irish in missionary work, notably Dante, making "money from the savages for the trinkets and chainies" through selling these worthless items to indigenous peoples (35), positioning the Irish in an uncomfortable juxtaposition to colonized peoples across the globe. This sublime movement relies upon earlier depictions of transcendence mixed with "primitive" desire for young Stephen. The link between longing and suffering for Stephen is evident even in his juvenile attempts to imagine his coupling with another. Joyce describes Stephen's desire as "savage" and counters it with the "sacred" even as he writes of "a tender premonition touched him of the tryst he had then looked forward to and, in spite of the horrible reality" (98–99) in which Stephen now lives at the end of the second chapter just before he loses his virginity with a sex worker. Stephen's psyche reflects the unknowing thought of a young man yet to experience any intimacy with another. He grows up and begins to reflect knowledge of desire and satisfaction in the infamous bird girl scene at the end of the fourth chapter. Stephen uses the image of the girl to fulfill his own desire. In a moment that seems evocative of Synge's avian images associated with women, Stephen notes "one whom magic had changed into the likeness of a strange and beautiful seabird" (171). The "beautiful" is also "strange" just as the moment is described as one of "profane joy" moments later (171). The tension between seeming opposites creates an enduring ambivalence that becomes deployed with even greater nuance in Joyce's increasingly sophisticated narratives. Joyce will merge these rhetorics of desire and otherness seen in *A Portrait of the Artist as a Young Man* as he creates his vision of the primitive sublime in *Ulysses* and *Finnegans Wake*.

In the twelfth episode of *Ulysses*, "Cyclops," which is set late in the day in Barney Kiernan's pub, the protagonist, Leopold Bloom, encounters a caricature of an Irish nationalist and Celtic Revivalist, named the Citizen. He lauds all Irish history and culture in a gauzy, hyperbolic, and (unintentionally) with overwhelmingly comic motifs. Because the name of the chapter indicates the narrowness of vision and exclusionary sentiments of the character, the Citizen is a figure of mockery for Joyce; the Citizen ends up attacking Joyce's hero, Bloom, and questioning Bloom's sense of national identity and belonging. "Ireland, says Bloom. I was born here" (*U* 12.1430–1431). Yet, within his myopic and limited vision related to Bloom's Jewishness the Citizen recognizes the import of the national identity of Roger Casement. Born in Ireland to a Protestant family, Casement was an officer in the British Foreign Office who had been sent to investigate Belgian atrocities in the Congo and report back his findings to London.[3] Joyce focuses on Casement in *Ulysses* on his political and diplomatic mission before the 1916 Rising. Joyce writes,

– That's how it's worked, says the citizen. Trade follows the flag.
– Well, says J.J., if they're any worse than those Belgians in the Congo Free State they must be bad. Did you read that report by a man what's this his name is?
– Casement, says the citizen. He's an Irishman.
– Yes, that's the man, says J.J. Raping the women and girls and flogging the natives on the belly to squeeze all the red rubber they can out of them.

(*U* 12.1541-47)

Joyce highlights the rabid abuses of the trade in rubber and the brutality of Europeans engaged in that endeavor as he overtly categorizes Roger Casement as an Irishman. Both the location of the Congo and the national identity of a British Foreign Officer, Casement himself, are presented as essential points of information for the Citizen to highlight. Joyce uses the key image of "the red rubber" from the Congo Reform Movement, a movement that was inaugurated due to the scandal and sensation that Casement's report creates, in his description of the industry to evoke the greater, bloody violence enacted during this time. Kevin Dunn explains: the Congo Reform Movement "developed the image of 'Red Rubber' to connect the wild rubber from the Congo with the blood spilled by the Congo's inhabitants, who were forced to gather it" (51). When Joyce describes the "red rubber," he uses the specific idiom of the Reform Movement to flag that the only thing characteristically red about the rubber from the Congo is the blood in which it is covered. Joyce's use of the phrase is significant because it not only underscores the substantial colonial atrocities in the Congo but also highlights the anti-colonial and pro-human rights campaign.

Casement's development as an anti-colonial voice was specifically related to his service in the British Foreign Office and his *Congo Report*, published in February 1904. Séamus Ó Síocháin and Michael O'Sullivan note that Casement's "alienation was largely due to a growing identification with the Irish nationalist cause and a corresponding negativity towards England's treatment of Ireland, both historical and contemporary" (20).

This identification, they write, ultimately led "to his involvement with the Irish Volunteers, to his mission to Germany during the First World War and, finally, to his capture, trial and execution in 1916" (20). Casement's political turn, away from his service in the British Foreign Office and toward the Easter Rising, grows directly out of his experience in Africa. More broadly, the exploitation that Casement delineates in his report motivated the Congo Reform Association because of its graphic descriptions of "punitive expeditions, hostage taking... shootings and beatings, maiming and other sadistic acts" that the Belgians performed (Ó Síocháin and O'Sullivan 36). The somewhat restrained description of "other sadistic acts" that the editors of Casement's report use refer to the mutilation of both living and dead, specifically the raping of women and the cutting off of a hand to evidence the killing or suppression of a "native" inhabitant in the Congo. These bodily mutilations of "natives" are well-documented and often occurred when the individual failed to harvest enough rubber for his or her quota.

Casement links the bodily mutilations to the "rubber wars," which replaced the quests for ivory, that captivated the *Heart of Darkness* author Joseph Conrad, and inscribed this heart of darkness within the European "gone native." Both the trade in rubber and ivory were built upon routes established for an earlier African commodity to interest Europeans: enslaved people. Ironically, however, trafficking in ivory and enslaved people required more specialized experience with hunting elephants and subjugating human beings, whereas rubber required relatively unskilled labor. European brutality arose amid the rubber trade not with the manner of the harvesting of the commodity, but in the cruel "management" of an ever-increasing demand and a shrinking natural resource. Therefore, while Casement's Congo Reform Association had much political and diplomatic impact, it was instead the over-harvesting of rubber that de facto ended it by 1913.

Joyce's reference in "Cyclops" thus alludes to this legacy of European brutality. In Casement's report of the public exhibition of violence in the Congo, he articulates his desire for emancipation not just in the Congo, but also in Ireland. Such is found in a letter, dated February 14, 1905, from the archives at the National Library of Ireland that Casement wrote to his friend, Alice Stopford Green, a historian and the author of the 1908 book on medieval Irish history, *The making of Ireland and its undoing, 1200–1600*.[4] Casement writes,

> I knew well that if I told the truth about the that devilish Congo conspiracy of robbers I should pay for it in my own future, but when I made up my mind to tell, at all costs, it was the image of my poor old country stood right before my eyes. The whole thing had been done once to her—down to every detail—she too, had been flung reward

to the human hounds, and I felt that, as an Irishman, come what may to myself, I should tell the whole truth... committing myself to no compromise.

(Casement)

Casement's view of Ireland as suffering the crude, animalistic brutality of colonialism, conquest, and commodity extraction and using those historical precedents and contemporary realities as a means through which to act for the freedom of both the Congo and Ireland exemplifies the complicated primitive alterities at work in Joyce's text. Casement later notes in that same letter that "no Irishman can do any good to Ireland by joining the unscrupulous gang of hypocrites who have played their evil farce hitherto without check, on the wretched savages of Central Africa" (Casement). Joyce's creation of this primitivist moment in *Ulysses* depends upon Casement's recognition of cultural similarity and a dread of indistinction with oppressed "natives."

Joyce's inclusion of Casement and his *Congo Report*, as well as using the Reform Movement's language to describe the heinous enterprise, implies his awareness of the European depravity described in that report. Joyce's primitivist rhetoric here becomes quintessentially modern: he focuses the lens of primitive constructs not on the pure, essentialized savages imagined abroad in his earlier works, such as *A Portrait of the Artist as a Young Man*, but alludes to the portrayal of the brutal, sexualized, and divergent practices of Europeans in the latter part of *Ulysses*. For Joyce, this development becomes one that grows from the naïvely essentialized romantic primitivism imagined by the Irish abroad in missionary service and into the brutal and troubled modern primitivism witnessed by the Irish abroad, outside of mission service, and reported as forms of modern physical, economic, and cultural savagery.

Joyce's use of modern primitivist rhetorics in *Ulysses*, from the romantic to the modern forms, is encapsulated in a preliminary draft of "Penelope," the final episode of *Ulysses*. What Sinéad Garrigan Mattar's labels as the peculiar paradox of "proper darkness" relates not simply to ownership and identity, but also to a kind of peripheral likeness that Joyce draws together in Irish and African terms (19). The British Museum Notesheets outline Molly's position as a primitive Irish model of a woman using images from abroad that seem reminiscent of the modern primitivism reached in "Cyclops," such as when Joyce writes of Molly: "her cunt, darkest Africa" (qtd. in Herring 484). The darkness, then, for Joyce and Bloom, and unlike Conrad's Marlow, lies not at a remove from Europe, within Africa, African peoples, a European man in Africa, or even in Bloom himself wandering in Dublin, but in the sexuality of an Irish woman spending the day in bed.

Joyce's increasingly sophisticated use of primitivism in his later works relies upon a comparative nexus between the Irish and other colonized peoples across the globe. For Joyce, his interest in these globalized networks becomes most pronounced when he compares the Irish to African others. In her *Trauma of History*, Christine van Boheeman-Saaf explains, "I see *Finnegans Wake* as a pedagogic attempt to inscribe racial darkness into western culture on the eve of World War II" (14). Boheeman-Saaf's poignant understanding of *Finnegans Wake* as an inscription of "racial darkness" highlights the import of the other for Joyce's final work and reminds us of the significance of these conceptions for his larger oeuvre. Ginette Verstraete makes a connection between the other and Joyce's sublime. She explains, "It is interesting to note that… the *Wake's* return to the sublime occurs in a context that Eagleton will many years later philosophically describe as 'a material implication with others'" in his *Ideology of the Aesthetic* (198). While the *Wake's* creation of Anna Livia as an African Queen has been well established by Sheldon Brivic in his work, *Joyce's Waking Women*, what becomes increasingly apparent is that Joyce's knowledge and use of both romantic and modern primitivist rhetorics were not only deployed well before the writing of *Finnegans Wake* or that they were often used to highlight freedom from religious servitude, European Imperialism, and sexual expression, but that these rhetorics also already existed inherently within Ireland herself, recumbent in bed, sleeping before the *Wake*.

The quest for origins remains paramount for Joyce; it facilitates his primitivist rhetorics, which in turn become models of cultural difference and temporal dislocation that evoke the sublime in *Finnegans Wake*. These primitive depictions often emerge within the contemporary moment, but use cultural interchanges between Ireland and global others to highlight the differences amid the empire(s) of various subject peoples. Joyce writes in *Ulysses*, notably, "Hold to the now, the here, through which all future plunges to the past" (9.89). The conception of the past is created with a contemporary retrospective arrangement, much like the arrangement of retrospection in all of Joyce's works. Even the future is about the now and the present remains a product of our relation to past events. Later, about the *Wake*, Beckett famously describes the novel's first book as a "mass of past shadows" (qtd. in Epstein 7). Examining how these past shadows emerge in the Joycean present will reveal the sublimity of Joyce's final encounters with the primitive. Joyce's vision of the primitive relates to the import of a sense of origin and the historical past. For Joyce, the veil of distinction between the past and present is reliably breached. In this breach of temporal flexibility, Joyce creates a space for his sublime. Reframing the past and questioning temporal constructions within fiction remains one of the central themes of the *Wake*, as when Joyce writes, "if there is a future in every past this is present" (FW 496.35). In his *Critical Writings*, Joyce explains,

> Often when a person gets embarked on a topic which in its vastness almost completely swallows up his efforts, the subject dwarfs the writer; or when a logician has to treat of great subjects, with a view to deriving a fixed theory, he abandons the primal idea and digresses into elaborate disquisitions, on the more inviting portions of his argument. Again in works of fancy, a too prolific imagination literally flys (sic) away with the author, and lands him in regions of loveliness unutterable, which his faculties scarcely grasp, which dazzles his senses, and defies speech, and thus his compositions are beautiful with the cloudiness and dream-beauty of a visionary …. When however the gift--great and wonderful--of a poetic sense, in sight and speech and feeling, has been subdued by vigilance and care and has been prevented from running to extremes, the true and superior spirit, penetrates more watchfully into sublime and noble places, treading them with greater fear and greater wonder and greater reverence.
> (CW 21).

Joyce's conception of the sublime relies upon the "vastness" and the sense of being made small in comparison to an overwhelming sensation as well as the "primal" revealing an "elaborate" or overwhelming conception of the idea of the self. Yet, Joyce argues that the "greater reverence" and the achievement of the sublime is possible when the writer or artist has been able to manage and control the sense of overwhelming sensation into more articulate and measured depictions.

Questions around the sublime and its relationship with sublimation and desublimation appear in *Wake* criticism with a certain habitual frequency.[5] Margot Norris shows how Stephen's sublimation of "savagery into romantic wildness" and the working-class feminine in *Portrait* and *Ulysses* develop into idealized aesthetic visions that emerge in *Finnegans Wake* as a negotiation between transcendent myth and material reality. Norris explains that Joyce "degrades myth from an instrument of desire" (144). Joyce's longing that debases yields both connection and horror at once. Joe Valente describes Joyce's "Cosmopolitan Sublime" in his article in *Joyce and the Subject of History*: "the dueling ambivalences of colonial and native discourse [that] make of decolonization both a perpetual possibility and a perpetual frustration, which is to say a properly sublime enterprise. Like the Kantian sublime, the prospect of decolonization tantalizingly promises and refuses to come into focus, tempts and balks" (60). The tension between the longing for and the refusal of an enterprise

50  *James Joyce and the Primitive Sublime*

creates an ambivalence related to the outcome or the object of desire. More specifically, if the traditional Burkean sublime is an encounter with something beyond the self that ultimately reveals a connection of the self with the infinite and is mixed with fear if not terror, then the *Wake* itself can be considered a sublime encounter. Yet, recently, Ginette Verstraete asserts, "of course by the time Joyce is writing the *Wake*, the question of the sublime as the presentation of representation in and for itself has been exhausted... According to Lyotard, this arrival of the sublime as the presentation of the unpresentable without nostalgia, opens up within modern art the condition of postmodernity" (216). The fundamental erasure of difference, however, becomes troubling as Verstraete continues, "by definition unrepresentable, Lyotard's (sublime) ... cannot distinguish between the impossibility of talking about one's experiences in Dachau on one hand and the impossibility of getting started on the *Wake* on the other. ... [it becomes a] homogenizing silence" (216-17). This erasure of difference within Lyotard's postmodern literary paradigm does not allow for the nuances of experience, as horrifying and/or overwhelming as they might be. Joyce's primitive sublime then is not merely operating in the traditional Burkean form, nor is it, per Lyotard, merely unrepresentable, but rather what is often obscured through brutality, violence, and sexuality becoming revealed to the Irish self through an "other" with whom the fear of indistinction provokes terror. Joyce's *Wake* evokes his primitive sublime in its very confrontation with language, culture, and meaning. His conception of sublime relies upon multivalent depictions of the primitive other both outside and within his coded categories of narrative personas as well as the permeability of temporal categories and cultural locations in his universal history. Verstraete explains that "the *Wake's* (egg)burst of meaning carries the concept of the sublime beyond itself. And it would become 'sublimer' (551.35) were it not for the laughter resounding from it. Indeed, what is not seen in Joyce—the disappearance of the sublime—can be heard in multiple peals of laughter, in the abundant presence of the Joycean pun" (200). Yet, I suggest that Verstraete overstates the case. The sublime does not disappear; rather, Joyce's sublime emerges in the *Wake* in an altered form through textual encounters that reveal the entanglements amid self and other, amid Irish and global subjectivity. Joyce's wordplay in the *Wake* offers not merely amusement, but often also subtlety reveals a profound degree of intersection and unease between the Irish and global others.

Joyce's movement beyond the romantic and modern primitivist rhetorics in his earlier works manifests in *Finnegans Wake* through three interrelated elements. Some of these elements do, in fact, appear in earlier iterations in *Portrait* and *Ulysses*, such as the Paris Colonial Exposition of 1931, the embodiment of Women through the Hottentot Venus, and Roger Casement's Africa. These elements, moments of vicious carnage and sexual desecration that are deeply rooted in the sacrificial Irish past and globalized others, are nonetheless repurposed in *Finnegans Wake* to evoke the primitive sublime.

Joyce began writing *Finnegans Wake* in Paris in 1923 and worked on it throughout the 1920s and 1930s.[6] While the construction of the *Finnegans Wake* is fascinating from a genetic standpoint, what is significant for cultural critics is the social milieu in which Joyce was living and creating. Paris during this time was a center for the *avant garde* art world, literary creativity, and cultural interchange. Metropolitan France also ran a global empire from the North of Africa to the Caribbean and Indochina. This was of particular interest to Joyce: *L'exposition coloniale de 1931*, the Paris Colonial Exposition, created a sensation in its celebration of colonialism, as well as inspired a vociferous condemnation of both colonialism and this exposition from the Paris literary world. The Surrealists famously signed a protest, the "*Ne Visitez Pas L'Exposition colonial*" (D'Alesandro and Cole 9)). They assert that French colonialism and the exposition have engendered a new form of slavery to the French national bank in service of the wealth derived from the Empire. They refuse in absolute and the most strenuous terms to support the exposition and assert a commitment to an alliance with the colonized peoples represented therein. According to David Spurr: "the *Exposition Coloniale Internationale*, held in Paris in 1931, combined displays of imperial wealth and achievement with imitation native villages and Oriental streets, complete with whirling dervishes and belly-dancers. The result was, in the words of one historian, 'the ordering up of the world itself as an endless exhibition'" (Mitchell 218; Spurr 877). This spectacle of colonial conquest in a circularized imperial exhibition organizes the world into a peculiarly ordered geographical zone. Spurr continues, "In *Finnegans Wake*, HCE's imperial conquest is followed by his construction of a 'city of magnificent distances' (539.25) complete with pageants, exhibitions, and pantomimes, and food imported from exotic lands. This imperial construction includes the vision of penetration, or the penetration of vision, into the interior space" of the colonial geography (877).

> In the context of late-nineteenth-century imperialism, it was arguably the employment of anthropology within the exhibitionary complex which proved most central to its ideological functioning. For it played the crucial role of connecting the histories of Western nations and civilizations to those of other peoples, but only by separating the two in providing for an interrupted continuity in the order of peoples and races—one in which 'primitive peoples' dropped out of history altogether in order to occupy a twilight zone between nature and culture. This function had been fulfilled earlier in the century by

the museological display of anatomical peculiarities which seemed to confirm polygenetic conceptions of mankind's origins. The most celebrated instance was that of Saartjie Baartman, the "Hottentot Venus."

(Bennett 90)

The museum imperative that took hold in Europe during this time privileged the art of collecting, of professional anthropology and archaeology, but it also privileged the amateur viewer in the role of spectator. Ms. Baartman was displayed in both her life and death as an example of the disparity between the races. Stephen, of course, remembers the Hottentot in *Portrait* in the final chapter where he is in a vibrant discussion with Lynch. Stephen remarks, "The Greek, the Turk, the Chinese, the Copt, the Hottentot... all admire a different type of female beauty. That seems to be a maze out of which we cannot escape" (183).[7] Yet, Stephen does ultimately suggest that while cultural conceptions of beauty are not universal, the esthetic value of what is seen in various cultures as beautiful is universally related to the visual sense of apprehension. The "Venus" of Hottentot or of de Milo are relationally linked but culturally distinct.

The exhibitionary complex and Joyce's repeated invocation of Hottentot highlights the depravity of the historical performative exhibition of African women and the subjectivity of the female form. Hottentot is used in *Finnegans Wake* just before Anna Livia's chapter. In a discussion between Justius and Mercius, Justius exclaims, "the overload of your extravagance and made a hottentot of dulpeners crawsick with your crumbs? Am I right?" (*FW* 193.1.3). According to Verstraete, "the 'feminine sublime' is what we get to see when beauty is unmasked as man's way of concealing as well as appropriating the female body. This self-critical stance of art, in which beauty extends its borders to incorporate what lies outside—or underneath—greatly contributes toward the aesthetic dissolution of both the beautiful and its traditional other, the sublime" (22). The use of the term Hottentot suggests a continued interest in Joyce's vision of desire associated with African women. That it emerges just in advance of Anna Livia's section is particularly striking. Sheldon Brivic finds that both "artist and woman [function] as nonwhite... [and] are defined as outside what is respectable or acceptable unless they imitate the dominant culture that suppresses them. Instead, they resist the ideology of that culture... to constitute one of the leading principles of the *Wake*, a principle of advancing consciousness continuously designated as African"[8] (171). The advance of such a global consciousness remains somewhat undervalued in *Wake* criticism. Joyce's inclusion of Anna Livia and his creation of her psyche as a representation of Africa suggests the import of the African continent in his creation of a relational dichotomy with Ireland amid a global colonial power structure(s). Yet, what also seems clear is that Anna Livia is also a representation of a temporally dislocated ancient, perhaps even primitive consciousness; the river runs eternally. Brivic asserts,

> The *Wake* closes on ALP turning back to a primeval identity that is feminist and Third World in ways that would be essentialist, except that other levels are present that make fun of these ideals. Anna rejects her man and realizes that his virtues were delusions—which, like any deconstructive move, tends to imply a higher standard. Then she returns to the memory of dancing with what she calls "my people," a female group of wild rivers. The two of these who are named, Niluna and Amazia (*FW* 627.28-30), stand for the two longest rivers in the world, the Nile and the Amazon—the latter also being a fierce woman. Anna fears that she may not be able to escape the terrifying attraction of her oceanic father, but she clearly does not want to return to submission.
> 
> (161–62)

If Anna Livia serves in the *Wake* as Joyce's Venus, he provides her agency and volition in her choice of exhibition and performance or, as Brivic suggests, submission or refusal of submission. Joyce references the Hottentot again much further into the novel: "Thank you, besters! Hattentats have mindered" (*FW* 540.28). Joyce acknowledges perhaps that the Hottentots mind much indeed. Anna Livia does not submit but other representations of primitive consciousness are deployed in the text in arresting, and yes, troubling ways.

The display of and desire for consumption of "other" cultures is familiar to Joyceans not only because of the allure of the Hottentot or even the exotic bazaar in "Araby," at which the young protagonist experiences desire and disappointment, but also because of more recent critical works by Vincent Cheng, Stephanie Raines, and Kathleen St. Peters Lancia. From Cheng's analysis of the "museyrooms" in *Finnegans Wake* to Raine's analysis of Araby, social class, and commodity culture in Dublin, to St. Peter Lancia's examination of the significance of the National Museum for Bloom and Joyce in *Ulysses*, it is clear that Joyce had an intense interest in representations of culture as consumption. According to Lyotard, "Culture is always transmission (whether it operates through tradition, institutions, or media) and because transmission demands inscription. A thing is cultural because it is exhibited, i.e., inscribed or 'written'" (148). Joyce's frequent links between sexual desire and the pleasure of voyeurism are captured in the *Wake*, as when he writes, "They were watching the watched watching. Vechers all" (*FW* 509.2-3).[9] Vechers, or lechers, the line appears in a challenging matrix of HCE's seeming display of himself to his daughter, which the text hints that he seems to have enjoyed. Yet, the violation of voyeurism mixed with a lecherous dream vision highlights the troubling link in Joyce's worlds of the sex, desire, objectification, and display. All these themes recur throughout the *Wake* in general, but also reflect the cultural milieu in which Joyce was writing, and in certain instances, specifically suggests The Paris Colonial Exposition of 1931.

While Saartje Bartmaan had long passed by 1931 (though, parts of her body would remain on display in Paris until the late twentieth century as anthropological curiosities), the cultural matrix surrounding the exoticized woman of African descent remains present at this time. Josephine Baker, the American performer who became a star in Paris and was well known for her lead role in *Siren of the Tropics* (1927) and would subsequently star in *Princesse Tam Tam* (1935), appeared at the exposition as the designated "Queen of the Colonies." She opened the festivities, saying, "L'Exposition colonial est un loisir du Dimanche, un spectacle de nuit, un rêve de voyage. Tandis que des milliers des visiteurs sont invites á faire 'le tour du monde en un jour' du Bois de Vincennes" [The colonial exposition is a place for Sunday leisure, a nighttime spectacle, a dream of travel. While thousands of visitors are invited to take a 'tour of the world in a day' in the park of Vincennes]. The use of an American dancer and actress to designate the colonial other in the metropolitan center of Paris appears not to have been critically examined by the French authorities. While it raises questions about the performance of race and globalized otherness, which are both issues at the heart of the exposition, Baker's position as a woman of African heritage remains unquestioned by the sponsors. Her overt markers of heritage and her ability to perform as a colonial subject brought to the metropolitan center simply make her a primitive other suitable for display, not so very unlike the Saartje Baartman, the Hottentot Venus from the previous century. A 1933 Government report published by the French National Printery states, "la manière plus instructive et la plus pittoresque, le double apport de la France à ses colonies et des colonies à la Métropole, de symboliser par des spectacles attrayants et devus l'histoire du progress humain à travers les continents et les siècles" [The most instructive and picturesque manner is the reciprocal symbolism from France to the colonies and from the colonies to the metropole that symbolized the inviting spectacles and to grow into (witness) human progress across the continents and centuries] (107). In other words, the French government's position viewed the exposition as a reciprocal arrangement for mutual benefit. They seem to have ignored the exploitation at the heart of such cultural displays, many of which were "altered" for visual import.

The International Colonial Exposition of 1931 was organized by the French Ministry of Colonies as an unashamed celebration and

promotion of the activity of colonialism, bringing a supposed experience of colonial life to Western populations. Held at Vincennes in Paris, May to November 1931, it was opened by the President of France (Third Republic), Gaston Doumergue. Originally planned for 1925 as a follow-up to the French Colonial Exposition of 1922 in Marseilles, it was postponed several times until 1931. By this time it had become an international event, with French colonialism located in wider colonial culture. It was intended to have a 'modern' concept, unlike the 'Oriental bazaar' and chaotic 'bric-a-brac' of the 1922 Marseille exposition. This Paris exhibition used modern methods of display, statistics, photographs, films, first-hand reports and above all, experience of actual native villages imported and rebuilt, complete with native inhabitants. Advertised as 'a tour of the world in a day' to show the 'formidable richness' of colonies, the Colonial Exposition was meant to be a total experience, where a spectator could sample a 'global village' of colonial life in the major empires of France, Denmark, Belgium, Italy, Holland and Portugal all in one visit. (British territories were present as a small medical exhibit.)
(Bate 210).

In 1931, Joyce spent a considerable amount of time with Nora in London arranging and preparing for a legal marriage to ensure the inheritance of copyrights for Nora and the children. Yet, they returned to Paris in the fall of 1931, when the Exposition Colonial remained a driving force of scandal in the political and literary establishments of the city. The exposition took place in an enormous woodland park, structured in a circular pattern. Visitors entered on the Eastern side of the park in front of the Art Deco architectural jewel, *the Palais des colonies*, designed specifically for the exposition. According to a guide, this "*Permanent Colonial Museum.—* Here are pictured the past, present, and future of France's colonization programme [sic]. In itself, the museum is a notable piece of architecture. Its wall is covered by the already famous 'Tapestry in Stone,' a work of A. Janniot, the French sculptor. This stone tapestry graphically portrays the interdependence of the colonies and the French motherland" (Elston 157). An enormous museum, it is covered in stylized reliefs depicting France's global colonial empire. This "tour of the world in a day" might also seem an apt, if inverted, descriptor of *Finnegans Wake*, Joyce's universal history as nightscape, just as the overwhelming architecture of a tapestry in stone evoke a sublime encounter with the globalized other in the modern European metropole.

The geographic layout of the Colonial Exposition was circular, around a central lake in the Bois de Vinceness, thus shaping the French Empire into mimicking that of the globe. In the *Wake*, this "coglional expansion"

56  *James Joyce and the Primitive Sublime*

(*FW* 488.31) so celebrated in the Colonial Exposition of 1931 begins with an invocation of time and age: "Their aggregate ages two and thirty plus undecimmed centries of them with insiders, extraomnes and tuttifrutties allcunct...from America Avenue and Asia Place and the Affrian Way and Europa Parade... his delightful bazaar and reunited magazine hall, by the magazine wall, Hosty's and Co, Exports" (*FW* 497.9-12; 24). The playful nature of integers becomes undercut with Joyce's use of "tuttifrutties allcunct" which evokes "all counting" but also a commonly derogatory term for female anatomy (that, in turn, conjures Joyce's embodied associations of Molly with Africa in his notes). His extensive catalog of global areas covered in the bazaar, as well as all of the anatomies on overt display, and the suggestion of the host's interests in exports are evocations of the Paris Colonial Exposition of 1931.

Various other installations from other global powers were also installed throughout the circular map of the world. Strikingly, a passage in *Finnegans Wake*, from a chapter that Jean-Michel Rabaté has called, "one of the most complex if not outright demented" chapters of the book ("The Fourfold Root" 385), imitates the installation:

> To nobble or salvage... busted to the world at large, on the table round, with the floodlight switched back, as true as the Vernons have Brian's sword, and a dozen and one by one tilly tallows round in ring-campf, circumassembled by his daughters in the foregiftness of his sones, lying high as he lay in all dimension, in court dress and ludmers chain...round him, like the cummulium of scents in an Italian warehouse... beswept of his chilidrin and seraphim, poors and personalities, venturous, drones and dominators, ancients and auldanicents, with his buttend up, exposited for sale after referee's inspection, bulgy and blowrious, bunged to ignorious, healed cured andambalsemate, pending a rouseruction of his bogey, most highly astounded, as it turned up, after his life overlasting, at thus being reduced to nothing.
>
> (*FW* 498.22-35-499.3)

The noble savage reference is arresting even as it overtly displays the type of, what Sínead Garrigan Mattar terms, romantic primitivist rhetorics that Joyce so clearly mocks. The global other is depicted as overwhelming the viewer, reducing the distinction between the Irish and other colonial subjects to a profoundly uncomfortable degree, evoking the primitive sublime. The remainder of the passage describes the type of exposition embalmed display of peoples and cultures at Vincennes. In fact, one Wakean reference, "as true as the Vernons," alludes to the estate of George Washington, Mt. Vernon, a model of which was built in Vincennes as a part of the small American display. *Cook's Traveller's Handbook to Paris, 1931* explains the American exhibit: "United States.—A replica of Mount Vernon, Washington's birthplace, has been erected. Annexes contain the exhibits of the Philippines, Hawaii, Porto Rico [sic], Alaska, Guam, Panama, etc." (155). This is followed by two other exhibits that would have been of note to Joyce, Italy due to his residence in Trieste and so briefly Rome, and the Congo due to his allusions to the Congo and Casement in *Ulysses* and *Finnegans Wake*:

> Italy.—Replica of the Basilica of Septimius Severus at Tripoli; also the Seven Towers of Rhodes. Architecturally speaking, these are among the outstanding features of the exhibition.
> Belgium.—A Congo palace, seemingly transplanted from the banks of the great African river. The exhibits reveal the development of art, industry, commerce and agriculture in the Belgian Congo.
> (155)

The descriptions from the *Cook's Traveller's Handbook to Paris* about the exposition would have been widely available to anyone, like Joyce, who resided in London in 1931.

During the fall of 1931, due to the popularity and scandal of the exposition, a large number of ethnographic films were shown in Paris. In a letter dated, December 7, 1931, Joyce writes to Harriet Shaw Weaver, "This is my son's wedding anniversary so I went out with Colum and Lee to see L'Afrique vous parle. I think I have done a good job for Lucia's. She has made initial letters for all the poems in P.P." ("Letter to Harriet Shaw Weaver"). Joyce's statement that they went to see "L'Afrique vous parle" in 1931 on his son's wedding anniversary is a conspicuous moment of Joyce encountering the primitive construction of Africa in Paris. The film that Joyce casually references is a documentary produced by Paul Hoefler and Walter Futter, which was shown in Paris that autumn and subsequently critiqued for its ethnographic depictions of Africans. Joyce was well into his writing of *Finnegans Wake* in 1931.[10] The film provides a striking lens into the primitive sublime encounter of the African other and the quest for cultural origins that remains an important aspect into African nexus of allusions that seem so present within the imaged past of the *Wake*. There are several salient elements about the film (and its associated book that was produced and marketed in the same year) that have suggestive links with the *Wake*. While the actual journey moved from east to west in the safari adventure, in the film (for dramatic purposes), the order of the journey was reversed geographically; the film's party instead moves from west to east. This inverse of expectation seems to be the creative decision that Joyce might approve given the circularity and transposal of the *Wake's* narrative structures. Yet, the geographic and cultural drama that is so apparent in the film that provides a climax for the journey is a troubling, graphic scene of a lion eating a Masai warrior guide.[11] The remainder of the film is filled with troubling depictions of Africans.

The book, released in conjunction with the film and written by the supposed "documentarians," includes equally racist representations; one passage reads, "Africa is a vast stage upon which savage men and millions of wild animals daily perform their allotted parts, and lucky indeed is the civilized man whom circumstances permit to visit this alluringly beautiful but primitive country" (137). The primitive encounter is described in terms of the typical relational dichotomy that operates in the modern period (the civilized, white, Western, and modern contrasted with the savage, Black, Other, and primitive). While there are moments of shock for the man who was eaten by the lion, the Masai are commonly depicted simply as others. For example, Hoefler and Futter write, "The Masai have no music of their own, but, like the people of all savage tribes, they go wild over American jazz. We had a great deal of fun with our phonograph. They could not understand where the sound was coming from and would gaze all about, looking for it. When we asked them what they thought made it talk, their reply was that we had cut off somebody's head and placed it in the box" (149). These warriors are depicted as ignorant fools and savages at once. They become mere objects of amusement, figurines on a playset, for these travelers.

Critically for Joyce's primitive sublime, at one point on the journey in the film, the group passes through the Congo. The descriptions of the Belgian Congo surely interest an Irishman like Joyce who used Roger Casement to great effect in the "Cyclops" episode of *Ulysses*. Hoefler and Futter describe their responses: "This was the Belgian Congo!.... the black men doing everything from piloting the boat to stoking the furnace. The white captain simply supervises and commands" Hoefler 307). The depiction of the Congo in the film is one entirely of colonial subjection. Hoefler continues his dominating narrative spectacle as he says, "considering that these Negroes are only a few years removed from raw savages who know nothing of boats except how to row a dugout, it speaks well of their adaptability and lends encouragement to our belief in their ultimate progress" (Hoefler 307). Joyce's depictions of the Congo, however, in both *Ulysses* and *Finnegans Wake* do not suggest the superiority of Europeans but rather that largely the Europeans are the corrupt and immoral practitioners of colonialism. Joyce makes an exception, however, within this structure of global power, for the Irish in general and Roger Casement in particular.

## James Joyce and the Primitive Sublime 59

The Congo is inherently linked with Roger Casement, who remains a specter both for Joyce and for Ireland. Roger Casement is for us a minor figure, yet for Joyce, he is a player on a stage worthy of comment in not one but two of his novels. Casement becomes famous during his lifetime for the report that exposed the Belgian atrocities and European depravity in the Congo. He would go on to become knighted and thus become Sir Roger Casement for these efforts. Hoefler and Futter depict the Congo and its inhabitants as primitive others whose "progress" can be hoped for and toward which they might make certain strides. Roger Casement appears overtly only once in the *Wake* during an account of history, four historians, four evangelists ("mamalujo," as Joyce terms them) are twisted and snarled in a mockery of progressive linear history that explodes of any easy notions of historical and literary inheritance. Yet in this chapter Joyce ponders, "how our seaborn isle came into exestuance" (*FW* 387.12) and continues a few lines later, "the blank prints, now extinct, after the wreak of Wormans' Noe, the barmaisigheds, when my heart knew no care, and after that then there was the official landing of Lady Jales Casemate, in the year of the flood 1132 S.O.S." (*FW* 387.20-23). Casement is no longer viewed only in the context of his Congo Report or Reform Movement, but he is immortalized and questioned at once for his "official landing" as an "official" of the British Foreign Office, landing with arms in advance of Easter 1916, *and* a call for help in the context of an island nation overtaken by water, a flood, sending out a signal of distress. His gender and title have been switched, in a disquieting conflation of sexuality and gender, perhaps in recognition of the whispering campaign undertaken against him for his homosexuality and the Black Diaries, as a means through which to forestall any likely defense or groundswell of public opinion. What remains salient, however, is his very presence within a section detailing world history.

Casement subtlety persists in *Finnegans Wake*: the reader finds him again within two paragraphs that draw associations with Africa, including in a likely reference to the film, *Africa Speaks*, a lion eating a man. This brutality and violence highlight Joyce's evocations of the primitive sublime. These references appear in a section in Book 3, in pages "laid out as a gigantic crescendo, which culminates in the heartrending release of the historical anguish of Ireland" (Epstein 193). Here, the cosmos is associated with sexual desire, which, along with punning, runs throughout the passages. The paragraph begins with an invocation of "Apep and Uachet" (*FW* 494.15), the male and female Egyptian snake gods. Sexual and gender identities are merged in the encounters that follow. Casement appears in an allusion to "Strombolo," which recalls the Bolobo, the port on the river in the Congo from where Casement begins his journeys. In an allusion that seems to indicate Casement's sexuality that would have been more generally known after his execution in 1916, to "I will confess

60  *James Joyce and the Primitive Sublime*

to his sins and blush me further. I would misdemean to rebuke to the libels of snots from the fleshambles the canalles. Synamite is too good for them" (*FW* 494.29-33), references the "sins" of Casement, the depiction of his sexual activities, and the "cannibals" for whom Casement's actions are "too good." Joyce's wordplay on "misdemean" and "libel" are suggestive of the anti-Casement whispering campaign British authorities undertook after his capture and the discovery of the so-called Black Diaries. Amid the Casement references to the Congo and the controversy over his sexuality, Joyce places a brief reference to African lions and eating. "Creeping through the liongraass... camouflaged as blancmange and maple syrop? Obeisance so their sitinins ins the follicity of the Orp. Her sheik to Slave..." (*FW* 494.19-23). The lion creeps through the grass to eat the white man, "blancmange," associated with the tasty North American maple "syrop," but it is the African—through folly and obedience, moving from a position of prominence, a Sheik, to one of servitude, a Slave—who is slaughtered and eaten. This reference is further supported by the "slanger," or serpent, representing the initially invoked African gods. While Joyce's vision of Casement in his fiction makes clear an anticolonial sentiment for both men. Casement writes in a letter from July 18, 1903 from Bolobo, Upper Congo to Harry Farnell, of the British Foreign Office. Casement remembers the era when he knew Conrad in the Congo and when the numbers of native inhabitants was in the several thousands, all evident from his journey into the Congo and the upper reaches of the river in 1887. He laments the vanishing of the inhabitants from the river and the land just as he clearly associates in equal terms being native and indigenous in the Congo with being fully human in this letter (Casement, Letter to Harry Farnell). Casement provides clear evidence for the brutality of the Belgians and the demands of the Belgian government to bring in human beings for punishment should the rubber quotas not be met (Casement, Letter to Harry Farnell).

At the time of this Congo controversy, Joyce was residing in Trieste. The Belgians had attempted to compel Italian military officers to serve in the Congo; however, the Italians, once aware of the brutality and exploitation, refused. "Many reports of the Italian officers employed in the Congo army were published by the Italian papers in 1905," writes Edmund Dead Morel," covering their experiences chiefly in the Eastern district. Summing up these reports the *Corriere della Sera* [a paper for which Joyce occasionally wrote] says: 'Slavery nominally established is rampant, cannibalism exists, and the sole desire of the native is to flee from the white man" (65). Decades after the Congo Report and its attendant human rights campaign, the primitive darkness, then, for Joyce and his heroes, unlike Conrad's Marlow, lies not at a remove from Europe within Africa, African peoples, a European man in Africa, or even in Ireland herself. The passages in the *Wake* that detail Africa and the Congo, Casement and man-eating lions, are in fact in a section that is more overtly about Irish history. The threat or the representation of Africa for Joyce and for Ireland are distinctly related to fears of what Van Boheeman-Saaf termed, "indistinction" in her *Trauma and History* work. The encounter with the other ultimately reveals troubling aspects of the self. Anxieties over indistinction within multiple systems of the global empires ensure a troubling relation between the Joyce's vision and depiction of primitives both at home and abroad. These troubling encounters, however, also uniquely provoke Joyce's primitive sublime.

What emerges consistently within the larger narrative structures in the *Wake* is a very peculiar indistinction of character formation. The self and the other, the father and the son, the mother and the daughter, the brother and sister become avatars of one another in a fluid matrix of identity formation. The fear of the other is most overt in the *Wake* when it becomes the fear of the self. What horrifies and delights, what voyeuristic pleasures and profoundly disturbing incestuous desires reimagine is the shape of and the very *possibility* of narrative. The worlds that Joyce creates in the circular structures of his Viconian cycles of history ultimately suggest that the other is much like the self, to a notoriously incestuous and thereby uncomfortable degree. The appearance of Roger Casement, and Joyce's use of his Congo Report, Black Diaries, landing, and ultimate sacrifice, clearly rely upon Casement's acknowledgement of the similarity in colonial oppressions between the Irish and the African. Joyce's seeming play upon colonial expositions, and, I suggest, even a particular exposition of 1931, the associated film *L'Afrique vous parle* (*Africa Speaks*), and its footage of a lion eating a man, joins the terror of death with the delight of a film viewing. The horror of the display of peoples and cultures as museum objects seems quietly reflected with the delight of watching the watchers watch back. As Joyce writes, "you would sublimate your blepharospasmockical suppressions, it seems" (*FW* 16.17) in a recognition of the need to suppress the desires that so disturb you. As he finally admits, "Sublime was the warning" (*FW* 517.10).[12]

The sublimity of *Finnegans Wake* emerges in its contradictions of identity. The tensions between character, self, and nation are not ignored but reveled in—the slippage of identity and of individual character formation in the *Wake* is a mechanism for engaging the Irish "fear of indistinction." As Verstraete notes in her *Fragments of the Feminine Sublime*, "the sublime as a presentation of a conflict beyond comprehension. *Finnegans Wake* pursues this to the very end" (22). This conflict of "indistinction" within the colonial Empire makes the Irish encounter with fellow colonial subjectivity unique in European modernism. According to Lyotard in *The Inhuman*,

> Burke wrote that for ... terror to mingle with pleasure and with it to produce the feeling of the sublime, it is also necessary that the terror-causing threat be suspended, kept a bay, held back. This suspense, this lessening of a threat or a danger, provokes a kind of pleasure that is certainly not that of a positive satisfaction, but is, rather, that of relief. This is still a privation, but it is privation at one remove; the soul is deprived of the threat of being deprived of light, language, life. Burke distinguishes this pleasure of secondary privation from positive pleasures, and he baptizes it with the name delight.
>
> (99)

Joyce does not remove "others" from his art; rather, he brings them forward to reveal the uncomfortable intersection and commonality between colonial subjectivities. In *Finnegans Wake*, in "Africa Speaks", and in the Paris Colonial Exposition, the depictions of the raw, material brutality and historic violence, the blood of the colonized is sacrificed to serve, to be eaten not by a cannibalistic tribe or the other, but the Irish self.

## Notes

1 For a full discussion of Joyce's early primitivist rhetorics see my article, "Primitive Emancipation: Religion, Sexuality, and Freedom in Joyce's *A Portrait of the Artist as a Young Man* and *Ulysses*." I thank Palgrave for allowing me to reprint a portion of this article in this chapter.
2 See Richard Ellmann and Ellsworth Mason's *The Critical Writings of James Joyce* for a reproduction of "Irelands, Island of Saints and Sages."
3 Casement's sexuality as a gay man places him outside of the official heteronormative culture in early twentieth-century Ireland and Britain, though this aspect of his being was not widely known until the 1916 Rising. When he was captured (having been given up by his Norwegian sailor lover when Casement attempted to bring arms into Ireland to support the Rising), his diaries, the so-called Black Diaries, were discovered. The British used their contents against him in a whisper campaign to avoid having his death sentence commuted (Casement was the last Knight of the Realm to be put to death). While scholars continue to debate the meaning of the diaries, it seems clear that they record sexual encounters. The British Government asserted in their campaign against him that the numbers recorded indicated the ages of his partners, making him into a child molester, a common homophobic slur that unfortunately endures into our present day. I suggest, however, that these numbers do not indicates ages, but rather the size of the endowments of his sexual partners. For a further information on Casement, his human rights endeavors, and his sexuality, see Lucy McDiarmid's *The Irish Art of Controversy* and "Casement, New York, and the Easter Rising."
4 Alice Stopford Green's work was condemned by the scholarly establishment but it is now increasingly seen as a useful intervention in advance of Ireland's

## James Joyce and the Primitive Sublime    63

emerging national identity and independent nation state. For further information, see Angus Mitchell's "Historical revisit: Mythistory and the making of Ireland: Alice Stopford Green's undoing."

5  See for example, Margot Norris's *Joyce's Web: the Social Unraveling of Modernism* and Joe Valente's "James Joyce and the Cosmopolitan Sublime."

6  Joyce famously claimed to have begun this *Work in Progress* in 1922, but genetic scholars have provided clear evidence to determine that he did not begin writing the book until 1923. See Crispi and Slote, *How Joyce Wrote Finnegans Wake*.

7  According to Verstraete, "Schlegel's aesthetics of the fragment has claimed our attention because it reformulates the Kantian sublime–as the presentation of the ideas of (moral) reason in the defeat of the imagination – in art historical terms, that is, as the presentation of the history of beauty in which artistic representation shows itself as itself... The sublime as the ongoing (re)production of beauty, and of the idea of beauty, opens up the truth about art, unmasks it so to speak." (215).

8  In articulating this principle, Joyce focuses on a terrible kernel of exaltation and debasement that had been ignored previously, exposing the root of future literary vision. The sublimity of this degradation will be expressed more fully through Morrison, who is more drastically afflicted and empowered by it.

9  As Verstraete explains of "Oxen in the Sun," "I have called the 'feminine sublime' as the counterdiscourse to man's self-empowering cultural narrative. Central to this discussion is again the plight of a maternal figure: Mina Purefoy's delayed pregnancy. Man's consciousness of superiority over nature now takes the form of a far-reaching subjugation of the female pregnant body to science (medicine) and technology. Horne's maternity hospital is the site of a fierce struggle for power between the male fetus and the child-bearing mother, but is so between the male doctors (students) and female midwives. If the traditional sublimes about the violent but self-assuring linkage between the world and the self, the outside and the inside, then this chapter is about a mother's liminal experience of having to expel a content that she does not control. The sublime 'influx of power' she is allowed to feel is that of man's technology invading her womb in order to secure his own origins" (21).

10  Anna Livia represents the river Liffey, but she is also described in Joyce' wordplay, as Sheldon Brivic has noted, as an African Queen. See his "Toni Morrison's Funk in *Finnegans Wake*."

11  All available copies that I have been able to track down both in the US and Europe (I consulted numerous archives in France specializing in film), none of the copies have the original run time with this scene included.

12  It is such a warning of the threat of the primitive Congo—and, in fact, for multiple forms of African primitives in Joyce's *Wake*—for Europe that seems strangely apparent in a map included in Morel's 1906 *Red Rubber* volume as a part of the Front Matter. While restrictions on images do not allow me to reproduce the image here, you can find it online at Project Guttenberg and other venues. The map is of Europe but "with a proportionate area covered by the Congo River and its affluents" that covers the landscape in red. The blood of the Congo and European savagery therein reimagines the cartography of Europe. The fear of indistinction within the modern primitivist rhetorics become actualized as a new imagined geography that adheres the blood of red rubber not to Africa alone, but also to Europe. The boundaries and waterways of each location are obscured and somehow newly revealed at once. The

position of Ireland, though, is notably not touched by the rivers of blood; it is the mainland, or continental Europe, that is truly corrupted by the Belgian Rubber trade and its attendant atrocities. In perhaps a movement of contagion and empire in the modern era and the chaos of the coming disintegration of empire with the World Wars, the blood remains an offshore threat for Ireland and safely away from brethren. Yet, in an ominous vision, the blood of the red rubber has begun to surge, just north of Conrad's ancient Thames, into the present geography of Britain proper. Here, he warns us not of the other, but of ourselves. We therefore encounter the primitive sublime when we recognize the indistinction between the Irish colonized and the African other, not on display for our visual pleasure but mirrored back in our own intimate reflections.

## References

Hoefler, Paul Louis. *Africa Speaks*. Mascot Pictures, 1930.

Bate, David. *Photography and Surrealism: Sexuality, Colonialism, and Social Dissent*. I. B. Taurus, 2009.

Bennett, Tony. "The Exhibitionary Complex." *New Formations*, vol. 4, 1988, pp. 73–102.

Brivic, Sheldon. *Joyce's Waking Women: an Introduction to* Finnegans Wake. U of Wisconsin P, 1995.

———.. "Toni Morrison's Funk at *Finnegans Wake*." *Joyce Studies Annual*, vol. 9, 1998, pp. 158–73, https://doi.org/10.5555/jsa.1998.9.158.

Casement, Roger. Letter to Alice Stopford Green. 14 Sept. 1914. Alice Stopford Green Papers. MS 10,464/10/2. National Library of Ireland, Dublin, Ireland.

———. Letter to Harry Farnell. 18 July, 1903. Roger Casement Papers. MS 13,080/6i/6. National Library of Ireland, Dublin, Ireland.

Cheng, Vincent J. "The General and the Sepoy: Imperialism and Power in the Museyroom." *Critical Essays on James Joyce's Finnegan's Wake*, edited by Patrick A. McCarthy and G. K. Hall, 1992, pp. 258–69.

D'Alesandro, Stephanie, and Matthew Cole. "The World in the Time of the Surrealists." *Surrealism Beyond Borders*. Metropolitan Museum of Art, 2021, pp.8–42.

Dunn, Kevin C. *Imagining the Congo: The International Relations of Identity*. Palgrave, 2003.

Eagleton, Terry. *The Ideology of the Aesthetic*. Blackwell Publishers, 1991.

Elston, Roy. *Cook Traveler's Handbook to Paris*. Simpkin, Marshall & Company, 1931.

Ellman, Richard. *James Joyce*. Oxford UP, 1983.

Epstein, Edmund Lloyd. *A Guide Through Finnegans Wake*. UP of Florida, 2009.

Exposition Coloniale Internationale et des Pays d'Outre-Mer, Paris 1931: Rapport general presente par le Gouverneur General Olivier (Imprimerie Nationale: Paris, 1933), vol. 6, pt. 1. "Metropolitaine."

Garrigan Mattar, Sinéad. *Primitivism, Science, and the Irish Revival*. Oxford UP, 2004. https://doi.org/10.1093/acprof:oso/9780199268955.001.0001.

Herring, Phillip F., editor. *Joyce's* Ulysses *Notesheets in the British Museum*. U of Virginia P, 1972.

Hoefler, Paul Louis. *Africa Speaks; a Story of Adventure, the Chronicles of the First Trans-African Journey by Motor Truck from Mombasa on the Indian Ocean to Lagos on the Atlantic, through Central Equatorial Africa*. John C. Winston Company, 1931.

Joyce, James. *The Critical Writings of James Joyce*, edited by Ellsworth Mason and Richard Ellmann, Viking, 1959.

———. *Dubliners*. Modern Library, 1969.

———. *Finnegans Wake*. Penguin Classics, 1999.

———. "Ireland, Island of Saints and Sages." *The Critical Writings of James Joyce*, edited by Mason, Ellsworth, and Richard Ellmann, Viking, 1959, pp. 154–74.

———. Letter to Harriet Shaw Weaver. 7 Dec. 1931. Ms Add 57350 Page 173, The British Library, London, UK.

———. *A Portrait of the Artist as a Young Man*. Viking Penguin, 1964.

———. *Ulysses: The Corrected Text*, edited by Hans Walter Gabler with Wolfhard Steppe and Claus Melchior, Random, 1986.

Lyotard, Jean-François. *The Inhuman: Reflections on Time*. Translated by Geoffrey Bennington and Rachel Bowlby, Stanford UP, 1988.

McDiarmid, Lucy. "Casement, New York, and the Easter Rising." *Ireland's Allies: America and the 1916 Easter Rising*, edited by Miriam Nyhan and Marion Casey, U College Dublin P, 2016, pp. 90–107.

———. *The Irish Art of Controversy*. Cornell UP, 2005.

McGarrity, Maria. "Primitive Emancipation: Religion, Sexuality, and Freedom in Joyce's *A Portrait of the Artist as a Young Man* and *Ulysses*." *Irish Modernism and the Global Primitive*, edited by Maria McGarrity and Claire A. Culleton, Palgrave, 2009, pp. 133–49. https://doi.org/10.1057/9780230617193_8. www.jstor.org/stable/25476083.

Mitchell, Angus. "Historical Revisit: Mythistory and the Making of Ireland: Alice Stopford Green's Undoing." *Irish Historical Studies*, vol. 44, no. 166, 2020, pp. 349–73, https://doi.org/10.1017/ihs.2020.40.

Morel, E. D. *Red Rubber: The Story of the Rubber Slave Trade Flourishing on the Congo in the Year of Grace 1906*. T. Fisher Unwin, 1906.

Norris, Margot. *Joyce's Web: the Social Unraveling of Modernism*. U of Texas P, 1992.

Raines, Stephanie. *Commodity Culture and Social Class in Dublin 1850-1916*. Irish Academic P, 2010.

Rabaté, Jean Michel. "The Fourfold Root of Yawn's Unreason: Chapter III.3." *How Joyce Wrote* Finnegans Wake: *A Chapter-by-Chapter Genetic Guide*, edited by Sam Slote and Luca Crispi, U of Wisconsin P, 2007, pp. 384–409.

Síocháin, Séamus Ó., Michael O'Sullivan, editors. *The Eyes of Another Race: Roger Casement's Congo Report and 1903 Diary*. U College Dublin P, 2003.

Slote, Sam, and Luca Crispi, editors. *How Joyce Wrote* Finnegans Wake: *A Chapter-by-Chapter Genetic Guide*. U of Wisconsin P, 2007.

Spurr, David. "Writing in the 'Wake' of Empire." *MLN*, vol. 111, no. 5, 1996, pp. 872–888.

St. Peters Lancia, Kathleen. "The Ethnographic Roots of Joyce's Modernism: Exhibiting Ireland's Primitives in the National Museum and 'Nestor' Episode." *Irish Modernism and the Global Primitive*, edited by Maria McGarrity and Claire A. Culleton, Palgrave, 2009, pp. 63–78.

Valente, Joseph. "James Joyce and the Cosmopolitan Sublime." *Joyce and the Subject of History*, edited by Mark A. Wollaeger, Victor Luftig, and Robert Spoo, U of Michigan P, 1996, pp. 59–82.

van Boheemen-Saaf, Christine. *Joyce, Derrida, Lacan, and the Trauma of History: Reading, Narrative, and Postcolonialism*. Cambridge UP, 1999.

Verstraete, Ginette. *Fragments of the Feminine Sublime: In Friedrich Schlegel and James Joyce*. State U of New York P, 1998.

## 4 Mid-century Malaise and Desublimation in Samuel Beckett, Flann O'Brien, Kate O'Brien, and Edna O'Brien

Mid-century representations of Ireland's desublimation reflect the disappointments of independence. Joyce's exile on the continent and the publication of *Finnegans Wake* in 1939 in some ways operates as a late marker of the primitive sublime in the early twentieth century. As we saw in the first two chapters, the primitive sublime manifests in both the Celtic Revival period and the works of James Joyce, yet the categorization of the primitive and the sublime is always contingent and remains in flux even as their deployment evinces a critical lens into the catalyzed eruption of their intersection. The period in question in this chapter, the late 1930s to the early 1960s, becomes complicated internationally due to the Second World War and its aftermath; as we will see, the mid-century period sees a profound decline, even a disappearance, of manifestations of the primitive sublime.

Ireland turns away from the cultural nationalism and the frameworks that privilege Irish indigeneity and primitivisms of the Revival during this period. For most Irish writers starting in the late 1930s, Ireland's disappointments of independence and the growing conservatism at home led not to flights of transcendence but to a troubling immanence of cultural provincialism. The desublimation at the core of the Ireland's tenuous cultural position from the late 1930s to the early 1960s emerges through intersecting tropes of the departure from (often to London), entrapment within, and return to Ireland evident through the lens of gender and the enduring anxiety of global others abroad. Ireland's prehistory and folklore are repeatedly questioned and sometimes mocked outright. For example, Samuel Beckett's *Murphy* finds his hero trapped in a labyrinth and seeking his final, ashen escape through being flushed down the toilet at the Abbey theater. In Flann O'Brien's little-known play, *Faustus Kelley*, the hero sells his soul not to save a starving peasantry as in *The Countess Cathleen*, but rather for a seat in the Dáil (the Irish parliament). In O'Brien's novel, *At Swim-Two-Birds*, interwoven circularity relies upon multiple layers of fractured consciousness and history mediated through an overt mockery of the Revival. In *Pray for the Wanderer*, Kate O'Brien shows how a return

DOI: 10.4324/9781003297390-4

to Ireland for any artist reveals the state to be an agent of oppression. Finally, Edna O'Brien's *Country Girls Trilogy* finds that for women, Ireland's emancipation from colonial rule leads only to their oppression. The engagement with globalized others becomes a reflection not merely of a "fear of indistinction" (Van Boheemen-Saaf 139) but in fact suggests a fear of the capacity for the "other" to become a part of an Irish "self." Ireland, after independence and the Second World War, became a nation of suppression.

During the mid-century period, Irish identity was in a process of dynamic renegotiation for both writers and the society at large. As Kelly Matthews explains, the "era has been widely viewed as a time of introversion and introspection in Ireland. Taoiseach Éamon de Valera had officially declared neutrality in 1939, cutting Ireland off from the war in Europe and the country was still experiencing a wave of postrevolutionary conservatism that affected many aspects of its literary and cultural life" (106). The writers of the era therefore strove to engage with the multiplicity of perspectives and the recalibration of social norms (Matthews 124). Matthews continues on to note that one literary magazine, "The Bell [,] ... attempted to document Irish life *without* idealizing its *traditional* or *primitive* elements" [emphasis added] (109). How, then, does the Countess Cathleen—Yeats's Revivalist heroine in her eponymous play of an aristocrat willing to sell her soul to feed starving peasantry—become in Flann O'Brien's *Faustus Kelly* a character who sells eternal salvation for craven political self-interest and a seat in the Dáil? The depiction of this transition engages Ireland's writers, providing them with a scathing opportunity for political and social commentary. Ireland in the post-war period, as Claire Wills has found in her *The Best Are Leaving*, is a nation that was formed and fractured. In doing so, from the Rising of 1916 to the Free State, the radicals too often became conventionalists. Within frameworks of a national government that moved far from the idealization of the peasantry to a post-war reality of "independence" that rejects primitive elements of Irish culture and desublimates them in a gesture that, amid earlier fears of indistinction, brings entanglements within the global British empire home to ensnare the Irish. The four writers examined in this chapter, Samuel Beckett, Flann O'Brien, Kate O'Brien, and Edna O'Brien, capture the malaise of the period particularly well, while also engaging in a questioning mockery of Revivalist and Joycean literary precedents as they negotiate the contemporary uncertainties of Irish life.

Perhaps no other writer captures the rejection of the sublime and its mid-century mocking of the Revival as Samuel Beckett's in his *Murphy*. Published in 1937, *Murphy*, epitomizes the mid-century movement against the primitive sublime. The text symbolizes a labyrinth through the imagery of enclosed spaces and self-contained worlds, the construction of interdependent relationships between the characters as well as the semiotics of chess game, the kite episodes, and most importantly, the sewer funeral. The trap of the labyrinth represents an inverse of the sublime to suggest degradation. This degradation manifests in profound, comic moments that, taking place in the toilet, link the epitome of the Celtic primitivism with the horror of urine and excrement. Even Murphy's name indicates a degree of denigration. Patrick Rafroidi sums up many critics when he notes that the "'Murphy,' patronyme si courant en Irlande qu'il devient, sinon 'Everyman' au moins 'Every Irishman' mais est aussi 'morphé' et 'mort-fou'" [Murphy, a common surname in Ireland that signifies the everyman and at least every Irishman but also suggests change and mad death] (75). Rafroidi extends the common everyman interpretation to include the protean-like morphé and the comically dead fool. Beckett locates his character in a city, London, and portrays other characters confusedly tracking Murphy throughout the city-as-labyrinth, though this attempt is ultimately futile. Caws notes that "because the design of the labyrinth simultaneously represents a puzzle and a solution, a journey and an arrival, it embodies the way in which urban texts can be seen as both maps and routes, as descriptions and projects, portraits of streets and guides within them" (38). Caws suggests that modern literary labyrinths contain within them an escape, a final solution that leads to the exterior. Beckett's maze, however, shows the reader no guide to the exterior; Beckett's portrait of his literary labyrinth paints no escape. While the first paragraph establishes the labyrinth motif for the entire novel, one critic explains that for Beckett, "freedom exists in the unseen of one's dark zones, i.e., in one's inner life; for in one's outer life, one is incarcerated. There not only is one's habitation a prison…but one's job is likewise an enslavement" (Steinberg 100). S. C. Steinberg also notes that Murphy's "first room is a 'cage' and a 'mew,' his second 'between Pentonville Prison and Metropolitan Cattle Market,' his third a 'trap'" (100). Beckett's second sentence introduces the idea of confinement and illusory freedom:

> Murphy sat out of it, as though he were free, in a mew in West Brompton. Here for what might have been six months he had eaten, drunk, slept, and put his clothes on and off, in a medium-sized cage of north-western aspect commanding an unbroken view of medium-sized cages of south-eastern aspect. Soon he would have to make other arrangements, for the mew had been condemned.
> (1)

Beckett begins his novel by describing his protagonist's daily routine and condition of life in which the tedium involved in the prosaic details of modern existence highlights the conditions of banality. Beckett calls the living quarts both a mew and a cage: places that represent seclusion, concealment, and confinement. Beckett's protagonist, trapped within the symbolic spaces in the second sentence, might move about throughout the novel, but he remains enclosed, bounded within a defined space.

Exploring desublimation in Beckett remains uncommon perhaps because of Beckett's desire to write "sans style" in his later work (Bair 21). The markers that indicate place and context (markers that, most obviously, indicate the use of labyrinth in literature) diminish in his work throughout his career. Murphy's view of this self-created and imposed prison becomes evident in his description of the cells in the MMM, which "surpass by far all he had even been able to imagine in the way of indoor bowers of bliss" (181). Here, Murphy finds that the cells exceed his expectations for the comforts of confinement. Though in his essay, "Dante… Bruno…Vico… Joyce," Beckett noted that "the danger is in the neatness of identification" (5), Murphy finds that the cells "lent colour to the truth, that one was a prisoner of air" (181). Beckett's prison, his labyrinth, ultimately may be constructed with nothing other than his psyche that envisions life as the final trap.

The peculiar request that Murphy leaves for his remains is certainly unique in literature, but it also indicates his desire to move from one labyrinth (the world, the MMM, London, etc.) to another: the labyrinth of sewer pipelines that run beneath Dublin. To this end, Murphy writes "with regard to the disposal of these my body, mind and soul, I desire that they be burnt and placed in a paper bag and brought to the Abbey Theatre… on the right as one goes down into the pit, and I desire that the chain be there pulled upon them, if possible during the performance of a piece" (269). Murphy wants to escape the land upon which he has walked, the labyrinth whose passageways he knows well, but he does not want to escape it to move to a transcendent, romantic, otherworldly realm, perhaps a seductive reading for any critic who seeks some consolation in Murphy's last wishes. Beckett, however, leaves his readers and his critics unconsoled. There is no sublime or transcendence for Murphy, who wants to become ash and explore the subterranean world beneath Dublin. He wants, in short, to be flushed down a toilet; to be spread throughout the literal underworld, the sewer. He winds up being "swept away with the sand, the beer, the butts, the glass, the matches, the spits, the vomit" (275). (This comic end apparently so amused James Joyce that he memorized these lines). This humorous finale provides Murphy not with his desired end of the Dublin sewer system but instead into a network of blind streets and alleys, a grid system to organize pedestrian movement that becomes itself symbolic of a labyrinth.

Beckett's final mockery of the novel is perhaps his stress that this act, the flushing down of the toilet of his hero/antihero, takes place not only at the Abbey, the theater founded to celebrate Ireland's indigenous culture and history, but, critically, during a performance meant to celebrate Irish identity. Beckett's flush is not only for Murphy's ashes, but for the clichéd depictions of the peasantry so associated with the performances of Irish identity of the primitive sublime at the theater. Beckett's flush that potentially sends the remains of his protagonist down the toilet simultaneously endeavors to send Revivalist conventions swirling down into the Dublin sewer system along with him.

If Beckett's mid-century desublimation uses the toilet at the Abbey theater as a final escape from his protagonist's entrapment in a labyrinth, Brian O'Nolan's desublimation relies upon the unstable narratives of novelistic mockery in his *At Swim-Two-Birds*. O'Nolan—or Flann O'Brien, the pen name he adopted for the publication of the novel of his most prominent in this chapter—creates narratives that undercut any conventional understanding of a stable reality. The novel, *At Swim-Two-Birds*, specifically, overtly "lampoons... mythologies of the Irish Revival" (McDonald 135). And in his *Faustus Kelley*, O'Nolan crafts a specific response to an Abbey production, *The Countess Cathleen,* that undercuts the idealization of Irish identity depicted in the early production of Ireland's national theater.

The salient issue for O'Nolan is the disappointment with the Irish state at large and the disenchantment of quotidian banalities of home life. This weary regret manifests throughout O'Nolan's writing despite, or perhaps because of, his concern with the material realities of Irish life after the establishment of the Free State and the ensuing Constitution. The focus on domestic realities in Ireland manifests in his *At Swim* in its anxious lodging and family arrangements mired in a revision of the Sweeny tale. In the novel, Conor Dowling writes, "Sweeny's recasting is not represented as a movement towards freedom, or a release into a sudden state of freedom." He continues: "It is a 'descent' from the 'genuine artistic expression' of *Buile Suibhne* recitals down into a 'narrative peopled by shames, imposters, plagiarizers and thieves. Sweeny, then, is not stripped of authority but loses any definite identity, as he is subsumed into the institutions of state" (Dowling 56). Sweeny, in *At Swim*, becomes a mockery of his ideal form at the same time that he becomes an encapsulation of the challenges within Irish culture and society. He becomes a figure lost amid the disappointing turns of the Irish government.

O'Nolan's most significant narrative focus in *At-Swim-Two-Birds* is the madness of Sweeny, a hero from myth who will be taken up later in the twentieth century by Seamus Heaney in his *Sweeney Astray*.[1] He is a mad king who believes he is a bird due to an imprecation cast against him. As Anne Clissmann explains,

> The version of *Buile Suibhne* as given by O'Brien in *At Swim* is very nearly a literal translation of the original Middle Irish romance. In

certain places, however, he departs from the original and gives a variant version which is usually chosen because it draws a parallel between Sweeny and Stephen, or rather between Sweeny as bird-man and Stephen as Icarus failing to his death… All the images of flight and falling in the Sweeny tale correspond with those implied by the Icarus-Daedalus theme in *A Portrait*. Stephen, in fleeing the 'nets' that are thrown to hold him down, is associated with Icarus fleeing the labyrinth. Sweeny too takes flight after a battle with the Church and has to strive to escape nets.

(112)

O'Nolan is responding not only to the medieval Irish tale of Sweeny, but is also engaging with the images of transcendent flight that Joyce himself relies upon as he gestures towards the primitive sublime at the end of *Portrait*.

The destabilization of any central reality in the novel seems to emerge from the conflicts at hand in the 1930s, when O'Nolan was writing. As Conor Dowling notes, the novel "is often framed as a carnivalesque rebellion against the attempt… to establish cultural and social norms for the Free State… just as de Valera's 1937 Constitution, despite formal repealing the Free State, entrench rather than rejected these norms" (49). O'Nolan's work undercuts any facile acceptance of the role of narrative and the nation. His narrative becomes a venue to mock the State and a means through which to satirize the received tropes and sacred images of the Revival. Clissmann notes, "the narrator's choice of language…His parodic and fantastic turn of mind, his awareness of the relativity of reality, make him an unconscious satirist, intensely aware of the lunacies of many aspects of Irish life and literature, in particular of the inordinate claims of the Irish literary renaissance" (88–89). The mockery of Irish Literature and particularly the vaunted past that so enraptured audiences and writers of the Celtic Revival is a particular specialty of O'Nolan.[2] His *At-Swim-Two-Birds* is a send-up of all things serious about the imaginative recuperation of lost Irish folk and literary lore. He mocks the Irish penchant for conversation and its associations with water, "A satisfying ululation is the contending of a river with the sea. Good to hear is the chirping of little red-breasted men in bare winter and distant hounds giving tongue in the secrecy of fog" (7). In this late 1930s text, the send-up of self-importance, the poor, florid writing is the point. The sacred tropes of Irish literature, from the sea to land, from sound to speech, are all put forth to amuse and undercut the seriousness of the endeavors of the writers of the Celtic Revival.

## Mid-century Malaise and Desublimation 73

The figure of mad Sweeny is especially ripe for ridicule in O'Nolan's novel. The figure of Sweeny even serves to mock the Revivalists use of bird imagery in their depictions of the primitive sublime. O'Nolan writes,

> Who could put a terrible madness on the head of Sweeny for the slaughter of a single Lent-gaunt cleric, to make him live in tree-tops and roost in the middle of a yew, not a wattle to the shielding of his mad head in the middle of the wet winter, perished to the marrow without company of women or strains of harp-pluck, with no feeding but stag food and the green branches? Who but a story-teller? Indeed, it is true that there has been ill-usage to the men of Erin from the book-poets of the world…
>
> (13)

The treatment of the tale of Sweeny is mocking both the ancient lore of the tale but also the contemporary effort to write about it. As O'Nolan drolly notes, "the upshot is that your man becomes a bloody bird" (88). The earnest elements of the Revival, and particularly those avian images that evoke transcendence, are reduced to a cursed consonance. The creatures that suggest sublime transcendence are now during the 1930s an opportunity for mockery.

Even the sacred terrors of lamentation become the subject of ridicule for O'Nolan in his novel. The terror at the center of the Sweeny tale becomes a focus for O'Nolan. He writes,

> Piteous was the terror of the wailing cries, and the din and the harsh-screaming tumult of the heads and the dogs-heads and the goats heads in his pursuit thudding on his thighs and his calves and on the nape of his neck and knocking against trees and the butts of rocks— a wild torrent of villainy from the breast of a high mountain, not enough resting for a drink of water for mad Sweeny till he finally achieved his peace in the tree on the summit of Slieve Eichneach.
>
> (91).

The cultural identity of Ireland is framed within clichéd visions of color and culture. Alana Gillespie notes, "this powerful critique of (or even attack on) a certain Revivalist discourse and canon formation also informs *At Swim-Two-Birds*, whose characters take matters into their own hands to fashion a narrative better suited to their particular cultural identity" (211). O'Nolan mocks the transition in Yeats's "Easter 1916" from a place where "motley" was worn to one where "green" is worn by suggesting the comic overreach of cultural nationalism: "All colors except green he regarded as symbols of evil and he confined his reading to books attired in green covers" (104). He additionally mocks Yeats overtly, "I will arise and I will slay thee with a shovel" (200). The symbols of Irish identity either in book or color are clearly targets of satire for O'Nolan at home. Yet, he even subtly marks Irish identity within a larger framework of global otherness abroad. He seems to satirize the kind of transnationalism and cosmopolitan identifications seen in Joyce's *Ulysses* and *Finnegans Wake* as essentializing tropes. O'Nolan writes of "Cuban love songs" (141) and African American "maids" (53) as clichés of otherness, using them to mock cultural earnestness beyond Ireland's borders. The writer suggests that the Irish penchant for identifying with cultural "otherness" is merely an opportunity for self-aggrandizement and cross-cultural misunderstanding.

All the figures of myth in *At Swim* end up in various forms of misery and in utterly dreadful conditions. In fact, the degradation of the writers and the heroes is framed as an apt end to the idealization of the Celtic Revival and full desublimation of the mid-century.[3] O'Nolan's ridicule even recalls Beckett's focus on toilets in *Murphy*. In *At Swim*, O'Nolan alludes to a vision of a dog on the street in terms of "a dog as to his legs is evil and sinful to attains sanctity at the hour of his urination" (194). The Irish state encounters a banal reality quite different from the vaunted idealizations of the Revival and 1916. According to Gillespie, O'Nolan's "engagements with the modern drives of mass culture but also to his deconstruction of the aura of history's authoritative texts and their place in cultural memory...[function to undercut] Revivalist discourse" (207).[4] O'Nolan's wild satire relies upon multiple encircling layers of narrative that evoke a multiplicity of facsimiles that incorporate subtle but discernable variance; these variances suggest the multiple perspectives on Ireland's cultural and political history. O'Nolan's framework includes varying generations and regenerations of writers and texts at once and it is this wildly propagative and inclusive technique that allows for new visions of the past and undercuts any facile mimicry of nationalistic or celebratory cultural memory. O'Nolan's endeavors in *At Swim* are not merely to mock the Revivalists or their seemingly received sacred tests and motifs. Rather, O'Nolan's efforts reveal that, while he would surely mock the "radical memory" endeavors of the Celtic Revival, he would also use them to reflect the banalities and disappointments of independence and a mid-century culture that he saw as profoundly lacking.

While the disappointments of independence are shrewdly if slightly evident in *At Swim* as they are mediated through Irish literary myths and conventions, they become powerfully overt in O'Nolan's *Faustus Kelley*. This play, which ran for just two weeks at the Abbey in 1943, was nonetheless considered by Patrick Kavanaugh to be O'Nolan's best work (Cronin 134). A parody of the Faust tale, the play, set in an unnamed town, charts the machinations of a local council member who bargains with the devil to obtain a seat as a TD, a *Trachte Dála*, in the Dáil, a member of parliament, as well as marriage to a prosperous widow. Patrick Kavanagh, the poet, famously ridiculed the 1943 play as a "major critical response" to "an Independent Ireland" (Brooker 95). Kavanagh's scathing indictment of the Dublin literary scene underscores O'Nolan's indictment of its political one.[5] A self-important and pathetic local functionary with ambitions beyond his talents, Kelley makes a deal with the devil, termed "the Stranger" in the play. Kelley, however, does not in fact have to accept damnation in the end; the devil determines that life in Irish politics is a fate worse than hell. Calling the devil "The Stranger," is O'Nolan's brilliant move to undercut Yeats's famous "Strangers in my House" from *Cathleen Ni Houlihan*. O'Nolan's Stranger has no wish to endure the company of Kelley, a corrupt political operative. O'Nolan writes in the first act of a conversation about selling out:

The Town Clerk confesses, "(*Again sotto voce.*) Be Gob, I'd sell my soul for half a crown"
    Kelley replies, "(Shouting *savagely*.) I won't be bought by gentile or jewman! I won't be bought! I'm not for sale! Do you hear me, Town Clerk? I'm not for sale! I'M NOT FOR SALE!"

(67, emphasis added).

Kelley's indignation will become his crime. O'Nolan's use of "savage" in the stage direction to note his style of address will be picked up throughout the play. O'Nolan adopts the old familiar colonial rhetoric of "civilized" vs. "savage" as a relational dichotomy to highlight the opportunistic deployment of those terms by the Irish political class after independence. Kelley's long speech that follows clarifies that he has been charged with a "scorn" for England (71). O'Nolan writes of Ireland's relation to Britain and Empire:

With what pitiless and inexorable terminology will I lash and lash again these debased minions who have presumed to tamper with our historic race, to drive millions of our kith and kin in coffin-ships across the seven seas to dwell in alien clime with the naked savage… who have not hesitated to violate the sacred tabernacle of our nation to steal therefrom, defile and destroy our melodious and kingly language—THE IRISH LANGUAGE—our sole badge of nationhood, our only historic link with the giants of our national past—Niall of the Nine Hostages, who penetrated to the Alps in his efforts to spread the Gospel…

(71–72)

When describing the position of Britain and Ireland, O'Nolan uses discernably dichotomous terminology (civilized versus savage) at the same time that he positions Ireland as an anomalous state, a colony of sophistication and refinement. The term, "civilised" [sic] emerges later in the play to further the engagement with the dichotomies of Empire (106). O'Nolan's litany of Irish exceptionalist victimization juxtaposed with an heroic Irish past becomes a comic moment that evokes the litany of Irish heroism promulgated by Joyce's Cyclops figure in *Ulysses* (and as moment of a clear departure from the reverential celebratory recuperation of those myths during the Revival). O'Nolan's characterization of Irish history is just as inflated and inaccurate as Joyce's characterization. For example, Niall of the Nine hostages, a fourth-century CE Irish king, is a figure more of myth than history.

Critically, O'Nolan has Kelley position the Irish among the global others abroad, from the English working classes to the subaltern others in India and New Zealand.[6] He writes,

> With what appalling and frightening curse, Captain Shaw, will I invoke the righteous anger of the Almighty against these wicked men who live in gilded palaces in England, cradles in luxury and licentious extravagance, knowing nothing and caring nothing for either the English masses, the historic and indefeasible Irish nation, the naked Negro in distance and distressed India or the New Zealand pigmy on his native shore?
>
> (72)

As the final revelation of the play emerges, the context is clearly one of otherness. The Stranger, or the Devil, insists on being able to speak with people so he can manipulate them to his own ends. The Town Clerk insists, however, that "You'll have to do your talking to the Mexicans, like the other fellow," Kelley's schemes are revealed to be shattered (112). The Mexicans serve as descriptors of transnational identification that end up revealing Irish political deviousness. The Devil holds the stage in a "green spotlight, a figure of great horror" as he mimics the human characters in the play (115). The machinations and exhortations of the Irish public man are no match for the Devil himself, as he notes finally,

> Not for any favour... in heaven or earth or hell... would I take that Kelley and the others with me to where I live, to be in their company for ever... and ever... and ever. Here's the contract, his signed bond. (He shows the document and tears it up savagely.) I WANT NOTHING MORE OF IRISH PUBLIC LIFE! (Pause; he turns away, suddenly weary.) I'm tired. I'm going home.
>
> (116)

The Devil has the last word, in which he rejects Ireland's political institutions. Weary and fatigued, he returns to his domain. The Stranger becomes the representation of the sad state of the Irish nation: disappointed and suffering from a malaise of self-disgust, the reality of self-governance had led to disappointment and conventionality. The dreams of sublime transcendence that seemed so possible earlier in the century are here revealed as false, misleading, and ultimately hollow.[7] The Devil prefers his own lair of damnation away from Irish politicians and considers a life in Irish politics to be a terrible enough fate for Kelley. O'Nolan himself had an 18-year career in the Irish Civil Service, and the play's satire of Irish political life seems clear. O'Nolan is known to have blamed the government for having the play shut down, but this is not supported by evidence. Instead, Anne Clissmann notes, "if the play failed, it was not because the government disliked it or because the satire was too savage; it was because it was tedious and badly structured" (260).

O'Nolan's two works, *At Swim-Two-Birds* and *Faustus Kelly*, evince the disappointments in the essentialized nationalisms of the Celtic Revival, the malaise of Irish independence, and the degradation of Irish political life in the 1930s and early 1940s. Unlike the London of Beckett's *Murphy*, O'Nolan's works portray life at home. Yet his depictions often indicate a sense of entrapment. Crucially, however, O'Nolan's novelistic and dramatic representations also question Ireland's globalized rhetorics of otherness that seemed so prescient in Joyce's works and powerfully re-emerge in the writing of Kate O'Brien.

In Kate O'Brien's novel of disappointment in the banality in De Valera's Ireland, *Pray for the Wanderer*, is published on the cusp of World War II and Ireland's neutrality (1938). Matt Costello, a former IRA operative, returns to Ireland as a successful writer, but finds the return home to be unwelcoming for a free thinker. He seeks welcome from and reunion with Ireland and its women (one in particular), but is rejected both personally and artistically in the staid society of de Valera's conservative vision of Catholic Ireland. Costello has been disappointed in what the dream of independence has become. O'Brien's vision of Ireland in the late 1930s is one of a limited and limiting society, which we also see in the novel's context: she writes it in a fury of only five months to overtly indict Ireland's censorship of her previous novel. This prior work, *Mary Lavelle,* published in 1936 and quickly banned in Ireland, celebrates a beautiful Irish woman living abroad in Spain as a governess who celebrates her own burgeoning sexuality and attraction to women.[8] O'Brien's response to its banning is to create a scathing indictment of the Irish state and the toll of its conservatism for artists in *Pray for the Wanderer*.

For O'Brien, *Pray for the Wanderer* is an attempt to counter the small-minded hypocrisies that become so prevalent in Ireland. The outrageous and intrusive mechanisms of the contemporary state are an inversion of the category of the sublime and certainly the primitivism in Ireland that so often creates the sublime encounter. In *Pray for the Wanderer*, she transforms the female protagonist of *Mary Lavelle* into the male protagonist of Matt Costello. Yet, despite this shifting of the character's gender into a more privileged masculinist role, Costello ultimately finds that he is unwelcome in Ireland, as is his work. Eibhear Walshe finds that "*Pray for the Wanderer* [is a] project being the realization of a viable defense against censorship and, by implication against the constrictions of a centralized and masculinist nationalism" (151). Accordingly, when Costello explains his new novel, he makes a haunting prediction: "Yes, it's coming out in a few weeks. But it will be censored in this country" (16). The statement is a matter of fact without melodramatic intrigue. His sister-in-law, Una, plainly states, "I wish you weren't always censored... What's the fun of having a famous relative if he's got to be so embarrassing" (16). O'Brien overtly engages with the role of the artist not only in society, but also in a family. Despite the fame and celebrity attendant with the accomplishments of an Irish writer in the 1930s. Ireland, it seems there will be a price expected and extracted for any kind of welcome at home. Una's husband, Will, Matt Costello's brother embodies this familial effect when he tells Una, "We'll make him settle down over here, Una, and learn sense'" (16). Yet, the novel explains, "Will's manner was very kind and a little embarrassed. He did not read his brother's novels and plays, though proud of his success, but he hated having to face, however lightly, the knowledge that a member of his family was frequently guilty of impropriety in print" (16). The struggle between artist and society endures in De Valera's Ireland. The ease with which the family accepts censorship and displays embarrassment about the returned exiled writer suggests the degree to which the state controls the apparatus of intimate, familial affection. According to Aintzane Legarreta Mentxaka the social control of the state necessitates the creation of a new type of esthetic scaffolding to counter its hegemony,

> O'Brien develops a new aesthetic marker which is also a category of knowledge: "shabby." Placing the shabby between the beautiful and the Burkean sublime, she politicizes aesthetics by striking an anti-capitalist match that makes neglect visible.... The shabby can indicate authenticity, the neglect caused by poverty, or both... it is more than a bohemian trait, indicating substance, or contempt for the culture of display associated with market capitalism.
> (*Kate O'Brien*, 2022 150–51)

The categorization of knowledge in O'Brien's novel as "shabby," a space between the beautiful and the sublime, however, is not merely a mechanism of countering market capitalism but of critiquing a society that, when it had an opportunity to fully emerge from its colonial hegemony, instead embraces a new form and mechanism of social control. What Mentxaka terms "shabby" is in fact a pronounced desublimation and a rejection of the delight and transcendence associated with the primitive sublime during the Revivalist period, as well as in the works of James Joyce.

For O'Brien in *Pray for the Wanderer*, the intersection of intimacy and state control extends toward matrimony. While women were key players in both the cultural Revival and struggles for political independence and nationalism, the 1937 constitution relegated them to the limited spheres of the domestic and maternal. The Irish state finds that sexuality and sexual expression are threats to be controlled and contained, "primeval" elements that need to be suppressed (Inglis 13); the primeval or primitive then become fundamentals that must be eliminated. The quest to eradicate all but the most traditional roles for women and any sense of independent sexual expression is foregrounded in O'Brien's text as a problem. Matt Costello explains to Nell with kindness and sympathy, "'She'll never forgive you if you manage to dodge the slavery of marriage. She's jealous of your freedom!'" (19). The question of slavery and freedom is not merely political, but personal.[9] O'Brien's artist figure celebrates non-traditional sexual and personal relationships. As Mentxaka notes, "Matt is happy to share Louise Lafleur [an actress he knows in London] with her husband Adam, but she decides she 'can't belong physically to two people' because of her Huguenot scruples" (2022, 138). These scruples become markers of social convention and traditional heteronormative marriage structures—both of which Kate O'Brien countered in her personal life and questioned in her characters. Curiously, it is not in the conservative landscape of Irish life that this character rejects a polyamorous arrangement, but within the presumably libertine London theater world. This British theater that Louise and Adam represent in the text stands in for the larger bohemian circles that O'Brien often subtlety lauds but here finds lacking. O'Brien celebrates Costello's free thinking even as she declines to depict his obtainment of satisfaction of any kind outside of the realm of his professional writing. Yet, while Costello has been rejected in Ireland, it seems his desires remain unbound and are more likely to be accepted abroad. Louise, the theater actress who is married already, considers but ultimately rejects Costello's offer of a polyamorous relationship. The labyrinth of entrapment for Costello is not the London mews of Beckett's *Murphy* but rather the sad, limited streets of de Valera's Ireland. The bohemian pleasures of London are unavailable to Costello in Catholic Ireland, even if O'Brien frames them within Protestant Huguenot morality. Crucially, Kate O'Brien sees both Protestant and Catholic morality as faulty and limiting, representing the troubling intersection and entrapment within Christianity and its position vis-a vis state control over personal relationships.

In a moment of high drama, a conventional Catholic marriage between Nell and Costello is discussed and rejected. Costello has been accused of still loving someone else. He says, "If you did marry me, Nell, I'd give you all my trust and faith and gratitude; I'd make a new kind of life with you, here in Ireland, bowing the knee to old Dev! I'd be a good husband, honestly—all the Costellos are!" (156). This is a pragmatic notion of an arranged union, not a love match. Mentxaka explains, "as described in *Pray for a Wanderer*... her characters are forced to develop their own ethics in response to a morality that fails them, when 'everything is a sin'" (2022, 121). Given its pragmatic notion, the inclusion of De Valera into the arrangement seems fitting for O'Brien's representative of the artist alienated from and returned to Ireland, accommodating the material realities of disappointment both in life and state. Nell rejects Matt. She exclaims, "Go back to your own world, Matt—you'll find some solution there. There isn't any in Ireland" (160). The rejection of matrimony is simultaneously configured as a rejection of the state. He is marked as "a womanizer and a pagan" (171). For Matt, the attempt to become engaged in conventional nuptials results only with a denunciation and a plea that he leave Ireland.

O'Brien sets her novelist, Matt Costello, as returning from the cosmopolitan center of London. He exists at home as a figure of the established literary world, but abroad he is considered a provincial. O'Brien details Costello's recollections of his time in London:

> He remembered what someone in Bloomsbury had said to him in disparagement of one of his novels which dealt with a problem of the Catholic conscience: 'It's esoteric, Matt; it's a book written by an Elk for the brother Elks.' A singularly ignorant comment, he had thought at the time, lacking in a sense of history. Now he smiled... Catholicism was not a secret society. Bloomsbury—now that was an esoteric entity. It might indeed have the truth in its beard—who was to say? But it certainly was an Ancient and Venerable Order of the Elks.
> 
> (141)

Costello's position in London is as an outsider. He is an interloper in Bloomsbury as much as he is revealed to be the same at home. It is at this moment that Costello, sophisticated and alienated, hears a hymn at mass: "Do thou, Bright Queen, Star of the Sea, / Pray for the wanderer, pray for me" (141). Matt is the wanderer who has returned, but who will venture forth again. If Catholic Ireland is a club, it is one to which he will not seek membership.

While he is rejected as a romantic partner, Matt Costello sees the censorship in Ireland as a greater threat to his personal autonomy and success. He has suffered the censorship of his work in Ireland and also sees a growing right-wing conservatism in Europe as a threat of cultural and artistic enslavement. He "recognizes the onset in Ireland of the mental slavery that is devouring Europe. The censorship of his novels in Ireland expresses the same disavowal of human rights that prevails in Russia or Germany" (Dalsimer 51). O'Brien's juxtaposition of the family and the state reflects extreme difficulty for the artist who seeks a way beyond the boundaries of the state and its incursions into artistic freedom. O'Brien asks, "Is De Valera as strong a brute as Mussolini then—or as Stalin?" (20) This question suggests that Ireland's past shadows its present and foretells the future, and the answer, according to Costello, is yes. Dalsimer explains, "De Valera wields his power subtly... with a writer's more subtle attention to its language, Matt's reading of the Constitution exposes its manipulation of Irish society; and his opinions clearly mirror Kate O'Brien's" (51). The growing repression of Irish society makes it one that is unwelcoming for creative expression.

This assertion of creative repression in turn shows, throughout the novel, that De Valera's Ireland is a source of disillusionment and apprehension. Dalsimer provides insightful context:

Eamon de Valera's Constitution of 1937, unveiled as Kate O'Brien worked on *Pray for The Wanderer*, was, in its social dimension, a codification of the Irish Catholic values to which the majority of the population subscribed and which Weir House [the somewhat modest Catholic Big House around which the novel centers] illustrates... In the new Constitution, the State 'committed itself publicly to upholding a pattern of life that the majority of its citizens,' none more than the occupants of Weir House, 'felt to be the right pattern for them.'
(48)

O'Brien's portrait of Irish society reflects a scathing social criticism. She is disappointed in the rejection of progress and the attendant embrace of conservatism at once. O'Brien's desublimation is a form of disenchantment not only of public life but also of the personal choices that are available to her protagonists. O'Brien questions the possibilities of a free artistic life in Ireland when she writes of Costello considering his choices:

Could he live in De Valera's Ireland, where the artistic conscience is ignored – merely because, artist or not, he loved that Ireland, its lovely face, its trailing voice, its ribaldry and piety and dignified sense of the wide spaciousness of time? Could he live here because here was the antithesis of her, because here was a morality that scorned and banished hers and his, a pious, Christian island where noise and applause and passion and the cry... would never thrill the quiet? Could he live here... And forget her? Forget the pagan Muse, the eternal Venus, the wild, great plays, the stirring, high abandon of ambition, the delight of unlawful love—and live like the decent son of his father, even the son of his Church, that he was born to be?

(98)

The choices that are possible for someone who thinks and wishes to live outside of social convention are limited for O'Brien and her character, Costello. The pleasures of Ireland for Matt are, however, fleeting: he is a figure of a man isolated from his community even as he attempts to reengage it. He is rejected. O'Brien explains how one character, "told Matt his literary work was a disgrace to Ireland, and that she had never read a word of it, she was happy to say. She wondered what had brought him to Mellick now, and assumed he wouldn't stay very long. She deplored Una's method of bringing up children" (40). The contrast between the returned and rejected artist and the home country in which he is entwined is notable given how the innovative fervor of the Revival period has degenerated into De Valera period of social conformity. O'Brien's use of children in the passage underscores the limiting heteronormative social expectations of fecundity that operate in De Valera's Ireland. In this way, O'Brien's portrait of Ireland in 1937 is one that, much like Joyce's *Portrait*, is one from which the artist must seek exile. De Valera's 1937 Constitution constructs a limited cultural warren, from which anyone seeking a free artistic life in Ireland must escape.

O'Brien's use of and references to Joyce are suggestive of admiration and identification as a fellow Irish writer who attempts to move beyond novelistic convention and social expectations in Ireland. Mentxaka, for example, "agree[s] with Ann Owens Weekes, who believes that O'Brien mirrors Joyce 'in a parodic female fashion,' in a 'deliberately revisionist treatment'" (105).[10] O'Brien's Joycean engagements, however, are less parodic than solemn. She writes the following exchange:

'Do you know *Ulysses* by heart?'

'No. But I know that conversation in the library. The best conversation Ireland has done yet.'

'I'm not the Bard—and there is no Anne Hathaway here—what is it? "And in New Place a slack, dishonoured body that once was comely—"'

'The *mobled queen*—stretched back in the *second-best bed*...'

[emphasis added] (42)

O'Brien focuses on a particular chapter in *Ulysses* where Stephen, Joyce's young writer/artist figure, argues about Shakespearean biography and creativity.[11] As a part of this episode, Joyce mocks Shakespeare and his wife, Ann Hathaway, and their "second-best bed." The marriage bed becomes a symbol of social convention that the young bard (possibly) and the young Joyce (most certainly) sought to avoid; Shakespeare's marriage to an older woman, the subsequent birth of an heir more quickly than a propriety of time would have expected, and his solitary move to London has suggested to scholars for centuries that the marriage was a strained one. In a similarly unorthodox fashion, Joyce's marriage to Nora does not take place until nearly two decades after their exile from Ireland and is undertaken to assure copyright inheritance for Nora and the children. The final line of the quotation refers to a "mobled queen." The phrase is used to describe Gertrude in Shakespeare's *Hamlet* and suggests a veiled figure of desire (Shakespeare 1023). In *Hamlet*, she is the wife who marries the brother of her dead husband. She betrays her marriage vows and breaks social taboos against such intimacy. O'Brien's returned exile, Matt Costello has attempted to counter social taboos related to intimate relationships but has failed. Costello offers a tempting target of the townspeople to critique. He defends himself, "I'm tired, I tell you man! I'm sick of town... I wanted to... find out what Dev is really doing for *Cathleen Ni Houlihan's* four green fields! How dated that phrase is, Tom! How old it makes us!" (45). Ireland and the vision of Yeats's and Gregory's *Cathleen Ni Houlihan* exist for him in the past; it marks his age and exile.

Despite O'Brien's description of Cathleen's "four green fields" as symbolic relics of a previous era, she nevertheless values more recent writers, specifically James Joyce (45). O'Brien defends Ireland's capacity to produce indigenous talent with a vivid conversation between Tom and Matt. Matt explains that "the native Irish literature has a character and strength which are downright impressive. The Bardic schools were good... and by no means naïve." (48). Yet, Tom replies, "Granted. We can, and do produce literature... because we are cerebral...and we're moralists and observers and mockers... words we have some master with... we've only produced one native giant so far... we've only got Joyce to measure against the immortals up to date. And his great spring seems to have dried up on him now" (48-49).[12] Although, Joyce's *Finnegans Wake*, his last novel, appears in 1939, a year after O'Brien published *Pray for the Wanderer*. O'Brien clearly identifies Joyce as a virtuoso and a considerable forebearer with which any Irish writer must contend, not only because of his talent, but also because he was a writer in exile who was censored at home. In any case, Matt laments: "He's banned, too" (49). As Dalsimer claims,

> When the Irish Censorship Board banned two of her books, Kate O'Brien learned, first hand, that the artist's need for freedom might

generate political as well as personal discord, and she began to explore the texture of Irish life in terms of the issues of her day. Although she sympathizes with Irish nationalism, Kate O'Brien decries its myopia and the isolationism and neutrality it produces among raging tyranny.

(xvi)

O'Brien attempts to define the place of an Irish writer at home in the face of an indifferent public and sometimes hostile state. She finds that the indifference of certain people toward art and writing is, in fact, a mechanism to perform a studied neutrality in the face of oppression, a cultural position for which O'Brien holds overt contempt.

O'Brien's contempt for those who do not support art also seems evident in terms of language and the performance of cultural identity. O'Brien's keen skewering of the Irish woman who makes a living off the language revival (a specific aspect of the Celtic Revival that sought to increase the fluency and use of Irish in Ireland) suggests a rejection of the past of Irish primitivism. In response to a question about teaching, O'Brien describes the characters of Nell, the surprising focus of Matt Costello's local romantic attentions, as a scathing opportunist:

> More of her nonsense, that. When she came back from abroad she became interested in perfecting her Irish—spent summers in the Gaeltacht. She speaks it fluently now—of course she has to for her work. She teaches world history in Irish, I'd have you know! Well, that brought her in touch with a lot of our native pedagogues, and she grew interested in education. She's a bossy character, you see... She'll be well off when her mother dies—and meantime, I've always tried to make her see that any sane female would take a salary for all the time and energy mother exacts from her one way and another. But you might was well be talking to Nelson's Pillar. She decided to have a job—and her dear old *alma mater* was delighted to give her one.

(54)

O'Brien undercuts the language revival through the acknowledgment of the disappointment with the language movement's efforts to resurrect from what she suggests is a linguistic past, a primitive relic with little utility in the contemporary world. O'Brien's desublimation revolves around the rhetoric of the dangers of the primitive are highlighted in this passage. She furthers her point: "It's an intellectual theory she has... that social duty demands certain taboos of speech and action, and that is that! I don't madden her at all nowadays... she has read your books, and says are anti-social, myth-creating and unnecessary" (58). The language revivalist and teacher finds no merit or even basic utility in Costello's literary endeavors. For O'Brien, the attempt to revive the Irish language is thus based on an unsophisticated and misguided insularity.

The discussion of myth-creating asserts that the primitive is a central tenant of the fiction created in and around Ireland. O'Brien chastens its creation as a false promise of seduction that leads only to an unnecessary production of deception. Matt laments the attack on his work:

> Matt felt uneasy now, and wished he were alone. Anti-social, myth-creating and unnecessary. Yes, indeed—and the gods be thanked. So might his work continue to be while the world remained the smug, dead colony of slaves he found it. Myth-creating. But his myth had vanished. Had beaten him off. Had grown common, cruel, practical, afraid. He was alone now and would always be alone—without his Muse.
>
> (58)

Matt understands in this moment that the Ireland he imagined is no longer the Ireland that exists. His muse, of Ireland, of *Cathleen Ni Houlihan*, has become ensnared in the servitude of De Valera's state apparatus.[13] The dream visions of the Revival become a form of mind-numbing enslavement.

In a shocking moment, O'Brien posits the role of the artist in society amid the turbulence of early twentieth-century Europe in a conversation between the local priest, Father Malachi, and Costello.[14] Malachi asserts that "Artists are dangerous fellows" (122). In response, Costello draws a scathing equivalence between Ireland and continental Europe as he exclaims, "So does Hitler... So does Stalin. So does Dev, I'll be bound!" (122). Indeed, Costello *will* be bound in the ties of social conservatism: the conversation evinces the strong pull of social convention that results in the artist being relegated outside of and entirely alienated from Irish society.[15] While Father Malachi asserts the falsehood of romantic love and fiction as focused on "a non-reality" (122), Costello goes further. He counters that the falsehoods inherent in his work serve as a form of imaginative revelation and a critique of society. Ultimately, Costello declares, "I'm not prepared to be saved on Ireland's dictated terms" (124). He refuses convention and questions state and religious control of society. Walshe suggests that "O'Brien articulates through the medium of a civilized after-dinner debate between the well-informed priest and the respectfully dissenting novelist a clear rejection of the control sought by Church and State over creative autonomy" (154). O'Brien moves the artist into a position not only of social critic, but also of outsider/truth teller. She also seems to highlight the threat of, and even reject, fascism and its growing prevalence on the continent within months of the publication of this novel. That she frames De Valera in the same image as that of Hitler is shocking; yet, the imposition of state control in Ireland in the late 1930s over much of the private lives of its citizens is clearly worrisome. Dalsimer finds that "Matt's negative feelings about his country commingle with positive ones that no amount of rejection or neglect can obliterate" (57). Nell has rejected his proposal in favor of one from her cousin Tom. Dalsimer continues,

> Matt leaves his lotus land wistfully, the dams in the outside world about to break. As much as the resemblances he perceives between De Valera and Europe's despots offend him, Matt—as well as his creator—understands the great differences. Deploring the entrenchment of the Church in the Irish State, Matt Costello and Kate O'Brien both know that the 'tricky constitution' they have reviled for its preservation of a Catholic society grants religious freedom not only to Catholics but to Protestants, and, considering its date, most importantly, to Jews. Both know that if de Valera's Ireland condones censorship it does not condemn difference of opinion.
>
> (57)

The rejection of Matt Costello's work and romantic overtures in Ireland suggests the degree to which a free-thinking artist is unable to live, work, and create there. Yet, O'Brien's comparison of de Valera's politics with that of the growing fascism on the continent shows the dangerous elements mounting within Europe are another even a greater threat.

Much like the comparative nexus in O'Nolan's *Faustus Kelly*, global rhetorics of otherness and social class seep into the O'Brien's *Pray for the Wanderer*. O'Brien writes that "the price of these two cigars would feed an unemployed man for the week—according to recent strange statistics! But we're callous as the devil, and we're going to smoke them! There's the labour question in Havana, after all!" (118). The Caribbean nation, a location of excess and of fulfilled desires, rests upon the exploitation of labor. The question of labor is framed within a broader international comparison rather than the internal labor struggles in Ireland during the period. The question of the unemployed man is seen as a jest when compared to the Cuban production of tobacco. The consumption of Caribbean stimulants is contrasted with Ireland's production of art. O'Brien mocks the Irish middle classes and highlights the power of the written word as a form of darkness. She writes,

> They were crude and small to be considered by the ancient and snobbish sophistication of Catholic Ireland. A sophistication which had

produced, but would by no means read, *Ulysses*—the most awful outcry ever raised about *the power of darkness*. A sophistication which held debauchery as a vile and private matter neither startling nor unlikely, but yielding nothing to the true purpose of life. A snobbery perilously over-nurtured—into cruelty and blindness—by the alarmist policy of the Church but having, too, its indigent graces... and usefully politically and racially.

(71, emphasis added)

The rhetoric of darkness becomes one of otherness within O'Brien's textual defense of *Ulysses* and her attendant condemnation of the conservative state. Her reliance upon conceptions of "darkness" then seems akin to those highlighted in the work of Sinéad Garrigan Mattar, who used the term, "proper darkness" to define the modern primitive in Irish writing of the early twentieth century—just as the juxtaposition of politics and race presages a turbulent postcolonial fracturing of the global British empire after the Irish Republic is established (19). The rejection of social norms, or, rather, their expansion, is clear. Importantly, O'Brien casually engages with the orientalist impulses of her age: "It isn't often the Mountain takes his car to find Mahomet. And I find you no less." (78). Mentxaka comments on O'Brien's orientalism, writing that "[her] work also presents an Islamophobic strain... this racist aspect is unexpected in a body of work known, as we have seen, for its plea for mutual respect" (*Kate O'Brien*, 2022 132).[16] The rhetoric of savagery emerges consistently, but focuses on the epistolary. O'Brien writes, "Apart, or among other people, they could drive each other mad, and work up agonies of loathing and confusion, write *savage* letters, stare at each other out of eyes like stones - but alone again and face to face in his rooms, even if quarreling still, even if weeping, even if shaken with *rage* and *terror*, the air was changed" (84, emphasis added). The implicit agony of otherness is made explicit in the passage. Yet, O'Brien posits a conception of savagery, as epistolary, that is so dull as to be banal. She must stress the possibility of "rage and terror" and even then only finds that the "air changed." This markedly underwhelming change undercuts the primitive sublime of Yeats's famous repetition of change in "Easter 1916" and becomes an example of the mid-century's unexceptional adjustment. The intersection with a primitive other for O'Brien is framed within the racial and social class expectations of her world. O'Brien reifies the broad social norms of the age while engaging with the personal alienation and despair of the artist.

The sense of entrapment and the need for escape pervade in the characters of novels into the Post-War period and reflect a development sense of encountering globalized others in Irish writing. From Beckett's Murphy, who desires to become ash flushed at the Abbey during a performance, to O'Nolan's Kelley, who agrees to damnation for political gain, to Kate O'Brien's troubled writer, Costello, these figures all become juxtaposed to some degree with globalized others in their texts. I find that these ethnographic interchanges are situated as the progeny of Synge's *The Aran Islands* and other treatments of inhabiting extremes in small isles. With this legacy in mind, I turn finally to Edna O'Brien's famed *Country Girls Trilogy*, which charts the confinement, escape, and disappointment of the era, particularly for women, as it ultimately envisions the potential of the global other within the Irish self.

Edna O'Brien's trilogy of novels, *The Country Girls* (1960), *The Lonely Girl* (1962), and *Girls in Their Married Bliss* (1964), remain notable even today for their radical treatments of sexuality and the female consciousness. O'Brien revised the final novel and included a new ending of *Girls in Their Married Bliss* in 1984, including a new epilogue. O'Brien's radically comprehensive vision of female desire and an intense critique of marriage shocked critics and readers in Ireland; all of these novels were banned in the Republic. While, as Claire Wills explains, "the development of new forms of realism in the 1950s and '60s... including the working-class novel, documentary, and sociological ethnographic texts, opened up a space where new types of experience including migration and labour could begin to be addressed" (109), this new form of social realism still manages to find female desire problematic. If there is a fear in O'Brien's work, it resides in the domestic space, such as the returning home of an alcoholic father in *The County Girls*. As one critic notes, "in this house surrounded by fields in the west of Ireland, Caithleen often wakes in terror because her father is once again missing from home... [When she considers the possibilities of his eventual return, she asks:] Would he shout, struggle, kill her, or apologise?... All this had happened so many times it was foolish to expect him to come home sober" (Brayfield 122). Unlike the primitive sublime terror of the Revival, or even that in Joyce's later works, the terror in mid-century writing is that of a desublimated domestic return of a deficient alcoholic and cruel father.

In *The County Girls*, O'Brien's character, Baba, mocks Joyce and Caithleen's admiration of him. Baba exclaims, "Will you, for Chrissake, stop asking fellas if they've read James Joyce's *Dubliners*? They're not interested. They're out for a night. Eat and drink all you can and leave James Joyce to blow his own trumpet'" (qtd. in Brayfield 88). According to Emer Nolan, "there is a tension in O'Brien between her attachment to popular women's culture and her sense of affiliating with early twentieth-century experimental or modernist Irish literature" (20–21). Yet, this strain is perhaps overstated. While O'Brien's actual reverence for Joyce as a writer is clear in her biography of him, *James Joyce*, published in 1999, she nonetheless mocks the cultural weight of both Joyce and the writers of the Revival period. Reverence for the past in O'Brien's work often reads as a kind of inherited cruelty that will emerge again, much like the alcoholic father in her first novel. While the coming of age tale in Ireland is somewhat conventional in the characterization of a stifling and homogeneous culture in O'Brien's work, she shatters expectation of the form through her female protagonists. The "grooming" of Caithleen as a very young girl by a grown man is deeply disturbing and is too often overlooked by scholars. Rather than achieve a transcendent sublime, the characters become ensnared within the quotidian banality of life, captured in O'Brien's characterization of female experience. What initially emerges as a fraught gendered and sexualized coming of age in the early narratives set in Ireland, later manifests with a profound connection with newly conceptualized and encountered "others" for O'Brien's London novel.

The final novel in the trilogy, *Girls in Their Married Bliss*, explodes off the page with the anxiety of the other and the intersection of cultures.[17] Much like Beckett's *Murphy* and Kate O'Brien's *Pray for the Wanderer*, the last book in the trilogy views London as a significant location; yet, O'Brien focuses not on the entrapment of city life, but rather the contact zone of the metropolitan globalized population of Windrush emigration. The questioning of identity of global others and the anxiety of the Irish place within London's social structures both remain salient throughout the novel. The peculiar experience of the Irish in Britain relates to the "ambiguous position of Irish migrants in post-war British society… [and] the shifting categories of race (and sub-racial types) and of class" (Wills 127). The dramatically hybridized society, however, still reveals an anxiety of otherness. Wills determines that the Irish can in some ways merge "with the urban English, their children indistinguishable from English youth" (Wills 134). Novel forms of identity become possible, even probable, as immigrants and their progeny ascend the ladder of the British class. Yet, the desire for difference or distinction between the Irish and other new immigrants yields extremely disquieting events. The 1958 Notting Hill riots in London were a dramatic and violent uprising against the Windrush generation of Caribbean migrants in Britain. Irish immigrants to Britain took part in the riots. Wills describes the reaction of one Irish young man to taking part in the violence. She explains: "the young man's confusion about where to place himself isn't edifying—what he wants is to be the same as his white mates, including in their racism, but what he articulates is his own uncertain racial designation, neither one thing nor the other" (135). The Irish migrant insult of being called a "Pat" is notable and offensive for the young man, but he does not see a commonality with the Caribbean migrants (Wills 139). In fact, he desires to make a distinction between himself and other immigrants. Wills notes, "the conflation of issues of race and nation skin colour, especially in the context of the end of Empire and the arrival in Britain of Commonwealth and colonial migrants, created a situation in which white people were perceived as part of the indigenous majority and black people were members of an immigrant population, whatever their origins" (137). A significant portion of the Irish living in London and Britain post World War II desire assimilation with the white power structure of Britain, courtesy of the privilege of their skin color to differentiate themselves from stereotypes and the underclass of recent arrivals, particularly those migrants from other parts of the British empire during and after its collapse.

The problematic encounters with the globalized others, particularly with the Windrush migrants, in O'Brien's work are discussed overtly in *Girls in Their Married Bliss*. O'Brien notes of this cultural intersection and its banality: "'Darling, just make yourself known to everyone,' the hostess said. Kate looked around. Two West Indians were arguing. Sophistication. She thought of telling them of a sign she'd seen in the Underground which said NIGS GET OFF OUR WOMEN, but they might not laugh. They might just tell her to hoof off" (in Brayfield 489). O'Brien's character is aware of the problematic racial hybridity in the contact zone of London's immigrant communities, West Indian and Irish. She acknowledges the social dynamics of fear that arise not only from the potential of racial mixing, but also the likely confrontation of addressing the issue. O'Brien explains Kate's response to a possible racial intersection, "He'd said he'd lived all over, in Australia and Mexico and places, and that he had Apache Indian blood. I thought, How the hell can you be so white if you have Indian blood, but that's not the sort of thing you can say [sic]. Indian blood is all the rage now" (424). Native American identity is questioned, but it is also seen as desirable, "all the rage," even as its existence without a discernable physical marker is seen as worrisome. Yet, the subtle fears of indistinction that so seem to emerge for the Irish in Britain and in a larger global context become overt for O'Brien's London-based characters. O'Brien's characters in some way become the progeny of those early twentieth-century depictions of cultural fear related to racial intersection that were evident in Joyce's works so clearly. Amid a discussion of race and identity for an unborn child, the protagonist explains:

'He's a Greek,' said I, 'and he's gone home.'
It was the only thing I could think of. Kate had her head out of the bedroom door. She was as inquisitive as hell.
'Will it be white?' said he. The eejit doesn't know Greeks from blacks.

'It might,' said I, 'if we're lucky.' He said he wanted no more cheek from now on and I had to do what I was told and nobody was ever to know the truth.

(469)

The chance of having a child who appears white, rather than of African descent or Greek (which is, nonetheless, a Mediterranean identity that would be seen as more suitable and likely to "pass" as acceptable in the social confines of London and Ireland) reflects the anxiety and fear of racial intersection. Crucially, the developing pregnancy represents not merely the fear of indistinction from an "other," but the fear of the capacity for the "other" to become a part of an Irish "self." During a social scene, the identity of the primitive versus the civilized emerges through movement as identity:

'I'm drinking,' she said.
'You're not swinging,' he said. He had a ruddy, affectionate face and golden eyelashes. She would have liked to talk to him. She would have liked to say, 'I can't dance. I drink instead of dancing, or I cry.' She would have liked to say, 'Teach me to dance,' or, 'How many of these people sleep together?' but he was exercising his shoulder and flicking his fingers to the beat of the very loud music. 'You won't,' he said. 'You're not a primitive?'

(492)

The primitive, figured here as the dance of and around sexual freedom, thus becomes for O'Brien an identity to refuse and reject. The primitive has no place in her conception of contemporary Irish identity, either at home in Ireland or abroad in London. In fact, the primitive other is removed entirely abroad and becomes a subject of pity. In the epilogue, added two roughly decades later, O'Brien writes, "Well, if they were meant, why weren't they together, is what I thought, and why was she looking like something from Ethiopia, all dugs and bone" (528). The contrast between the acceptable identity for an Irish woman in London and the portrait of a contemporary famine victim upends any vision of either the primitive or the sublime. The other, here, is not a primitive figure, either within Ireland or in the larger world. O'Brien's point of contrast is a contemporary one. Unlike Terry Eagleton's assertion of the Irish famine as a sublime event, here there is no sublime attached to this depiction or reference, but rather immanent aversion and refusal of connection (Eagleton 31). O'Brien uses the Ethiopian as a point of contrast and exclusion for the Irish. The emergence of this figure in mid-century Irish fiction, as revised and included in the 1984 epilogue, suggests the degree to which the anxiety and fear of indistinction evident earlier in the century stubbornly begin to reappear at its close.

The four writers in this chapter, Beckett, O'Nolan, Kate O'Brien, and Edna O'Brien, all navigate the complexities of the Irish position in the mid-century. From Beckett and O'Nolan's overt mockery of the idealized primitivism in the Revival, to the more subtle questioning of Irish identity and positionality of Kate O'Brien and Enda O'Brien in the increasingly globalized world, the banalities of existence highlight the troubling disappointments of De Valera's Ireland and its Constitution. Women were put squarely in the domestic sphere and, after the brief liberatory moments of the Rising, were once again relegated to support positions. Both female writers in this chapter overtly acknowledge the limitations of those roles for women, whereas male writers seem to ignore them entirely. Yet, as Kelly Mathews notes Irish identity is always influx. It remains a process of "becoming" rather than a static ideal or one that is preserved in the amber of the Revival. Finally, as Sophia Hillan notes in her essay on Edna O'Brien in the collection *Wild Colonial Girl*, "In her first trilogy she carved out the novelistic equivalent of Seamus Heaney's digging down and back into her own past and that of the island of Ireland. As with Heaney's early work, this digging took the writer beyond itself to the wider world, and then back to Ireland, described by O'Brien as 'a state of mind as well as an actual country'" (144). What I suggest is that this "digging" is not merely the key to this one, or even all, of the mid-century writers in this chapter, but in fact, it becomes a more critical mechanism of return and renewal for writers of the late twentieth century such as Seamus Heaney, Eavan Boland, and Brian Friel. As we will see in the following chapter, this digging uncovers nothing less than Ireland's Living Dead.

## Notes

1. Readers will notice the slight difference in spelling between O'Brien's Sweny and Heaney's Sweeney. I have kept to the original spellings in each textual citation rather than norming them and losing the specificity of the authors' individual choices.
2. In the Flann O'Brien archives in Boston College's Burns Library, an untitled dialogue regarding the core of *At Swim-Two-Birds* suggests both the influence and powerful legacies that O'Nolan was negotiating (Box 4 Folder 4/33 p 2).The notion of plagiarism is significant in *At Swim*; yet, this notion represents not the anxiety of influence, but rather the overt rejection of knowledge of writers working in similar modes and/or characters. O'Nolan's knowledge of both Saroyen and Eliot's endeavors will not surprise readers.
3. Clissmann asserts that "the heroes are fallen, unable to serve in the modern world. Writers are punished by rebellious characters who will no longer tolerate the liberated imagination but wish to impose the tyranny of fact and detail and require that all possible ends should be tied up" (149).

## Mid-century Malaise and Desublimation 93

4 According to Alana Gillespie, "O'Nolan's treatment of time and the insistence on the mutability of {interpreting} narratives represent a radical critique not only of historical authority itself, but also of a non-critical attitude to history" (205).
5 Kavanagh notes that when "he came to Dublin... the Irish Literary Affair was still booming. It was the notion that Dublin was a literary metropolis and Ireland as invented and patented by Yeats, Lady Gregory and Synge, a spiritual entity. It was full of writers and poets and I am afraid I thought their work had the Irish quality." (qtd. in Boland. "Article" 20). He explained, "in those days the big thing besides being Irish was peasant quality. They were all trying to be peasants. They had been at it for years but I hadn't heard" (qtd. in Boland, "Article" 20).
6 Kelly explains to his paramour, Margaret, who has accused him of selling liquor on Sundays at his Off License: "Ah, they would be the language workers—the Gaelic League. I give them a room free of charge for their classes, you know. I do what I can to encourage the old tongue" (93). The degree to which the advocacy and instruction of the native language is used to mask the depravity of commercialism and alcohol on a sacred day of rest is notable.
7 In "Rhapsody in Stephen's Green: the Insect Play," the empire and otherness reflect again. The Keeper exclaims, "I don't give a damn if yer de Valera... or one of them lads out of the Kildre Street club... or (tremendous effort) the Bishop... of... Bangalore—OUT—OF—THIS—PAIRK—YOU'LL—HAVE—TO-GO—AND THAT'S All" (163). The insects debate empire and language:

> 2nd Engineer: In stap with the Awnt Empiere.
> Chief Engineer: On which the sun never sets.
> 2nd Engineer: Tha grawndest empiere in the world (217).

The British Empire is mocked throughout. The language of Rome, Latin, is used as a foil against the language of the British, English. Language therefore becomes a marker of identity and belonging even among the insect classes. Finally, as the play closes, a Petulant Voice asks, "Do you not know your own language, you ignorant man? He is proclaiming our great victory. At this hour he becomes emperor of all the earth. History is at an end. Our glorious destiny is achieved after seventeen hundred years".

8 Vivian Mercier indicated quickly that the banning of *Mary Lavelle* was surely at the root of the discussion on censorship in *Pray for the Wanderer*, a novel written in just five months (qtd. in Dalsimer 47).
9 Emma Donoghue finds that "Many of O'Brien's characters resist marriage, seeing, with Matt Costello in *Pray for the Wanderer*, that 'life might fruitfully be a lonely track or a jealously personal adventure.' It would be interesting to read O'Brien's novels as a series of interrogations of the institution of matrimony, and to analyze the figure of the independent, nunlike spinster who crops up in so many of her novels" (37).
10 For further reading, see Anne Owens Weeks, *Irish Women Writers: an Uncharted Tradition*, Kentucky UP, 1990.
11 The closing pages of the novel provide a Joycean reverie: "How odd if the distressful country, the isle of Saints and Doctors from which Patrick banished snakes, should prove a last oasis, floating Lotus Land when the floods rise!" (184). Matt, "thinking of Tom's ironic quoting of *Ulysses*...." (183), injects his own pseudo Joycean prose: "Merely write, and in due course die. Oh, green and trim Free State! Smug, obstinate and pertinacious little island, your sins and ignorances are thick upon your face, and thickening under the authority of your 'sea-green incorruptible'" (183).

12 This description of Joyce's well of talent drying up suggests that the character is unaware of the publication of sections of Joyce's "Work in Progress" that ultimately becomes *Finnegans Wake*. For further information, see Dirk Van Hulle's *James Joyce's 'Work in Progress': Pre-Book Publications of Finnegans Wake Fragments*, Routledge, 2016.

13 O'Brien mocks central tenants of Irish myth in the discussion of a fishing rod. She writes, "Nonsense. The royal salmon or nothing. The salmon of knowledge, Liam. Aunt Nell's an Irish scholar and known his noble place in Irish literature. Who in God's name wants to catch a trout?" (99). O'Brien continues, "it was bought at last, with reel and line. Liam was in raptures, In a shop famous for its salmon-rods this was the pick, it seemed. A dream, a beauty. Matt paid for it, and asked to have it sent to him at Weir House" (99).

14 The issue of a defrocked or soon to be priest seems keen at certain points. O'Brien writes, "In the day of battle, his problems will be solved. They'll ship him off to Madagascar or Patagonia, and by the time he has re-established his power and personality there he'll be old, he'll even be dead. It's easy enough, Matt. Saints are so few and so humble, and the world is wide. His vow of obedience will solve this problem." (121)

15 "I expect the old horror haunts of the neighborhood! I'm not so sure about my house!" (112). The sublimation of class and otherness become explicit when the priest say, "mockingly. 'And I'm not wanting to argue the distribution of wealth. I want to talk about Mellick's returned celebrity.' He turned to Matt. 'Have you come back, like Saint Patrick, 'to dwell amongst us?' 'And preach you a new conversion?' 'To neo-paganism? That would be an enterprise" (118). O'Brien emphasizes that this conversation is about class: "He was feeling arrogant and cheerful. The artist is always 'myth creating, anti-social, and unnecessary', in Nell's sense" (118–19). Later, O'Brien again engages with rhetorics of class and identity: "'He's as near a militant Communist as a consecrated priest has ever been – and in the class war that's coming.' 'Is there to be a class war in Ireland?' 'As sure as I'm sitting here,' said Tom. 'And if Dev and the hierarchy go on keeping their heads in the sand it'll be sooner than later'" (120–21).

16 I characterize O'Brien's work as an example of what Joyce Zonana terms "feminist orientalism" in her Sultan and Slave article, which charts the feminist use of orientalist tropes through Wollestonecraft to Charlotte Brontë.

17 According to Celia Brayfield, at the end of *Girls in their Married Bliss*, "Baba brings news that her husband has suggested Kate move in with them. 'She was glad at being able to make the offer[...] They would have each other, chats, moments of recklessness, they could moon over plans they'd stopped believing in, long ago'" (141). Brayfield continues, "The first edition of the novel ended there, with the promise that the lifelong friendship would be sustained. When the trilogy was reissued in 1980s, however, O'Brien wrote a tragic epilogue to the story of Kate and Baba. Kate, 'proned to the old Via Dolorosa' has died from drowning like her mother, although she may well have ended her life deliberately. It falls to Baba to organize the funeral and to evade her son's questions 'because there are some things in this world you cannot ask, and oh, Agnus Dei, there are some things in this world you cannot answer.'" (141).

## References

Bair, Deirdre. *Samuel Beckett: a Biography*. Harcourt Brace Jovanovich, 1978.
Beckett, Samuel. "Dante… Bruno.Vico. Joyce." *Our Exagmination Round His Factification for Incarnation of Work in Progress*. New Directions, 1972 [1929], pp. 1–22.
———. *Murphy*. Grove Press, 1957.
Boland, Eavan., editor. *Irish Writers on Writing*. Trinity UP, 2007.
———. *Ordinary People Dancing: Essays on Kate O'Brien*, edited by Eibhear Walshe, Cork UP, 1993
Brayfield, Celia. *Rebel Writers: The Accidental Feminists: Shelagh Delaney, Edna O'Brien, Lynne Ried Banks, Charlotte Bingham, Nell Dunn, Virginia Orinisde, Margaret Forster*. Bloomsbury Caravel, 2019.
Brooker, Joseph. "Ploughmen Without Land: Flann O'Brien & Patrick Kavanagh." *Flann O'Brien and Modernism*, edited by Julian Murphet, Rónán McDonald and Sasha Morrell, Bloomsbury, 2014, pp. 93–106.
Caws, Mary Ann. *City Images: Perspectives from Literature, Philosophy, and Film*. Taylor & Francis, 1991.
Clissmann, Anne. *Flann O'Brien: A Critical Introduction to His Writings*. Gill and Macmillan, 1975.
Cronin, Anthony. *No Laughing Matter: The Life and Times of Flann O'Brien*. Grafton, 1989.
Dalsimer, Adele. *Kate O'Brien: A Critical Study*. Gill and Macmillan, 1990.
Donoghue, Emma. "Out of Order: Kate O'Brien's Lesbian Fictions." *Ordinary People Dancing: Essays on Kate O'Brien*, edited by Eibhear Walshe, Cork UP, 1993, pp. 36–58.
Dowling, Conor. "Carnival and Class Consciousness: Bakhtin and the Free State in *At Swim-Two-Birds*." *Flann O'Brien: Gallows Humor*, edited by Ruben Borg and Paul Fagan, Cork UP, 2020, pp. 48–60.
Eagleton, Terry. "The Irish Sublime." *Religion & Literature*, vol. 28, no. 2/3, 1996, pp. 25–32, www.jstor.org/stable/40059661.
Garrigan Mattar, Sinéad. *Primitivism, Science, and the Irish Revival*. Oxford UP, 2004.
Gillespie, Alana. "In Defense of 'gap-worded' Stories: Brian O'Nolan on Authority, Reading and Writing." *Flann O'Brien: Problems with Authority*, edited by Ruben Borg, Paul Fagan and John McCourt, Cork UP, 2017, pp. 204–218.
Hillan, Sophia. "On the Side of Life: Edna O'Brien's Trilogy of Contemporary Ireland." *Wild Colonial Girl: Essays on Edna O'Brien*, edited by Lisa Colletta and Maureen O'Connor, U of Wisconsin P, 2006, pp. 143–64.
Inglis, Tom. "Origins and Legacies of Irish Prudery: Sexuality and Social Control in Modern `Ireland." *Éire-Ireland*, vol. 40, no. 3/4, 2005, pp. 9–37,
Joyce, James. *Ulysses: The Corrected Text*, edited by Hans Walter Gabler with Wolfhard Steppe and Claus Melchior, Random, 1986.
Mathews, Kelly E. "'Something Solid to Put Your Heels On': Representation and Transformation in *The Bell*." *Éire-Ireland*, vol. 46, no. 1–2, 2011, pp. 106–27, https://www.doi.org/10.1353/eir.2011.0000.

McDonald, Rónán. "An Astonishing Parade of Nullity': Nihilism in *The Third Policeman*." *Flann O'Brien and Modernism*, edited by Julian Murphet, Rónán McDonald and Sasha Morrell, Bloomsbury, 2014, pp. 135–48.

Mentxaka, Aintzane Legarreta. *Kate O'Brien*. Edwin Everett Root, 2022.

———. *Kate O'Brien and the Fiction of Identity: Sex, Art and Politics in Mary Lavelle and Other Writings*. McFarland, 2011.

Nolan, Emer. *Five Irish Women: The Second Republic, 1960–2016*. Manchester UP, 2019.

O'Brien, Edna. *The Country Girls Trilogy*. Faber & Faber, 1984.

———. *James Joyce*. Penguin, 1999.

O'Brien, Flann. *At Swim-Two-Birds*. Dalkey Archive Press, 2005.

———. "Faustus Kelly." *Collected Plays and Teleplays*, edited by Jernigan, Daniel Keith. Dalkey Archive Press, 2013.

———. Flann O'Brien Papers. Boston College Burns Library. Box 4 Folder 4/33 p 2.

———. *Rhapsody in Stephen's Green: the Insect Play*, edited by Robert Tracey. Lilliput, 1994.

O'Brien, Kate. *Pray for the Wanderer*. Penguin, 1951.

Rafroidi, Patrick. "Pas de Shamrocks pour Sam Beckett? La dimension irlandaise de 'Murphy.'" *Etudes Irlandaises*, no. 7, 1982, pp. 71–82, https://doi.org/10.3406/irlan.1982.2670.

Shakespeare, William. *The Complete Works of Shakespeare*. Oxford UP, 1928.

Steinberg, S. C. "The External and Internal in *Murphy*." *Twentieth-Century Literature*, vol. 18, no. 2, 1972, pp. 93–110, https://doi.org/10.2307/440722.

van Boheemen-Saaf, Christine. *Joyce, Derrida, Lacan, and the Trauma of History: Reading,Narrative, and Postcolonialism*. Cambridge UP, 1999.

Van Hulle, Dirk. *James Joyce's 'Work in Progress': Pre-Book Publications of Finnegans Wake Fragments*. Routledge, 2016.

Walshe, Eibhear. "Lock Up Your Daughters: From Ante-Room to Interior Castle." *Ordinary People Dancing: Essays on Kate O'Brien*, edited by Eibhear Walshe, Cork UP, 1993, pp. 150–57.

———, editor. *Ordinary People Dancing: Essays on Kate O'Brien*. Cork UP, 1993.

Weeks, Anne Owens. *Irish Women Writers: an Uncharted Tradition*. Kentucky UP, 1990.

Wills, Claire. *The Best Are Leaving: Emigration and Post-War Irish Culture*. Cambridge UP, 2015.

Zonana, Joyce. "The Sultan and the Slave: Feminist Orientalism and the Structure of *Jane Eyre*." *Signs*, vol. 18, no. 3, 1993, pp. 592–617, www.jstor.org/stable/3174859.

# 5 The Living Dead

## The Late Century Resurgence of the Primitive Sublime in Works by Seamus Heaney, Eavan Boland, and Brian Friel

The reemergence of the primitive sublime begins in the 1960s with the increasing presence of rhetorics of global otherness in Ireland and amid the Diaspora. The encounters of the Irish abroad reverberate at home with the fraught dichotomies in Ireland/Northern Ireland and the eruption of the Troubles in the late 1960s. The figures at the forefront of this movement, such as Seamus Heaney, Eavan Boland, and Brian Friel, touch upon the enduring tension and fear of indistinction within the Empire and reveal disturbing insights into the vexed positions of the Irish at home and abroad at once. They look back to the period of the Revival, and, to a certain degree, the works of James Joyce, and recast their broadly abstract, and sometimes nationalist, tropes from the late nineteenth and early twentieth century into profoundly intimate and often familial portraits of the primitive sublime. Amid the turmoil of the cultural "debate [that] Heaney dubbed song versus suffering" (Clark 34), the poet fractures any facile understanding of duality by relentlessly moving between the two. In fact, he shows that for Ireland in the twentieth century, "song and suffering" are one. Eavan Boland's language of displacement and Friel's exploitation of the priest "gone native" in "Dancing at Lughnasa" evince ways in which the global primitive trope endures in the Irish creative conscious. For these writers, the dead become reanimated and walk again in the late twentieth-century consciousness; these reanimations become identified within comparative notions of the other but reveal primitive sublime manifestations within the Irish self. The primitive encounter that provokes the sublime is central not simply for literary culture, but also for Ireland's pressured conception of the modern nation in the wake of the eruption of violence in the North/Northern Ireland after the late 1960s. The violence of the late century in some ways refracts that of the early century; the manifestations of the primitive sublime emerge again as avatars of the undead. This resurgence of the primitive sublime centers on the reanimation of the Irish corpus serves as a means to raise the dead and inform the living in the enduring struggle for cultural liberation.

DOI: 10.4324/9781003297390-5

98  *The Living Dead*

Seamus Heaney, a poet from the fraught partitioned geographies of The North or Northern Ireland, would find a powerful symbolic network for his own art and for Ireland at large with his encounters of the bog bodies and the Viking incursions of Ireland, which often engaged with human sacrifice and enduring suffering. For Heaney, the return of the violence of ancient world within his contemporary one likewise brings back the powerful rhetorics of the primitive sublime. Conor Carville notes, "nationalist variations on the idea of temporal disruption read the Irish landscape itself as a kind of theatre of memory which made the past visible in the present, a mode of seeing that has its origins in late eighteenth-century antiquarianism, although it can also be found later" (46). The temporal dislocations of the Irish landscape serve as repositories of history and cultural memory for Heaney. More specifically, this chapter explores how his poetic reanimations of the bog bodies, a literary practice evoking the primitive sublime once more, bring ancient victims of human sacrifice into a powerful comparative dialectic with his contemporary moment.

Heaney's relationship with the landscape of Ireland reaches back to his own childhood. The poet famously writes, "I'll dig with it" when he compares writing poetry to the digging in the turf of Toner's bog and the violence of a "gun" ("Digging" 31; 2). As much as he defines poetry as akin to excavation, he also sees himself as embedded in a practice formed within the deep past. He explains, "I feel myself as a member of an archaic tribe. Maybe the archaic has something to teach us" ("The Usual Suspects"). The ancient—the "archaic," as the poet says—offers lessons to the contemporary world. This legacy of instruction becomes defined for Heaney within the Irish landscape, in general, and the bog, in particular. In this vein, Carlanda Green explains that "as a young child Heaney and a friend stripped naked and bathed in a mossy bog." She continues:

> The event was a *seminal experience* in Heaney's life, so central that he says that he still feels 'betrothed' to 'watery ground.' His descent into the bog became the abiding metaphor of his poetry, and the female principle is inseparable from that metaphor whether he is delving into the depths of the earth, the bog, the womb, or the Celtic unconscious of the Irish people.
>
> (151, emphasis added)

Green's use of the "unconscious" to explain Heaney's relentless attraction to a generative, soggy landscape that reveals the preserved corpses of ritualistic violence—drawn as both the ancient victims of human sacrifice and also imagined as the "disappeared" victims of the Troubles in his contemporary world—becomes suggestive of Heaney's dance around the primitive sublime. Green's use of "seminal" as an adjective to describe

Heaney's "experience" rightly suggests the opportunity of procreation in the endeavor. Not until 1969 would Heaney encounter images and texts that revealed his unconscious preoccupations, such as P. V. Glob's *The Bog People*. Heaney explains his fascination with the work:

> [The book] was chiefly concerned with preserved bodies of men and women found in the bogs of Jutland, naked, strangled or with their throats cut, disposed under the peat since the early Iron Age times. The author, P. V. Glob, argues convincingly that a number of these, and in particular the Tollund Man, whose head is now preserved near Aarhus in the museum at Silkeburg, were ritual sacrifices to the Mother Goddess, the dosses of their ground who needed new bridegrooms each winter to bed with her in her sacred place, in the bog, to ensure the renewal and fertility of the territory in the spring. Taken in relation to the tradition of Irish political martyrdom for that cause whose icon is Kathleen Ni Houlihan, this is more than an archaic barbarous rite; it is an archetypal pattern. And the unforgettable photographs of these victims blended in my mind with photographs of atrocities, past and present, in the long rites of Irish political and religious struggles.
>
> <div align="right">(<i>Preoccupations</i> 57–58)</div>

Heaney's acknowledgment of archetype joining the Scandinavian and Irish sacrifices to a maternal goddess remains an important key for understanding his bog poems. His turn toward the primitive elements in Northern European history relies upon both archeological and textual accounts.[1] For Heaney, the Scandinavians that came to Ireland were, in fact, Viking ravagers. The only known textual account of an encounter with Viking raiders and traders comes from the ninth century. In this period, an Arab traveler and scholar, Ibn Fadlān, left Baghdad for a journey that would lead him to an encounter with the Rus, who were Viking traders on the Volga River. This journey would lead him to write one of the only known first-hand accounts of Viking cultures and rituals. In his report home, sent to the Caliph of Baghdad, Ibn Fadlān describes the Viking practice of ritual sacrifice, an angel of death, and a forest filled with the corpses hung from trees. The text is a useful corrective to the relational dichotomy of civilized and savage that conventionally appears after the fifteenth century to reflect the power of European empires and their colonial possessions. For Ibn Fadlān, it is the Rus who are savages in comparison to his Middle Eastern civilization, an apex of learning and sophistication. During the ritual of a ship burial preparation, he writes of an enslaved girl, supposedly willing, but not convincingly so (she is given what appears to be alcohol and/or a hallucinogenic), who is sacrificed to enter the afterlife with her master. This brutality occurs only after the freemen all take their turns raping her, giving her the message: "tell your master I only did this for [my/your] love of him" (49–54).[2] The female body in a ritualized rape becomes a means of communication and adoration among men, she becomes the vessel through which male power becomes negotiated and proven.

Ibn Fadlān's horror at the ritualized rape and death is, in turn, equally both horrifying and strangely familiar to Heaney's encounters of human sacrifice in his bog and Viking poems. In his "Bog Queen," the poet takes on the perspective of a woman who is killed, transformed, and preserved,

I lay waiting
Between turf-face and demesne wall,
Between Heathery levels
And glass-toothed stone.
My body was Braille
        (lines 1–5)

The woman's consciousness remakes her own body as a text. She is in "braille" bodily form, to be read not by sight, but by touch. The development of her preserved state reveals the bumps and lumps of her being and, ultimately, the gifts of her burial, both of which are precious elements that link her with the ancient world revealed in the twentieth century. Heaney continues to emphasize her body as a symbol of writing and reading when he calls forth the "The illiterate roots/Pondered and died/In the carvings/Of stomach and socket" (lines 12–15). The figure is encapsulated in her "Dreams of Baltic amber" (line 21). She is adorned with Phoenician textiles that would have been brought from the Mediterranean to Northern Europe through Viking trade, and the "Baltic amber" and the "fjords" (lines 21;35) overtly link her with the Scandinavian landscape and elements. Amber itself is a fossilized tree resin that achieves a stabilized state due to chemical changes when buried. It endures and remains beautiful, and sometimes even translucent despite its often incorporating and remnants of carbon and thus aspects of life. Heaney writes,

In the peat floe
Like the bearings of history.
My sash was a black glacier
Wrinkling, dyed weaves
And Phoenician stitchwork
        (lines 27–31)

The symbol of Ireland's figure of feminine sacrifice is adorned in the threading of the ancient Middle East.

The poet's creation of the mythic bog woman and island repository rests upon ancient paradigms. She is a martyr to Ireland, a sacrifice to the island nation. This is a trope that reaches back to the "the aesthetic politics of nationalism" and "which finds its most intense symbolism in martyrdom" (Lloyd, "The Indigent Sublime" 127). Yet, she has a kind of preserved eternal being and rebirth as her body is revealed and excavated from the landscape: "A slimy birth-cord/Of bog had been cut/And I rose from the dark" (51–53). She has been dead for centuries, and yet she rises once more. She has become not a new thriving being per se, nor has she reached the status of a full living being, but she is a corpse that has become preserved and rises again courtesy of an Irish bog. She has no agency and is unable to either consent or counter this rising; she occupies the liminal zone of the living dead. Heaney's treatment of the "Bog Queen" reveals the poet's preoccupation with the landscape and his reverence for the inherited position of female subjectivity as central to Ireland's history. According to David Lloyd,

> To this cultural tradition, it is true Heaney seeks to give an Irish "bend," grafting it on to roots which are identified as rural, Catholic, and, more remotely, Gaelic. That grafting is enabled by the return to place, a reterritorialization in a literal sense initially, which symbolically restores the interrupted continuity of identity and ground... The putative sameness of place supplies an image of the continuity underlying the ruptures so apparent in the history of language usage in Ireland... In all its functions, language performs the rituals of synthesis and identity.
> ("The Indigent Sublime" 124)

Lloyd suggests that Heaney's inclusive vision of body and island is an elemental syncretism that reaches back to the "remote" Gaelic past seems evident. Yet, Heaney's vision includes Ireland's Scandinavian elements.[3] Heaney's inheritance then becomes not merely the landscape and cultural memory of Ireland, or even the bog itself, but rather the simultaneous past and present event of the boggy union of slaughter, sacrifice, and ritualized violence. Such an event emerges in Heaney's contemporary moment, deriving not merely from Ireland, but from the wider Scandinavian world, which he subsequently draws upon for his allusions and metaphors.

In his description of the Irish landscape, Heaney paints a vision overtly inclusive of its inheritance of a Viking raider past. For his "Bog Queen," Heaney writes of "the nuzzle of fjords/at my thigh"(lines 35–36). The passage links the comfort of intimacy of the nuzzle and thigh, yet evokes the cruelty and violence of the Viking Age, with a culture of conquest that commonly included rape. The word "fjord" comes from Scandinavia, "[especially] on the coast of Norway a long narrow inlet of the sea between high steep cliffs formed by glacial action.C17: from Norwegian, from Old Norse *fjörthr*; see firth, ford" (Dictionary.com accessed June 1, 2020). Yet, it is a term that marks not just the landscape, but also Irish geography. Towns and cities in Ireland today, such as Wexford and Waterford, carry the suffix "-ford," indicating that they were originally Viking settlements. The violence, however, that such settlements indicate is notably in the historical past for Heaney. The poet clearly suggests that the spade of the contemporary turf digger and poet has once again torn open the body of the female persona suggestive of the Irish bog-scape. The violence of the past emerges into the present. Heaney is drawn to such turmoil, concluding the poem with a powerful moment of regeneration, "And I rose from the dark,/Hacked bone, skull-ware,/Frayed stitches, tufts,/Small gleams on the bank" (lines 53–56). The emergence of this figure from the dead, an ancient, if disquiet sleep, provides a spectacle of rapture for the late twentieth-century poet. The "gleams" on the bank serve as beacons for the poet as witness.[4] Critically, for Heaney, however, his reanimated corpses do not perform conflict, or even undertake any movement, in their reanimation. In Heaney's world, the corpses emerge from their graves but remain immobilized.

In his depiction of the female embodiment of sacrifice for the nation, Heaney evokes the sacrificial sublime memories of *Cathleen Ni Houlihan* and the *Countess Cathleen*. Heaney's consciousness of the ancient bog woman is brought forth again in "Punishment." Yet, it is now the poet himself who is persona whose subject speaks as the "I" on history and of memory. He becomes overtly more uncomfortable with the ancient presence of human sacrifice in the contemporary world, as its resonance disturbs him and yet clearly also evokes a kind of recognition. In "Punishment," perhaps the most famous of his bog poems, he notes once again the Viking resin that marks the female body. He writes, "It blows her nipples/to amber beads" as he confesses a witnessing: "I can see her drowned/body in the bog,/the weighing stone" (lines 4–5; 9–11). He places himself within the realm of a kind of awed silence. He explains, "I am the artful voyeur" and "I who have stood dumb," even as he will "understand the exact/and tribal, intimate revenge" (lines 32; 37; 43–44). The poetic persona is slightly removed from the action as a "voyeur," yet he also reframes the violence with a highly personal and "intimate" vengeance at once (Lloyd 131) The tribalism of Heaney's poetic consciousness links his contemporary moment with the historical past.[5] Yet, Heaney's ineluctable drive toward historical memory and contemporary witnessing does not suggest mere identification, but rather the invitation of a shocked, silent encounter with the primitive sublime when the historical and the contemporary amalgamate as a form of poetic resin.[6] Heaney links his present with the ancient past to reveal the fluidity of connection between the two periods and realms. Heaney himself comments on "an encounter between the archaic and modern… natural creatures and forces of civilization" in a radio program during which he remembers his time as a boy hiding in nature ("Sunday Feature: The Last Inheritor"). Heaney's aggregation of the two realms, archaic and modern, and his insistence that the dead rise and occupy the zone of the living, creates the conditions of a fascinated and seductive terror critical for a late twentieth-century primitive sublime encounter.

Heaney's preoccupation with the landscape and the historical past becomes one of embodied historical struggle. The bog serves as a "repository" that encapsulates, preserves, and ultimately yields a powerful symbol of the shaded and fluid boundaries between past and present and extends beyond the poet's usual tropes of historical realms of problematic Irish indigeneity, moving not only to the ancient Irish, but also to the Hellenic and Early English worlds (Johnston 199). His "Sweeney Astray" reimagines a Celtic tale for the modern era, portraying a mad king cursed to take refuge with birds in trees and who finds the terrestrial horrors of humankind to be peculiar. *The Cure at Troy*, a re-imagination of the ancient Greek Philoctetes tale, serves as a Hellenic example, in which he moves beyond convention to examine indigenous forms of ancient history. Even in his translation of *Beowulf*, published in 1999, a year after the Good Friday/Belfast Agreement brought an unsteady peace to the North, Heaney incorporates Hiberno English into the famed Old English epic in a shockingly inclusive vision of identity in his archipelagic island-scape.[7] His model is accretive and syncretic. According to Dillon Johnston, Heaney's poetry incorporates "his relation to *primal* forms of life, and, in his fidelity to the perceived natural object" (198, emphasis added). This powerful primitivist trope within Heaney's writing reveals an unrelenting awe and recognition that creates momentary ruptures during which Heaney's poems conjure a highly seductive, if horrifying, form of sublime. Nathalie F. Anderson suggests that in Heaney's bog poems, "the association of earth, grave, womb, vagina, and corpse manifests itself gradually, by this seducing the reader into sensual complicity, by displacing intimacy to Glob's preserved victims…Heaney shapes a context in which revulsion might understandably be shared, and convincingly links revulsion and fascinated devotion" 149).[8] Heaney's ambivalence suggests a profound disquiet with the intimate aspects of violence and the troubling regeneration or rebirth of the dead in his contemporary moment. On a BBC radio program when Heaney introduces his poem, "The Tollund Man," he says,

> They were sacrificed and put into the bog. They have beauty about them too and a hell of a lot of violence with them too. They were

killed ritualistically. And they draw out and make external [pause] they take out of the Irish context and out of the bewildering particularities of everything that is happening into a larger pattern things that I think I feel. So if I am *lying down beside them or rising them up* I don't know which at the moment.

(Interview, emphasis added).

Heaney is doing both: placing the contemporary self among the dead *and* reanimating them. As Heaney ends the poem, he explains that he is "lost,/Unhappy and at home" (lines 43–44). The poet's discomfort with the unsettling allegiances between the ancient and contemporary victims of sacrifice emerges from the recognition that these figures are both recognizably close and disturbingly prevalent.

In his "Viking Dublin: Trial Pieces," originally published in the 1975 collection, *North*, Heaney describes the excavations of the city that profoundly emerge within the modern era. The excavations yield both plunder and rage, expertise over the seascape and the mining of the landscape, from the first millennia of the Christian era to his own. Within the haunting poetic imagery, the body is dissected and takes flight, the Viking traverse of the seas is met with murderous delight on the land. The body becomes configured as an aspect of the ruined landscape that emerges with fragments of the Viking settlement of Ireland. The lungs of the long-buried figure become externalized as wings, once again evoking transcendence and flight. Yet, there is a welcoming and reunion as well when the braids, the sinews, and the beads, all serve as relics, which, in turn, become talismans that shape an encounter with the past. Heaney is drawn to these items and uses them to construct his present. "Viking Dublin: Trial Pieces" maintains the same archeological approaches and northern theme evident in Heaney's larger works, but does so in an ostensibly random technique based on the musing of a Viking child's microscopic carvings on a bone.

Notably, in Heaney's "Viking Dublin: Trial Pieces," the poet historically locates his repository in James Joyce's figuration of Dublin, but uses different terms. Alluding to *Portrait*, Heaney invokes not the mythological Dedalus, an old artificer, but the murderous Vikings, as a "cunning assessor" (line 73). This development seems remarkable for a poet whose *The Cure at Troy* centers on the ancient Greek myths; instead, Heaney now places his Vikings on the same level as those Greek epics and myths. He asks of his Vikings: "Old fathers be with us/Old cunning assessors/Of feuds and sites/For ambush or town. (lines 72–75). The link between Heaney and Joyce's *Portrait* is readily evident in this passage. Yet,

Heaney constructs a hemispheric myth, inherent in the Viking foundations of Dublin, of man's homicidal nature, with is as inexplicable as nature's unconscious processes from which it is derived. Heaney associates war rites, ritual sacrifice, and sacrificial victims with the return of spring, sexuality, generation, and attachment to the mother, as they are associated in the ancient Celtic worship... to suggest that current Ulster killings are conditioned by preconscious forces.

(Johnston 204)

The "preconscious forces" that Johnston imagines are the drive toward, or rather back, to the primitive. The work lust is the toil that brings delight, the immanence of self uniquely tied to the transcendent. Heaney's poetic technique and subject matter reanimate the ancient victims of ritual sacrifice, transforming them into the contemporary victims of sacrifice in the Troubles of the North. What emerges is a powerful current moving through the centuries that ultimately rises up through the new bog corpus and provokes visions of terror that also suggest the sublime. The slippage between the present and the past seems to resonate with his poetic technique throughout his life.[9] Heaney's encounters with these ancient bodies evoke the primitive sublime.

While Heaney's specific metaphors and images are radically original as they, drawn from Scandinavia, emerge in the 1970s, other poets and writers *also* take on this practice of reanimation of the body and move this in new directions in and beyond Ireland. When Seamus Heaney digs into the earth, he discovers the very liquid juices that preserve ancient bodies and reveal their contemporary insights into a boggy union.[10] As Sidney Burris observes of Seamus Heaney's Irish pastoral in *The Poetry of Resistance: Seamus Heaney and the Pastoral Tradition*, pastoral poetry since Virgil has sought to counterpoint "the joys of the landowner with the miseries of the dispossessed" (18) The "dispossessed" suggests not only land, but also the bodily forms encased within it, which Heaney reanimates as corpses of both the individual and the nation; they rise again not despite, but because of the violence surrounding their demise, which characterizes their very being(s). Irish sovereignty requires the sacrifice of the ancient body, typically female; but this female body will not only rise, but also begin to write back in the works of Eavan Boland.

Eavan Boland's poetry overtly subverts the patriarchy, the heroic Irish past, and the Revivalists. This sense of possession and dispossession recur throughout her work but is particularly evident even in her early poetry such as "A Cynic at Kilmainham Gaol" and "Yeats in Civil War," both in her 1962 volume entitled, *23 Poems*.[11] "Boland's sense of dispossession arises not merely from her status as an Irish writer, but also from her status as a woman, dispossessed by patriarchal structures" (Potts 101). Boland's engagement with the primitive past manifests as nostalgia for the Irish poetic and historical legacies, as well as its late twentieth-century judgments on Irish identity. Lucy Collins notes that her

> yearning for origins is also the yearning for self-knowledge. ... This need to construct the self ...from a barely reclaimable past, and from the personal histories of one's parents and grandparents, is itself a source of challenging inspiration ... Especially important is her formation of the female continuum that will later provide her with a personally and politically sustaining narrative.
>
> (27)

Her political and historical narratives are often framed within domestic concerns. Yet, much like Heaney's evocation of the susceptibly liquid territory of the bog as a repository of Irish history, Boland positions Ireland in a watery frame of Atlantic seepage in her poetry. The land is both contested and at risk of constant watery incursion. Even in the paved city streets of Dublin, the potential for the fog to become sea is ever present. Boland asserts ultimately that the water that is most present in the heroics of 1916, however, is not the broad Atlantic frame, but the intimately profound tears that martyrs both shed with one eye and refuse to shed with the other. The split body and mind of the evocation of tears and their refusal suggests the painful wrenching that emerges in Ireland with partition. In "A Cynic at Kilmainham Gaol," she positions Ireland amid the Atlantic and the executed leaders of 1916 as figures imagining watery symbols in their urban prison. She talks of "ghosts" and a "gaslamp in the dark seems to make sea/Water in the rising fog" as she notes the "Atlantic hearts" of the men whose blood sacrifice has become a national elegy, courtesy of Yeats (lines 3; 4–5; 11). Yet, Boland acknowledges that the "Sight—seeing from one eye with the tears they chose/Themselves the magic, tragic town, the broken/Countryside, the huge ungenerous tribe/of cowards" (lines 15–17). She writes of both the shocking sacrifice and the mockery of the "jibe" (line 19). This language choice suggests that she is inhabiting Yeats's "Easter 1916" elegy with a modernization of his poetic personas memory of the club and "mocking tale or a jibe" who live "where motley is worn." (lines 11; 15) Yet, Boland focuses on the poor souls who lost their lives and condemns the cowards who did not fight. The jesters of the early twentieth-century poem become secondary for Boland, an afterthought with a sad retrospective gaze of cowardly recrimination. Those who refused to fight are no better than the lauded Yeats, who shields himself with his idiosyncratic spiritual system of the occult and automatic writing. In "Yeats in Civil War," she condemns the lauded poet who found his "escape/Aboard a spirit-ship which every day/Hoisted sail out of fire and rape,/And on that ship your mind was a stowaway" (lines 8–11). Boland's condemnation of Yeats's turn toward the spiritual realm as a means of avoiding direct confrontation with the raw material brutality of war is followed with a more nuanced "Whatever we may learn/You are its sum, struggling to survive -/A fantasy of honey your reprieve" (15–17). The "sum" of the "reprieve" then becomes not just Yeats, but the desire to transcend into another realm. Boland's insistence on holding Yeats to account for his escape becomes fraught with a recognition of the necessity of "fantasy" amid Ireland's fraught postcolonial cultural turmoil.

Boland oceanic vision of Ireland's cultural and political position is evident in both her early poem, "Atlantic Ocean" in the 1975 collection, *The War Horse*, and her now iconic mid-career "Mise Éire," published in the 1987 collection, *The Journey*. In Boland's "Atlantic Ocean," the poet positions Ireland both in the aquatic realm and firmly within a cultural and political revolution that frames Ireland's transnational identity with that of another European Revolution. She writes,

> Out of the ocean now, its menacing storms,
> Out of its cryptic structures, its tribal
> Tides, out of its secret order, from the cabal
> Of trade wind and water, look, a Soviet forms
> (lines 17–20)

The political council or body forms amid a Revolution in both Moscow and Dublin. The framework of the Revolution calls forth her well-known "Mise Éire" poem in an unexpected way. "Mise Éire" is conventionally understood to place the poetic persona and the island of Ireland in one location, at home. The self and the island-scape are one. Yet, crucially, when Eavan Boland proclaims "Mise Éire" (I am Ireland), she does so within the broader fluid zone of the Atlantic world.[12] The pronoun refers to Ireland, a land of the past, from which the persona flees. She continues on to write,

> land of the Gulf Stream,
> the small farm,
> the scalded memory,
> the songs
> that bandage up the history
> the words
> that make a rhythm of the crime
> where time is time past.
> (lines 8–15)

Boland's Ireland is one from which the persona escapes; the island-scape remains eternally soaked with the seepage of the Atlantic and the transnational affiliation from its largest and most dynamic current, the Gulf Stream. The Gulf Stream originates in the Caribbean, particularly with the currents of the Florida strait, that links Cuba to the southernmost tip of the continental United States.[13] Yet, Boland's late twentieth-century exiles then become more than just Irish in a traditional European framework: they transform into transnational migrants taking the waves across oceans and currents at their peril. When reading both the "Atlantic Ocean" and "Mise Éire" alongside each other, it becomes clear that her revolution is not merely the Irish Revolution or even the Russian Revolution but in fact the Cuban Revolution. Collins finds that "the complex relationship between self and other in Boland's work emphasizes at once the sameness and the difference that the singular subject, located in time, can encompass." She notes that this "also creates an important sense of proximity to past generations and a commitment to understand and represent them with care," which emphasizes Boland's preoccupation with the "complex relationship" between "the past and history" (33). In this sense, Boland sees the transnational affiliation within the Atlantic's Gulf Stream as one of profound possibility, even as she acknowledges the presence of the "new language/is a kind of scar/and heals after a while/into a passable imitation" (lines 41–44). Her call toward the primitive is an abstract connection to the transatlantic other as that of an affiliative opportunity for generation.

Her desire to engage the Irish historical past and of the history of revolution becomes salient through metaphors of an uneasy birth, painfully delivered and endured, of a lingering labor to bring forth a new nation in its possibilities, yet to be fulfilled, even as it emerges from the "precincts of the garrison" and its "quick frictions,/the rictus of delight" (24–25). Even in this poem, which does not overtly deal with the Revival, she suggests an aging Yeats when she writes "where time is time past./A palsy of regrets" (lines 14–15). Such recalls Yeats's "Sailing to Byzantium," in which he confesses, "an aged man is but a paltry thing," even as the persona confesses a desire to escape temporality and decay within the "artifice of eternity" (lines 9; 24).

Boland's foregrounding of personal subjectivity reframes the tropes afoot in the primitive sublime. She does not go elsewhere to determine a secondary body, but rather finds her own self and its own physical experience as primary. In fact, in Boland's "Oral Tradition" (also from the 1987 collection, *The Journey*), she responds to both the orality within Irish culture and reaches back to question the corpse within Irish poetry and a longer oral tradition that shapes the national identity. She responds to Heaney's bog victims, corpses of Irish identity, who cannot speak and thus hold the potential to reflect whatever image is pressed upon them. Boland's powerful "I" statement, "I was standing there," foregrounds not a vessel for, but an agent of language (line 1), experience, and witness. She writes,

> the oral song
> avid as superstition,
> layered like an amber in
> the wreck of language
> and the remnants of a nation.
>                (lines 71–5)

She evokes the amber of Heaney's bog victims as she merely says that semi-precious resin in fact holds the "remnants" of and "wreck of language" (lines 74–75). She counters Heaney's mark of preservation with her own images of a fractured linguistic legacy. She continues,

> and I had distances
> ahead of me: iron miles
> in trains, iron rails
> repeating instances
> and reasons; the wheels
>
> singing innuendoes, hints
> outlines underneath
> the surface, a sense
> suddenly of truth,
> its resonance.
>
>       (lines 80–90)

For Boland, it is the Irish woman in her contemporary embodiment who is ill-treated and abused. The poet responds to the "iron" of the Heaney's external victim to achieve a sense of mastery of her own. This also reveals a powerful resonance of repetition and buried forms ascending to sing—to transcend and achieve a sense of momentary sublimity. Boland herself comments on the dangers of the imagined past as distinct from the historical record in a 1997 interview in *Éire-Ireland*:

> The past—in its silence and inconvenient completeness—should not be remade. It should not be open to version-making. That is what history is. The past is not a version of events. It is a record of reality. For that reason, if we are to be true to the experience of a people, the past must remain the past. It must remain in the suffering, powerless place it surely was and is. Let me repeat myself. The relation between

the past and history—that awkward, charged, and sometimes mysterious distance—should be a crucial care of postcolonial studies.

(13)

Boland's identification of the critical nuances between the past and history reflects the space that she creates in her poetry to reclaim the past and insert the feminine perspective and the woman-as-agent into the nexus of identity and belonging. In doing so, however, she does engage her masculinist forbearers.

Boland's invocation of Joyce and Heaney reappears in the 1994 volume, *In a Time of Violence*, in her "Anna Liffey." The Joycean wake/wave speech that creates the narrative stream of central female consciousness in *Finnegans Wake* is critiqued as an inadequate and superficial depiction of a female persona. Instead, Boland asserts the complexity and gradations central to the experience of womanhood. According to one critic, "Boland's concern for the exclusion of women from cultural and political history in Ireland reveals her awareness of the effect this exclusion has on all acts of representation: it is thus 'neither marginal nor specialist' but 'concerns all of poetry, all that leads into it in the past and everywhere it is going in the future'" (Collins 27). Boland proclaims, "A river is not a woman./Although the names it finds,/The history it makes/And suffers—" (lines 65–68). She foregrounds the agency of the female persona through suffering and the creation of history itself. Her portrait of Anna Liffey is generative and creative, rather than passive and accumulative (a routine critique of Joyce's limited and limiting embodiment of Irish womanhood in *Finnegans Wake*). She then engages the Viking past of Ireland:

> The Vikings blades beside it,
> The muskets of the Redcoats,
> The flames of the Four Courts
> Blazing into it
> Are a sign.
> (lines 69–73)

In this moment, the Irish past of Viking incursions creates a window into the distant historical records of the first millennium of the Christian era. Boland then moves onto the late eighteenth-century Redcoats and their musket balls during the Age of Atlantic Revolutions that reverberate so profoundly for the United Irishmen, and finally to the burning of the Four Courts in 1922. She joins these historical ruptures through her textual edging. She invokes the "black peat and bracken" of the river, a seeming nod to Heaney's boggy union of corpse, territory, and nation, and says simply "Make of a nation what you will/Make of a past/What you can" (lines 14; 56–58). Her call to the relics of a primitive Irish past is associated with the waters of the river and the narrative of woman. She turns, much like the Revivalists, to birds:

> The seabirds come in from the coast.
> The city wisdom is they bring rain.
> I watch them from my doorway.
> I see them as arguments of origin—
> Leaving a harsh force on the horizon
> Only to find it
> Slanting and falling elsewhere.
>
> Which water—
> The one they leave or the one they pronounce—
> Remembers the other?
>
> (lines 95–104)

Boland's vision of the birds and their association with water suggest the sublime. Her depiction of the primitive sublime posits, familiarly, the avian as the symbol of a personal consciousness that determines both perspective and memory. Her "arguments of origin" and the "harsh force on the horizon" seem distant and near at once, a momentary sense of release and perhaps elation, that leads to a recognition of personal loss.

In "The Muse Mother," from 1980's *Night Feed*, Boland again foregrounds female perspective and subjectivity. She responds to Heaney and seems to presage Paula Meehan's "Not Your Muse" from her 1994 collection, *Pillow Talk*. In "Not Your Muse," Meehan writes, "In my twenties, I often traded a bit/of sex for immortality. That's a joke./Another line swallowed, hook/and sinker" (lines 14–17). Meehan's refusal of the muse as a role for women is associated with both the "swallowed" and the swallows, a punning on the birds of flight and the frequent depiction of Irish women as idealized avian objects (see, for example, Joyce's *Portrait* and the famous bird girl scene). Like Meehan would do, Boland refuses the role prescribed for women as objects. Instead, she demands and creates agency for her poetic identity. Boland again positions her "I" as the persona, a female voice, an intimate perspective of caring and maternity. Yet, the tension for Boland is in the desire to reject maternal care and pressures to be able to sing the song of her own muse. She exclaims:

> she might teach me
> a new language:

> to be a sybil
> able to sing the past
> in pure syllables,
> limning hymns sung
> to belly wheat or a woman—
>
> able to speak at last
> my mother tongue.
>
> >     (lines 28–36)

Boland's nostalgia is one of desire for an escape from the bonds of maternity and enter the temple of the muses. She wants to be her own muse, not someone else's object, "to sing the past" as her "mother tongue" (lines 31; 36). As she engages, like Meehan, with the essentialized feminine trope of muse, she counters it with the creative memory of her lost language, a maternal linguistic inheritance. She creates agency and critiques masculinist notions of inspiration at once.

The presence of ancient history in Boland's work reflects not simply her Irish subjectivity, but also her exile from it as a child in Britain. She was the child of a diplomat and lived in both London and New York before returning to Ireland. Later, as a successful poet, she lived in California and taught at Stanford University. She reflects on this exile in her 1994 collection, *In a Time of Violence*, specifically in her poem, "In Which the Ancient History I learned is Not My Own." In the fourth stanza, Boland encapsulates an enduring terrestrial aquatic nexus:

> And the waters
> of the Irish sea,
> their shallow weave
> and cross-grained blue green
> had drained away
> to the pale gaze
> of a doll's china eyes—
> a stare without recognition or memory
> >      (lines 26–33)

While her teacher claims that the Imperial Roman empire was the precursor to the current British empire and its only known predecessor, Boland asserts a counternarrative written in the waves of the sea that knows a different route outside of the received and imposed narratives of empire. The use of "pale" becomes a marker of identity outside the area of control of British domination in Ireland, just as her use of "weave" to remember her own country relies upon the ancient technique of Penelope to resist domination and remember her true course. For Boland, that course is Ireland.

Finally, in Boland's "I Colony," from her 1998 collection, *The Lost Land*, she brings together the personal and the political in a tribute to Ireland's present and past. We find again that birds are symbolic of the primitive sublime as Boland uses them to negotiate her own position. She writes,

> empire and arrogance and the Irish sea rising
> and rising though a century of storms
> and cormorants and moonlight the whole length of this coast,
> while an ocean forgot an empire and the armed
> ships under it changed: to slime weed and old salt and rust.
> City of shadows and of the gradual
> capitulations to the last invader
> this is the final one: signed in water
>
> (lines 36–43)

The poet's cormorants recall Synge's birds in his "Riders to the Sea," when Cathleen laments that there is "no one to keen him but the black hags that do be flying on the sea" (12). In Boland's work, these birds are ever present and move between land and sea. Boland's flight of negotiation evokes the primitive sublime as she addresses the most recent of Ireland's invaders and foregrounds the watery borders that signify belonging and perspective. Her shadows suggest the perspective of centuries—the history of an emerging Irish nation—that casts a long specter.

Boland's spectral image of the emerging Irish nation powerfully turns to her own imagining of the living dead. She reanimates the symbolic island corpus through her poetic vision of what it means to be "I Colony" in a section called "Witness." Boland simply asks:

What is a colony
if not the brutal truth
that when we speak
the graves open.
And the dead walk?
    (lines 60–64)

The vision of the dead rising from their graves in a zombie-like state of alienated labor evokes the colonial condition of subjectivity, where people are forced to labor with their bodies, not their minds, and have limited or even no autonomy.[14] According to Collins, "Boland's endless return to the processes of representation, then, may be seen as a desire to keep the past always in motion, always in productive exchange with the present" (45).

## 114  *The Living Dead*

In fact, Boland's witnessing of the meaning of colony as self suggests that the past of the dead rise and their troubled strides are a manifest part of the colonial/postcolonial present. Elizabeth McAllister explains:

> The mythmaking surrounding the zombie… originates from sensationalized descriptions of a set of Afro-Caribbean mystical arts. The word zombie appears in writing as far back as colonial Saint-Domingue [now Haiti], glossed by travel writer Moreau de Saint-Méry as the slaves belief in a returned soul, a *revenant*. Twentieth century reports describe… a returned body—a person bodily raised from the grave and turned into a slave worker.
>
> (64)

Yet, the primitive relic of the dead body rises in Boland's poem to achieve the primitive sublime. Like Heaney's bog bodies, Boland's dead rise from the grave in a state of poetic reanimation. For Boland, the primitive corpse body reaches sublimity through the truth telling of the contemporary poet confronting the colonial subjugation. Importantly, unlike in Heaney's vision, in Boland's work, the risen bodies move again and walk upon the earth, which creates not just an enslaved subject, but rather cultivates an ongoing horror of enduring and witnessing continued colonial oppression. Boland's unique deployment of this trope sees the powerful witnessing of maternity and colonial subjectivity at once. "That a female creature," writes Joanne Feit Diehl, is the occasion for this unprecedented experience "is itself not unexpected: such a gesture participates in the reaffirmation of maternal power," a power embodying "a female strangeness that constitutes an inherently subversive notion of the Sublime" (qtd. in Potts 107). Boland's primitive sublime critiques tawdry colonial expression, forced intimacy, and brutality. Her Atlantic imaginary is suggestive of the Cuban theorist, Antonio Benítez-Rojo who explains, that "the Atlantic today is the Atlantic… because it was the painfully delivered child of the Caribbean, whose vagina was stretched between continental clamps" (5). There is, for Boland a monstrous tribalism that continually calls back the island body of the "aqueous kingdom" for impregnation. The question remains, however: what will the sacrifice, blood, and water create, preserve, and yield? Boland's depictions of Ireland and its Revolution, imperfect and yet enduring, reinscribes the motifs of the Revival even as it questions the Revivalists' depictions as one-dimensional. Eavan Boland's gift to twentieth-century Irish poetry is the refusal to imagine a static past and to insert the sublime into the space between past and history. Her primitive sublime at the end of the century harkens back to the "reliably breached veil of distinction" in the context of the early Revivalists as a fundamental primitive characteristic of Irish Modernism (McGarrity and Culleton 5).

The so-called "veils of distinction" and the "tension between the archaic and the modern" (McGarrity and Culleton 5; Castle 207) manifest in Brian Friel's profoundly intimate family drama that makes overt the more subtle tropes of the living dead, reanimation, and voodoo/vodou that Heaney and Boland deploy.[15] Brian Friel's plays are frequently set in the historic past, like his 1990 play, *Dancing at Lughnasa*, which portrays a rural Ireland of 1936. In this retrospective play, Friel returns to the currents of the primitive sublime established during the Revival period, but updates them for the late twentieth century. Martine Pelletier, in her "New Articulations of Irishness and otherness" writes:

> In recent years Ireland has undergone something of a revolution... has given the country a new confidence whilst challenging or eroding the old markers of Irish identity. The election of Mary Robinson [in 1990] as the first woman President of the Republic came to symbolize that rapid evolution in the cultural, social, political and economic spheres as Ireland went on to become arguably one of the most globalized nations in the world.
> (98)

Pelletier's context frames Friel's depiction of the rural Donegal of 1936 within the highly challenging national and international cross-currents of the late century. While the setting of the play is in the past, much like the Revivalist dramatists, Friel uses the historical past to comment upon the present. Pelletier continues,

> The undeniable exhilaration felt by many as Ireland set itself free from former constraints and limitations, waving goodbye to mass unemployment and emigration, has nonetheless been counterpointed by a measure of anxiety. As the old familiar landscape, literal and symbolic, changed radically, some began to experience what Fintan O'Toole has described as "a process of estrangement [whereby] home has become as unfamiliar as abroad." If Ireland changed, so did concepts of Irishness.
> (98)

In fact, what I would like to suggest is that the concepts of Irishness depicted on Friel's stage rely upon the rhetorics of the primitive sublime of an earlier period. However, much like Heaney and especially Boland, Friel's late-century depiction of the primitive sublime takes place in an acutely intimate family setting. What Friel's play reveals is that the distinction between the primitive sublime at home relies upon a cultural nexus from abroad to suggest a more inclusive globalized definition of what it means to be Irish in the late twentieth century. This relation between Ireland and the globalized other reveals a radical inclusivity of the globalized other as it creates a reanimation of the body and reveals the "voodoo" of the Irish at home (Friel 2).

In *Dancing at Lughnasa*, Friel foregrounds an Irish priest who has served in an African mission for many years; Father Jack returns to find an Ireland much changed since his departure, and yet, at first, it seems that the person who has changed most is Father Jack himself. However, Father Jack's adoption and even celebration of Ryangan (a fictionalized African tribe in Uganda) cultural practices reveals a deep layer of connection between the performances of cultural identity in Ireland and in Uganda. He praises the merits of "love children," polygamy, and polyandry, and finds that the Ryangans have a mode of being that the Irish can recognize amongst themselves.[16] Father Jack says, "in some respects they're not unlike us" (48). The desire for cultural connection and new forms of social and family structures seem clear. Yet, the desire of Father Jack is held off as somehow inappropriate by his sisters, as well as the Church hierarchy, which sends him home in quasi disgrace as his health fails him. He has forgotten his own language, English (though of course, Irish was a relatively common language in Donegal in 1936); specifically, the English that Jack has forgotten is Hiberno-English, a language created through the cultural fractures of colonial occupation. Jack's alienation from Hiberno-English also suggests the community's alienation from a previous national language, Irish. After this forgetting, he relies upon an African language, Swahili, as he grasps for English words. Mistaken language is an indicator of the transformation of identity, perspective, and even people. He continually mistakes one of his sisters for his African servant, Okawa. The conflation of identity confuses the sisters, but Friel is perhaps suggesting a cultural affinity within that seeming error. Martine Pelletier elaborates,

> Africa is endowed by Jack with life-affirming possibilities, thanks to its continued link with the sacred, its paganism that has resisted all efforts at Christianization, his own included. The Irish Catholic Church has sought to repress the pagan rituals of the ancestral Celtic culture, represented in the play by the Lughnasa festival and its bonfires and animal sacrifices, but in Ryanga, pagan rituals and ceremonies still permit a spiritual communion which does not deny the body. Jack's tales of African customs—in which dancing, polygamy and love-children feature prominently—holds out an image of a world in which the sexual energy of women is neither feared nor frustrated, though that image itself may owe as much to Jack's imagination as to fact, as Michael's own memories of that golden summer of 1936 do. It is nonetheless striking that Friel should pit the sterility of Irish culture, deprived of any continuity with its pagan Celtic

roots, against the joyous celebrations and dances of Africa perceived as a repository of a universal sense of the sacred.

(102)

The disconnection of language in turn reveals the cultural disconnection that Jack exhibits. As one sister says, "Swahili has been his language for twenty-five years; so it's not that his mind is confused" (11). Yet, the key element of the play is the representation of the Ryangans specifically and Africa generally as similar to Ireland at its core. Both locations feature symbolically, for Friel, as resisting the globalized British colonialism that undercuts any facile notion of colony/colonizer. As a missionary priest, Jack has participated in the colonization of the non-Christian Ryangans, but, he seems delighted to explain, he has failed. He celebrates the Ryangan culture within which he has lived for decades and, when he responds to his contemporary Irish culture, it is to draw parallels between the two. Friel draws comparisons between British and Italian colonialism in Africa through one of the sisters, Rose, singing:

Will you come to Abyssinia, will you come?
Bring your own cup and saucer and bun...
Mussolini will be there with his airplanes in the air,
Will you come to Abyssinia, will you come?

(3)

While Rose's song is an invitation to venture to Africa (Abyssinia is modern-day Ethiopia), it is also a reminder that European powers continued to exploit this location in the early twentieth century for their military and colonial maneuvering: Mussolini invaded Abyssinia in 1935 and the British were neighboring colonial occupiers in Kenya. The contest over East Africa between the British and Italians, between fascist and democratic governments, both exploited these proxy outposts to establish power in Europe in advance of the Second World War. Even now, the invocation of "Abyssinia" serves as a rallying cry for African and anti-colonial cultural movements. Rose's song is therefore an overt acknowledgment of the shared colonial conditions, Ireland and Abyssinia, and their mutual subjectivities amid the Empires of two European powers.

Set within the large framework of the globalized Empires, Friel focuses attention in the play on an intimate family network. The position of the sisters in the play, all unmarried, and supported by Kate, the school teacher, is precarious. The family initially enjoys a certain small renown in the parish due to their brother serving abroad in an African mission. Yet, one sister, Chris, has become a mother outside of marriage with a notoriously unreliable man, Gerry. Rose, described as "simple" in Friel's set directions, is being groomed to succumb to the attentions of a neighbor, Danny Bradley (iii). Meanwhile, another sister, Agnes looks after and works with Rose to try to contribute to the household expenses with their meager earnings from knitting. The final sister, Maggie, serves as housekeeper. Their occupations and relationships reveal their economic and social precarity, but the family nonetheless enjoys a close bond and the atmosphere in the home is jovial and loving. Within this largely idealized scene of a rural Irish family cottage that seems reminiscent of the plays of Synge and Gregory, Friel places a palpable threat to the status quo. As the play opens, Friel sets the scene through the voice of the narrator, Michael, the lovechild of Chris and Gerry, and Michael's childhood memory:

> I recall my first shock at Jack's appearance, shrunken and jaundiced with malaria, at the same time I remember my first delight, indeed my awe, at the sheer magic of that radio. And when I remember the kitchen throbbing with the beat of Irish dance music beamed to us all the way from Dublin, and my mother and her sisters suddenly catching hands and dancing a spontaneous step-dance and laughing—screaming!—like excited schoolgirls, at the same time I see that forlorn figure of Father Jack shuffling from room to room as if he were searching for something but couldn't remember what. And even though I was only a child of seven at the time I know I had a sense of unease, some awareness of a widening breach between what seemed to be and what was, of things changing too quickly before my eyes, of becoming what they ought not to be. That may have been because Uncle Jack hadn't turned out at all like the resplendent figure in my head. Or maybe because I had witnessed *Marconi's voodoo*.
>
> (2, emphasis added)

The symbolic position of the radio in the play is compared overtly to African/Caribbean folk spiritual practices. The radio Marconi refers to Guglielmo Marconi, born in Italy of an Italian father, Giuseppe Marconi, and Irish mother, Annie Jameson, and inventor of the wireless telegraph (and winner of the 1909 Nobel prize in physics with his collaborator, Ferdinand Braun). If Marconi's work is voodoo/vodou, then all of the sisters, the brother, and the son/nephew are its adherents. Ironically, Declan Kiberd explains that it was the Roman Catholic church that encouraged the installation of radios in Irish homes so that the devoted could listen to the 1932 Dublin celebrations of the Eucharistic Congress (20). What Friel ultimately suggests, however, is not that the Marconi has brought the voodoo/vodou to Ballybeg, but rather that the voodoo/vodou is already present, gestated through a Wexford mother, if to some degree sublimated officially by the Church, in Ireland all along.

*The Living Dead* 119

The presence of the radio is evidence of a kind of technological sublime: it disrupts and transports the family across space and time into an ethereal ecstasy of dance and delight. It is seen as a threat, but that potential cannot overcome its transcendent possibilities for the family as a means of escaping the difficulties of their present circumstances. In fact, the "Marconi" described as "pagan" and "voodoo" in the play offers a means of experiencing the sublime. One critic claims that "'voodoo' finds an answering chime in Kate's favorite adjective 'pagan,' which comes promptly to her tongue whenever she is describing activity she considers indecorous... when the body is at one with the spirit and rapture ensues" (Cave 114). The conception of paganism as something other is shown to be a false binary for the Mundy sisters and their society. As Richard Allen Cave notes,

> And dance as formal ritual is described in detail: Rose's excited account of the age-old Lughnasa celebrations in "the Back Hills" where, in an annual re-enactment of Celtic rites, fires are built and leapt over, which is paralleled by Jack's equally lengthy tale of the festivals in Uganda honoring the Great Goddess, Obi, involving sacrifice, incantation and communal celebrations. Significantly, though both festivals are times of thanksgiving for plenty and harvest at a turning point of the year, the former is a secret occasion and largely the preserve of the young while the latter is open and available to all… the dialogue is focused on the pressures and anxieties of social change and the private tragedies these bring in their wake, while movement evokes experiences which are either ageless (being traditional rituals) or seemingly outside the dictates of chronological time (the dancing).
> 
> (115)

The rhetoric of paganism becomes one not of an external, far-off place but rather a timeless yet local space, the festival of Lughnasa. The building of the fire and the potential injury to young, largely unknown figure, Sweeney, who has partaken in the ritual is initially described as fatal, but ultimately marks the young man only with some burns. Sweeney has no direct appearance or dialogue in the play. He is significant because of what is reportedly known of him and his injuries. He survives his present difficulties and endures into the future, just as pagan Ireland endures. His flight of fire becomes one which is ritually reenacted every year at harvest time in the "back hills" away from the more conventional Christian expression in the town (16). Rose, the "simple" sister, explains,

> It was last Sunday week, the first night of the Festival of Lughnasa; and they were doing what they do every year up there in the back

hills... First they light a bonfire beside a spring well. Then they dance around it. Then they drive their cattle through the flames to banish the devil out of them... And this year there was an extra big crowd of boys and girls. And they were off their heads with drink. And young Sweeney's trousers caught fire and he went up like a torch.

(16)

Sweeney has become part of the fire himself. While this Sweeney is not Heaney's vision of his namesake, gone astray (*Sweeney Astray*), nor Flann O'Brien's depiction of circular narration in *At Swim-Two-Birds*, this young man is a talisman for an enduring cultural practice. Yet, he will be renewed and endure his injuries, despite the belief that he would succumb to them as he was "anointed" with the Last Rites of the Dead (16). The body is renewed as the land is celebrated through the harvest festival. The use of cattle as a kind of sacred object evokes not only the *Táin Bó Cuailnge* (*Cattle Raid of Cooley*), but the Swahili language as spoken by the cattle herding Masai of East Africa, who clear brush on their cattle roads with fire. Kate is horrified by the reports of the Lughnasa spectacle. She exclaims, "And they're savages! I know those people from the back hills! I've taught them! Savages—that's what they are! And what pagan practices they have are no concern of ours—none whatsoever! It's a sorry day to hear talk like that in a Christian home, a Catholic home" (17). Kate's refusal to acknowledge that the veil of distinction between her Catholic home and the pagan back hills is reliably breached to a significant degree suggests the interest she has in maintaining the appearance of a conventional Catholic household, especially since she is beholden to and must support the official teachings of the Church as a teacher in the local parish school. Yet, the existence of the "love child" Michael and her sister Chris's evident flouting of the prohibition against sex outside of marriage shows the seemingly impenetrable wall between Catholic and pagan has already been breached, if, in fact, it was ever reliably established.

Instances of voodoo/vodou/pagan animal sacrifices appear in the play, including a ritual of possession/dispossession often associated with zombification. The living dead, or zombies, are commonly associated with societies of enslaved and formerly enslaved peoples. As evident in the discussion of the semiotics of the living dead in Heaney and Boland, the zombie figure is representative of the anxiety associated with extreme forms of alienated labor related to the colonial condition of displacement from the land, dispossession from social and religious structures, and, ultimately, of the enslavement of people. These figures of the dead who rise have no ability to exert control over their movements or actions. The general understanding of "the zombie... arises out of stories connected to Haitian Voodoo... From the time of the Haitian Revolution [1804] onward, stories of Voodoo circulated throughout the Americas and Europe. Anxiety about Haiti in the United States translated into an anxiety about Voodoo [and] underscore[s] supposed Haitian *primitivism*" (Kee 9, emphasis added). Friel's use of these images and tropes in his play associates Irish rural life in 1936 Donegal with the colonized Africans (and by association those of the African Diaspora) whom Father Jack was sent to convert.

The complexity and nuance of Friel's play resists facile binaries, but it does revel in the links between the "primitives" of Ireland and Africa as they enact and evoke the capacity to uncover a sublime encounter. In the portrayal, the sublime is achieved through ritual performance. Kate is aware of the ritual sacrifice that has injured Sweeney on a subconscious level, though she claims she is unaware of how she has acquired that knowledge. Kate explains that Sweeney was injured not as Rose explained: "his trousers didn't catch fire... They were doing some devilish things with a goat.—some sort of a sacrifice for the Lughnasa Festival; and Sweeney was so drunk he toppled over to the middle of the bonfire. Don't know why that came into my head" (35). In the final scene, Rose's white rooster has been found dead. She believes in her innocence that the fox has attacked the rooster, but somehow not the hens. The rooster, however, is symbolically placed on the center of the family's modest table, alluding to animal sacrifice. Immediately following this dramatic placement of the dead bird, a ritual ownership transference takes place. Jack's ceremonial dress exchange, of possession and dispossession, of his colonial dress hat for a straw hat with Michael's visiting father, the Welshman, Gerry, is completed. Gerry's name recalls not only the tales of the Welsh collection, *The Mabinogian,* which include a Celtic form of ritual reanimation and combat, but also suggests a comic inversion of Giraldus Cambrensis, Gerald of Wales, the medieval cleric and historian who wrote *Topographia Hibernica (The Topograny of Ireland)* and *Expugnatio Hibernica (The Conquest of Ireland)*. Gerry's only conquest and knowledge of topography in Ireland seems limited to an understanding of Michael's family. Yet, the allusion to Cambrensis suggests that within his name and provenance, Friel is subtlety mocking the Anglo-Norman colonial conquest of Ireland. Jack and Gerry are jeeringly described as "peacocks" (69). Maggie asks, "let me finish off Lughnasa... put on Marconi" as Chris exclaims, "possessed that thing, if you ask me" (69). In fact, it is not the radio that is possessed, but Jack, the dying and yet undead brother who has performed a ritual of transference of ownership, of possession and dispossession. This functions as a moment highly evocative of the rituals of African Caribbean spiritual practice in which individuals no longer control their own bodily autonomy. Father Jack's transference of his hat is an emblematic gesture of the transference of his autonomy; he undergoes a process of personal dispossession. Jack explains it is "a symbolic distancing from what you once possessed. Good. now turn round once—like this—yes, a complete circle—and that's for formal rejection of what you once had" (69). Cave notes,

> This is difficult territory to explore without succumbing to the sentimentality of either nostalgia (old ways are best ways) or romanticism (the attraction of the exotic, the pagan; or the cult of the noble savage, whether African or Celt), while the concern for the contrast between the sacred and the profane might lead to too easy a resorting to binary oppositions. The strength of the play lies in Friel's refusal to take such simplistic ways with his material.
> 
> (116)

Crucially, the ritual of possession and dispossession of the hat is cyclical, a "whirling" action of bodies, that evokes the dancing of the play's title.[17] Friel's figure of encirclement from the dervish of the dance to the ritual of possession and dispossession relates to the divine as a form of transcendence. One critic asserts, "bodily expressiveness ... contain[s] both release and mania, expertise and impulse, sensuousness and sensuality, frenzy and transfiguring ecstasy" (Cave 117). What seems like transfiguration—and, certainly, traditional Catholicism is familiar with that trope—in fact what this scene seems to suggest is that Jack is practicing a form of African Caribbean spirituality of dispossession. One of the main spiritual differences, aside from mono/polytheism, between traditional forms of European Christianity and of that practiced in voodoo/vodou is that the latter's practitioners believe that they can control the gods or *loas*. It is not merely a religious practice of devotion or adoration, but it incorporates the priest/priestess as an agent of control over the gods/loas and the zombies they create in service of the gods and themselves. The practitioners can deploy the gods to their ends and, in doing so, create a form of agency for themselves. Jack's final words in the play as he adjusts to his new hat and a new identity form a question to his family: "like this? Or further back?" (69). Jack asks his family for their response to not only his positioning of his hat, but his own selfhood.

The final moments in the play incorporate the tropes of primitivism and ritualized cultural memory of Donegal as they evoke the sublime. At the play's conclusion, the narrator, a young nephew Michael, now long having left rural Donegal for his fortunes in city life, describes his memories of his aunts' performance of cultural identity and belonging:

> In that memory atmosphere is more real than incident and everything is simultaneously actual and illusory. In that memory, too, the air is nostalgic with the music of the thirties. It drifts in from somewhere far away—a mirage of sound—a dream music that is both

heard and imagined; that seems to be both itself and its own echo; a sound so alluring and so mesmeric that the afternoon is bewitched, maybe haunted, by it. And what is so strange about that memory is that everybody seems to be floating on those sweet sounds, moving rhythmically, languorously, in complete isolation responding more to the mood of the music than to its beat. When I remember, I think of it as dancing. Dancing with eyes half closed because to open them would break the spell. Dancing as if language had surrendered to movement—*as if this ritual, this wordless ceremony, was now the way to speak, to whisper private and sacred things, to be in touch with some otherness.*

(71, emphasis added)

His uncle, Father Jack, posits that the African natives are really more akin to the indigenous Irish peasantry than the racial politics of Ireland and the British Empire (whether that is of 1936 or 1990) might initially reveal. Friel's interest in Ireland's internal otherness or primitiveness becomes most salient with the expression of the festival of Lugh, the pre-Christian Irish god of the harvest, and the realm in which the sisters delight in their pagan pasts. The sublime, then, for these characters is achieved not within a dramatic island-scape on the sea coast, but in the ritualized dance surrounding a harvest festival fire, achieving a form of intimate, yet collective transcendence. According to Slavoj Žižek, the sublime represents "the fissure, the gap" in representation and "is therefore the paradox of an object which, in the very field of representation, provides a view, in a negative way, of the dimension of what is unrepresentable" (230). Friel's play evokes an intense nostalgia for what seems to have been lost, only to reveal that the loss is, in fact, a manifestation of the primitive sublime: a "fissure" of "representation" shaped within a transnational framework of Empire.

What emerges as unrepresentable for Irish writing at the end of the twentieth century is an anxiety of otherness not along the broad nationalistic frameworks of the Revival or Joyce's European cosmopolitanism, but rather the disquiet of the primitive sublime that arises *within* Ireland and the Irish family itself. Heaney comments upon Joyce's influence on Irish literature after the Revival when he says, "in one way he took away the angst of earnest representation of our noises. It [style] abides as a question" and describes *Finnegans Wake* as "language is in a state of meltdown" ("The Usual Suspects"). Heaney's undead—the bog bodies that emerge after centuries of being held and preserved in a peculiarly liquified form of earth—are not the dead of past centuries, but his contemporaries sacrificed in the Troubles. He is conscious of writing after independence and partition, claiming, "independence has something to do with an Irish relaxation about speech… obviously Northern Ireland isn't independent"

("The Usual Suspects"). Boland's dead are also her contemporaries: her sisters, mothers, and the feminine self, who refuse to be confined or limited. Heaney's Irish metaphors and symbols are drawn through Ireland's connections to the Baltic sea and Scandinavia, whereas Boland's reach across the Atlantic to the Caribbean and the so-called New World. Ultimately, however, Friel's metaphors and symbolic systems inhabit Europe, Africa, and the Caribbean. His Marconi, his voodoo/voodou, while of a transnational provenance, is revealed to actually be Irish, and he is, and has always been, right at home. The question of a home, however, as it relates to the depiction of Ireland and connects to the traditional folk spiritual practices commonly known as "voodoo/voodou," will have an astonishing presence as we will see in the following chapter of the Irish writing of New York in the wake of 9/11.

## Notes

1 Archaeologists and historians now generally use the term "Scandinavian" for this group of people(s), and instead see the term "Viking" as a profession of raiders and traders, rather than as a useful ethnic or social designation. Yet, given Heaney's use of Viking as a term, I will generally follow his usage when analyzing his poems, but use "Scandinavian" as a broader term for the larger culture(s)/people(s).
2 The translation of the pronoun in the phrase varies. I have included both variations here.
3 Lloyd continues on to explain of Heaney's work, "From oral culture and territory to the abstract form of the land… the immediacy of a primary relation to origins and ground can be replaced by a cultural medium, though in sublimated form and with a gain of pathos… That which is forgone is the most efficient myth of integration, supplying the lost object by which the work of mourning is transformed into the work of identification, specifically, here, identification with an inheritance" ("The Indigent Sublime" 130).
4 Heaney's images suggest the reanimated corpses that rise from the dead to fight through a process undertaken in a cauldron in the Welsh tale, "Branwen, Daughter of Lyr," in the *Mabinogian*. While Welsh, rather than Irish, this Celtic tale seems to represent the closest appearance of a reanimation of the dead in medieval Celtic literature(s). The vampire in Bram Stoker's *Dracula* also suggests an Irish provenance for connecting the living and the dead in an in-between, potentially reanimated, state.
5 As Green notes, "the poems of North which describe the victims… reflect a loss of consecration and peacefulness, a condition Heaney relates to the victims of the Irish strife… Many female sacrificial victims have been beheaded, their golden hair clipped short. In the poems, the poet identifies with the victims he refuses to become accustomed to the horror of death" (156).
6 Stallworthy's description of Heaney's work here seems apt. He writes that "the ancient and modern come into sudden conjunction" (180).
7 For a full account of my vision of Heaney's Beowulf, see my "Ancient Myths for the Modern Nation: Seamus Heaney's Beowulf" in *The Medieval Cultures of the Irish Sea and the North Sea: Manannán and His Neighbor*.

*The Living Dead* 125

8 She furthers, "Heaney draws his archaeologist-persona into absorbed relation with the personified land—Ireland—in order to convey the profound ambivalences at the heart of that bond—a sexual ambivalence which recognizes its own devotion as intrusion, a punitive ambivalence which perceives an implicit insatiable violence"(149).

9 Carolyn Meyer notes, "inasmuch as Heaney resists politicization and the active role it implies, the litany of violence and suffering rehearsed not only in Ulster's present-day sectarianism but in the equally unconscionable barbarities of ancient Ireland's bogland is something which merits sympathy yet also necessitates detachment" (207). In his "Station Island," Heaney remembers James Joyce at the end: "the pleasures of sexual love are not only celebrated in the fourth section but also intimated in James Joyce's affirmation of a creative as well as procreative 'work-lust' at the end of the poem" (210).

10 For a useful comparison, Potts explains, "Boland's suburban pastoral melds the labor-saving technology of the contemporary household with images of traditional pastoral: classical pastoral's herds of sheep have been replaced by the "switch and tick" of "new herds"—modern appliances such as dishwashers, washing machines, toasters, dryers, and irons. Whereas Heaney [is] nostalgic for the more primitive implements of the rural world, these labor-saving devices, in freeing women from many domestic responsibilities, have enabled women to approach the condition of pastoral harmony that was previously the provenance of men"( 107).

11 While I am noting the specific poetry volumes published during her career to give a sense of the scope of her work and its development in terms of the primitive sublime, all quotations of Boland's work are based on her *New Collected Poems*, Carcanet, 2005.

12 For a further discussion of Boland's engagement with gender and national identity formation, see Collins (33).

13 Flann O'Brien mocks Ireland's affinity for its transatlantic current, the Gulf Stream, in his "Faustus Kelly" in his mid-century desublimation.

14 Please note, I am using the term zombie as a semiotic found in colonial and postcolonial societies, particularly its usage associated with Haiti and Caribbean, as a manifestation of alienated labor and the colonial condition. I am not using the term in its popular definition(s), found most commonly in horror films and television series of monsters that appear undead in human form and attempt to murder and then consume their victims in a cannibalistic frenzy. Zombies as cannibals are commonly read as semiotics commenting upon the mass consumerism and economic precarity of late stage capitalism, particularly in the United States.

15 The writers in this and the following chapter all use the now defunct spelling of voodoo. I have incorporated the new critical/scholarly spelling of vodou as a marker of the change in language but have retained the original spelling in all textual quotations.

16 The change to Friel's depiction of nontraditional family structures as a possibility in the late century markedly contrasts the Ireland of mid-century when polyamory in Kate O'Brien's *Pray for the Wanderer* is rejected.

17 Cave furthers that "Friel chooses to evoke the effect he is after by referring in his stage directions to a 'dervish,' presumably to determine in the actress's performance a quality of abandoned whirling… For a true dervish, the whirling is not 'frantic' but an experience of union with the divine through the medium of the dance" (117).

## References

Benítez-Rojo, Antonio. *The Repeating Island: the Caribbean and the Postmodern Perspective*. Duke UP, 1997.
Boland, Eavan. "Daughters of Colony: A Personal Interpretation of the Place of Gender Issues in the Postcolonial Interpretation of Irish Literature," *Éire-Ireland*, vol. 32, no. 2/3, 1997, pp. 7–20, https://doi.org/10.1353/eir.1997.0013.
———. *New Collected Poems*. Carcanet Press, 2005.
Burris, Sidney. *The Poetry of Resistance: Seamus Heaney and the Pastoral Tradition*. Ohio UP, 1990.
Carville, Conor. "'Keeping That Wound Green:' Irish Studies and Trauma Culture." *What Rough Beasts? Irish and Scottish Studies in the New Millennium*, edited by Shane Alcobia-Murphy, Cambridge Scholars Press, 2008, pp. 45–71.
Castle, Gregory. *Modernism and the Celtic Revival*. Cambridge UP, 2001.
Cave, Richard Allen. "Questing for Ritual and Ceremony in a Godforsaken World: 'Dancing at Lughnasa' and 'Wonderful Tennessee.'" *Hungarian Journal of English and American Studies*, vol. 5, no. 1, 1999, pp. 109–26, www.jstor.org/stable/41274035.
Collins, Lucy. "Lost Lands: The Creation of Memory in the Poetry of Eavan Boland." *Contemporary Irish Women Poets: Memory and Estrangement*, Liverpool UP, 2015, pp. 23–48, https://doi.org/10.5949/liverpool/9781781381878.003.0002.
Fadlān, Ibn. *Ibn Fadlān and the Land of Darkness: Arab Travellers in the Far North*. Translated by Paul Lunde and Caroline Stone, Penguin, 2012.
Friel, Brian. *Dancing at Lughnasa*. Faber & Faber Ltd, 1990.
Glob, P.V. *The Bog People: Iron-Age Man Preserved*. Faber & Faber, Ltd, 1969.
Green, Carlanda. "The Feminine Principle in Seamus Heaney's Poetry." *Critical Essays on Seamus Heaney*, edited by Robert F. Garratt, G.K. Hall, 1995, pp. 151–154.
Heaney, Seamus. Interview. *BBC London*. The Seamus Heaney Centre at Queen's Broadcast Collection, Queen's University Belfast, FFBBC 013., Queen's University Belfast, Belfast, Northern Ireland.
———. *Preoccupations: Selected Prose, 1968–1978*. Farrar, Strauss & Giroux, 1984.
———. *Selected Poems, 1966–1987*. Farrar, Strauss & Giroux, 1990.
———. "Sunday Feature: The Last Inheritor." Produced by Charles Warmington. *BBC Radio Three*, August 6, 2006. The Seamus Heaney Centre at Queen's Broadcast Collection, FFBBC031-T1. The Seamus Heaney Centre, Queen's University Belfast, Belfast, Northern Ireland.
———. "The Usual Suspects." *BBC Scotland*, August 12, 1995. The Seamus Heaney Centre at Queen's Broadcast Collection, Queen's University Belfast., FFBBC038 TRACK 1. Queen's University Belfast, Belfast, Northern Ireland.
Johnston, Dillon. "Irish Poetry after Joyce (Heaney and Kavanagh)." *Critical Essays on Seamus Heaney*, edited by Robert F. Garratt, G. K. Hall, 1995, pp. 196–207.
Joyce, James. *A Portrait of the Artist as a Young Man*. Viking Penguin, 1964.
———. *Finnegans Wake*. Penguin, 1999.

Kee, Chera. "'They Are Not Men… They Are Dead bodies': From Cannibal to Zombie and Back Again." *Better Off Dead: The Evolution of the Zombie as Post-Human*, edited by Deborah Christie and Sarah Juliet Lauro, Fordham UP, 2011, pp. 9–24. https://doi.org/10.5422/fordham/9780823234462.003.0002.

Kiberd, Declan. "Dancing at Lughnasa." *The Irish Review*, no. 27, 2001, pp. 18–39.

Lloyd, David. "The Indigent Sublime: Specters of Irish Hunger." *Memory Ireland, Volume 3: The Famine and the Troubles*, edited by Oona Frawley, Syracuse UP, 2014, pp. 17–58.

———. "'Pap for the Dispossessed': Seamus Heaney and the Poetics of Identity." *Boundary 2*, vol. 13, no. 2/3, 1985, pp. 319–42, www.jstor.org/stable/303105.

McAllister, Elizabeth. "Slaves, Cannibals, and Infected Hyper-Whites: The Race and Religion of Zombies." *Zombie Theory: A Reader*, edited by Laura Sarah Juliet, U of Minnesota P, 2017, pp. 63–85.

McGarrity, Maria, and Claire A. Culleton., editors. *Irish Modernism and the Global Primitive*. Palgrave, 2009.

McGarrity, Maria. "Ancient Myths for the Modern Nation: Seamus Heaney's Beowulf." *The Medieval Cultures of the Irish Sea and the North Sea: Manannán and His Neighbors*, edited by Joseph Falaky Nagy and Charles W. MacQuarrie, U of Amsterdam P, 2019, pp. 143–59. https://doi.org/10.1515/9789048541959-010.

Meehan, Paula. "Not Your Muse." *Pillow Talk*, Gallery Books, 1994, pp. 24.

Meyer, Caroline. "Orthodoxy, Independence, and Influence in Seamus Heaney's Station Island." *Critical Essays on Seamus Heaney*, edited by Robert F. Garratt, G. K. Hall, 1995, pp. 207–217.

Pelletier, Martine. "'New Articulations of Irishness and Otherness' on the Contemporary Irish Stage." *Irish Literature Since 1990: Diverse Voices*, edited by Scott Brewster and Michael Parker, Manchester UP, 2009, pp. 98–118. https://doi.org/10.7765/9781526125149.00012.

Potts, Donna L. *Contemporary Irish Poetry and the Pastoral Tradition*. U of Missouri P, 2012.

Stallworthy, Jon. "The Poet as Archaeologist: W. B. Yeats and Seamus Heaney." *The Review of English Studies*, vol. 33, no. 130, 1982, pp. 158–74, www.jstor.org/stable/517203.

Yeats, W. B. "Easter 1916" in *Yeats's Poetry, Drama, and Prose: Norton Critical Editions*, edited by James Pethica, W. W. Norton & Company, 2000.

Žižek, Slavoj. *The Sublime Object of Ideology*. Verso, 1989.

# 6 Primitive Sublime Terror

Writing New York after 9/11 in Joseph O'Neill, Colum McCann, and Colm Tóibín

As the twentieth century closes with the Good Friday/Belfast Agreement that brings an uneasy, but enduring peace to the partitioned North of Ireland/Northern Ireland, global terror events move Irish writers to focus significantly on the other side of the Atlantic. New York had been a central diasporic location for the Irish imaginary centuries before the Twin Towers collapsed in explosive ash against the bright, clear morning of the 11th of September 2001. The production of Irish writing and art surrounding that event, though, begins to reframe New York within a broader tradition of the Irish experience, while also incorporating allusions to the terror of the event and manifestations of the primitive sublime. These novels seem to leverage the conception of the Irish in New York that Jim Sheridan establishes in his 2002 film, *In America,* which locates the other within the wounded cityscape. In these post-9/11 Irish novels, protagonists encounter the primitive sublime as the writers dramatically memorialize the anguished metropolis. Joseph O'Neill's *Netherland* highlights the immediate before as well as the aftermath, whereas Colum McCann's *Let the Great World Spin* begins when he temporally dislocates the trauma to the early 1970s; Colm Tóibín's *Brooklyn* dissociates from the contemporary world entirely, though movingly refracts historical trauma. Finally, in a postscript to this final chapter, I address Doireann Ni Ghriofa's *A Ghost in the Throat,* a mixture of poetry and memoir that examines the missing aspects of the life of the eighteenth-century Irish language poet, Eibhlín Dubh Ní Chonaill, as she laments her murdered husband in a famous poetic mourning. Her *"Caoineadh Airt Uí Laoghaire"* or "Lament for Art O'Leary" is a keening-in-verse, incorporating loss and enduring memory. Ni Ghriofa's work shows how more recent twenty-first-century Irish writing serves as a pivot within the manifestations of the primitive sublime.

The production of a Jim Sheridan film set in New York City in the late 1970s to the 1990s encapsulates the experience of the primitive sublime for Irish writers and artists in the late twentieth century and early twenty-first century (although, the film does not appear in theaters until 2002). It

DOI: 10.4324/9781003297390-6

charts the fictionalized story of the Sheridan family's arrival in New York in the late 1970s. They live in a tenement apartment in the Hell's Kitchen neighborhood of west Manhattan, which is certainly then, and to a lesser extent now a globalized contact zone. The Irish family, with the fictionalized name of Sullivan, befriends a neighbor: an artist named Mateo who is suffering with AIDS-related illness. Mateo is drawn as a Jean-Michel Basquiat figure, the noted Haitian-American painter who died of a drug overdose. Mateo's origins are obscure in the film, but he, a black man, serves as a foil to the white Irish family. In an interview about the film, Sheridan explains:

> I have to write with the *adrenaline of terror*... You need to be on the edge when you write. Mateo was not as violent as Djimon. [Djimon Honsou is the actor who portrays Mateo] But once I had that inherent nobility and sensitiveness of Djimon—I consider him the John Wayne of Black actors—I knew I could take him anywhere. I could push it and wouldn't lose the audience even though they'd be scared... I've never seen painting work well in films. There's something inherently un-cinematic about a visual medium... I wanted an emotional moment. I was going, "This guy is gonna put his *blood on the canvas*. Like a painting in a cave." I wanted it to be totally *primitive* and, in a way, that's kind of me dealing with death.
>
> (134, emphasis added)

The "adrenaline of terror" in the film relies upon both a depiction of the primitivism of the Black artist figure as well as the moment of sublime transcendence for both him and the white Irish family. Sheridan, though, seems unaware that his depiction is one of creating a twenty-first-century update of the old trope of the "nobility" of the "primitive" or savage. One critic writes that "culture in Ireland has... evolved from being the articulation of an aspiration (revolution), to the expression of a collective identity (the stabilization of the nation-state), to a means of fracturing that identity (postmodern identity politics)" (Barton 9). The postmodern, fractured identities at the root of contemporary politics at the turn of the millennium in Ireland also seem to chart the development of the primitive sublime for Irish writing in New York after 9/11. In the Sheridan film, the moment of death for the black artist is also when the white Irish child is saved. In this scene, freshly fallen white snow blankets the family in a shielding layer of health (and economic well-being, as the dead artist turns out to have paid the hospital bill for the white Irish child's illness). The closing scenes of the film juxtapose this snowstorm, a weather event that would have been unusual for the Irish family before moving to New York, with the black artist's painting of the white Irish child within a black body. One of the final primitivist images of Mateo has him reclining in a hospital bed wearing a leopard robe, an unsubtle image of the man of African descent wearing a modern animal skin/print. Yet, the final moments of the film include transcendence of the sublime with a second image of Mateo on a child's swing set gliding through the snowstorm. Crucially, this formation of the sublime is not merely about the terror of the primitive, but an overt encounter with death.[1] Specifically, these final scenes of the film suggest a transfer of spirit from one character to another: one body dies as another rises, an image of the reanimation and possession/dispossession that becomes increasingly overt in the fiction of the early twenty-first century. Sheridan's primitivist tropes of blood, terror, and death coupled with the depictions of death and regeneration become central African-Caribbean spiritual practices to which both McCann and O'Neill will allude.

Writing about the sublime after 9/11 seems counterintuitive if conceptualizing the sublime in terms of its traditional eighteenth-century Burkean esthetics, but, in fact, the sublime occupies an almost prototypical archetype of the postmodernist and technological sublime. One critic, Elizabeth S. Anker, explains that "it would not be a stretch to conceive of 9/11 as a, if not the paradigmatic postmodern event, given that it casts open the competing desires mobilized by the spectacle, lays bare the intimacy between art and terror, and reveals the violent underside of the postmodern sublime" (476). What characterizes the novels examined in this chapter is their retrospective arrangement of terror. These three works collectively span the latter half of the twentieth century; if we are to read the twentieth century, and Irish writing in the twentieth century, as a temporal condition of alterity and aftermath (the post in postcolonial, the post in postmodern, the post in post-independence Ireland), then we must necessarily reframe post-9/11 Irish writing, particularly that which is set in New York. The question then becomes: how does the primitive sublime emerge out of the trauma of those events in New York (and Washington and Shenksville, though critically these events do not appear as represented in Irish writing of the period)? Not surprisingly, these three writers focus on the typical New York Irish cityscape that has welcomed generations of immigrants, but ignores the other critical geographies of that day.[2]

Three twenty-first century novels published after 9/11 by Joseph O'Neill, Colum McCann, and Colm Tóibín encounter the primitive sublime as they vividly imagine representations of the anguished city in distinctive periods. O'Neill's *Netherland* (2008) focuses on the most proximate reverberations after 9/11, McCann's *Let the Great World Spin* (2009) moves the focus of the trauma to center on the Philippe Petit tightrope walk between the Twin Towers in 1974. Tóibín's *Brooklyn* (2009) detaches from the immediate events and location completely, though he incorporates the horrifying trauma of a twentieth-century conflict as he centers his novel across the

East River, in the emigrant enclaves of mid-twentieth century Brooklyn. All three novels engage with the wounded body, rapture, and anxiety, and ultimately reveal a primitive sublime strikingly not within the indigenous Irish primitivist manifestations of the twentieth century, but using figures of "otherness" drawn in relief outside of them in the New World. Often in the three novels in this chapter, the sublime is initially and traditionally represented as a moment of awe and personal, even aerial transcendence in view of a landscape that provides a heightened vision and sense of communion with something beyond the self. As Sara Suleri notes, "a historical reality evokes the horror of sublimity... such intimacy provokes the desire to itemize and to list all the properties of the desired [or sublime] object" (28). This creation of a kind of litany of the sublime object serves as a framework within which these writers engage with the terror of the sublime after 9/11. According to Luke Gibbons in his *Edmund Burke and Ireland* as he invokes Lyotard, "Writing about the resurgence of the aesthetic concept of the sublime as a key term in contemporary cultural debates... and to the contradictory feelings of 'pleasure and pain, joy and anxiety, exaltation and depression' that have characterized modernity in the aftermath of the Holocaust and the nuclear age" remains an Irish cultural imperative (1). Analyzing the primitive sublime in novels published after 9/11 reveals a depravity at the root of human experience so disturbing that it cannot be directly represented. Such a rhetoric of the sublime is based upon psychological catalogs of feeling and response and serves as a model of an index of horror, a primitive emotive intimacy with the body of otherness at the center of twenty-first-century Irish writing set in New York (Mellor 87).

Tóibín's *Brooklyn* creates a portrait of the city after the Second World War that is nostalgic for the mid-twentieth century and yet reflects the twenty-first century in its concerns. Written in the early twenty-first century, after 9/11, and published in 2009, Tóibín's retrospective placement of trauma within his narrative occurs outside of the immediate geographies in the text. Eilish, a recent immigrant from Ireland who will engage with a dynamic variety of peoples and histories in New York City, ultimately marrying an Italian American, represents both innocence and the possibility for growth through meaningful cultural exchange. Her significant moment of transcendent aerial sublime pleasure is captured in Eilish's memories of Ireland early in Tóibín's novel: "She was flying, as though in a balloon, over the calm sea on a calm day. Below, she could see the cliffs at Cush Gap and the soft sand... The wind was propelling her towards Blackwater... and Enniscorthy. She was lost so much in the memory of this dream" (71). These initially uncomplicated visions of sublime transcendence ultimately fall away and reveal primitive sublime encounters that resist comprehension both literally and metaphorically in the text.

For Eilish, this recognition of horror resides in an encounter with a living embodiment of the Holocaust in New York. This critical encounter becomes a representation of the postmodern sublime in its acknowledgment of what is unrepresentable. The Holocaust remains a complicated historical event in terms of Irish history and political positioning during and after World War II. In this way, the ongoing reckoning with the greatest depravity at the heart of Europe reemerges thematically within the early twenty-first century. Tóibín's novel, looking back to the twentieth century, seems to examine quietly the perverse commonality of brutality. The distortion of the body that the Holocaust created—from the tattoos on forearms to the emaciated skeletal survivors, the body erased and transformed into ash—is presented within *Brooklyn* through a fleeting encounter at a bookstore. The erasure of bodily trauma within the text masquerades as an Irish girl encountering an "other": Eilish isn't buying history books, but accountancy texts recommended by her professor at Brooklyn College, Mr. Rosenblum.

She encounters an acknowledgment of Rosenblum's identity in a bookstore on 23rd Street in Manhattan. The figure of Rosenblum is introduced with his renowned intellect. His name, discernably Jewish, marks him, and his reputation as possessing great intelligence differentiates him from others that Eilish has encountered. The store clerk and the Irish girl agree on his exceptionalism. Yet, after his brilliance is acknowledged, the clerk invokes the horror of the Holocaust in the following exchange:

> Joshua Rosenblum? The man asked. Can you imagine a country that would want to kill him?
> Eilish stepped back but did not reply.
> Well, can you?
> What do you mean? She asked.
> The Germans killed everyone belonging to him, murdered every one of them, but we got him out, at least we did that, we got Joshua Rosenblum out.
> You mean in the war?
> The man did not reply... Can you imagine a country that would do that? It should be wiped off the face of the earth.
> He looked at her bitterly.
> In the war? She asked again.
> In the Holocaust, in the Churben.
> But was it in the war?
> It was, it was in the war, the man replied, the expression on his face suddenly gentle.

(124–25)

Eilish is here confronted with the madness and horror of the Holocaust, repeating, as if in disbelief, "in the war" as a question, twice. Her unknowing related to the war and the question of genocide is met with sympathy. Her lack of knowledge reflects the limited if not complete absence of information in Ireland related to the war and the Holocaust during and after the war due to the censorship of the Irish state.[3]

The Irish position in the Second World War remains unique: officially neutral, the Irish response to Hitler and his slaughter of the Jewish people (and other minorities) remains a difficult chapter in the nation's history. The Germans, however, repeatedly bombed the partitioned North, the port of Belfast specifically, because of its strategic significance for the British navy and its ability to ship provisions to the island of Great Britain. Claire Wills elaborates:

> The most damaging [aspect of the Irish position]... was de Valera's refusal to acknowledge—publicly, at any rate—the moral dimensions of the war. He never appeared to see the war in broad terms of European morality but concentrated on Ireland's destiny within a domestic framework far removed from the struggle against Nazi Germany. In this he was aided by the extremely strict censorship in operation throughout the war, which forbade publication of any story that could be deemed partial to one side or the other, thus in effect banning any news.
> (123)

The Holocaust is occluded in the text. Eilish begins to understand the Nazi atrocities and genocide through which she retrospectively asserts meaning, trauma, and horror. These moments reflect the operation of the postmodern sublime. Eilish's consideration of and confusion about the depravity exhibited in the heart of Europe reflects a sublime failure of representation.

The sublime, obscured objects of ideology, and the representation of the bodies of those murdered in the Nazi genocide are not present in Tóibín's novel. Their absence reflects the core of the unknowing and unrepresentable and that characterizes the postmodern sublime. That Tóibín uses the figure of Joshua Rosenblum as symbolic of the primitive other and as a catalyst for this discussion suggests that his vision of primitivism, unlike as we will see McCann's and O'Neill's, operates not in relation to the globalized others from European empires but rather that it resides in the heart of so-called European civilization as it turns to excessive state violence as well as social exclusion and depravity against the Jewish people. Tóibín's vision of the primitive sublime then operates to undercut any sense of Irish knowledge of these events in either Ireland during Eilish's upbringing or during her life in Brooklyn. Tóibín's novel published after 9/11 moves the discussion of trauma to an earlier period and one in which the Irish have little or no direct encounter or understanding of it. The absence of any direct representation of the primitive sublime becomes strangely conspicuous in relief against the sublime objects and the bodies of the "primitive other" in Colum McCann's *Let the Great World Spin and* Joseph O'Neill's *Netherland*.

McCann's vision of the primitive sublime also reaches back, like Tóibín's version, to the Holocaust and the Second World War. Like Tóibín's depiction, which is momentary yet weighty, McCann's novel merely glances at the event but endows the narrative with a sense of the legacy of trauma. In a chapter when the Park Avenue matron considers her position and marriage, a burning image of cigarette smoke creates an opportunity for this character, Claire, to consider her husband's family and cultural history:

> Hope they [the ladies she has invited over] won't smoke inside. Solomon hates smoking. But they all smoke, even her. It's the smell that gets to him. The afterburn. Ah, well. Maybe she'll join them anyway, puff away, that little chimney, that small holocaust. Terrible word. Never heard it as a child. She was raised Presbyterian. A small scandal when she married. Her father's booming voice, *He's a what?*
> (80)

Claire, the Park Avenue Presbyterian housewife who has lost her son in Vietnam, casually compares the smoking and smell in her deluxe apartment, with its chimneys, to the charnel houses of concentration camps. McCann's use of "afterburn" highlights the legacy of European brutality. Much like Eilish's unknowing, Claire too is depicted as unaware of the terrible history of the Holocaust. While Claire's ignorance might seem unbelievable, it is squarely described as a reflection on her childhood innocence. Her use of the term Holocaust, small h, might appear callous, but she ultimately makes a connection between her present and the past. Claire references the unexpected marriage she has made and her family's, and particularly her father's, hostility toward the Jewish Solomon. McCann's depiction of Claire and Solomon's connection brings forth significant issues of ethnic and religious strife in postwar America. McCann is connecting 1970s America with 1940s Europe in terms of war and brutality.

The opening images of Colum McCann's *Let the Great World Spin* take place in 1974. Philippe Petit, a Frenchman and a tightrope walker, is perched between the Twin Towers of the World Trade Center. He is, as a New York City Policeman reports plainly, a "man on wire." The narrative continues:

> Those who saw him hushed. On Church Street. Liberty. Cortlandt. West Street. Fulton. Vesey. It was a silence that heard itself, *awful*

*and beautiful*. Some thought at first that it must have been a trick of the light, something to do with the weather, an accident of shadowfall. Other figured it might be the perfect city joke... But the longer they watched, the surer they were. He stood at the very edge of the building, shaped dark against the gray of the morning. A window washer maybe. Or a construction worker. Or a jumper.

(3, emphasis added)

The image of a man suspended alone between the towers provides an extraordinary image to open the novel. What is critical in this scene is the language denoting the sublime; with the mixture of "awful" and "beautiful," McCann's post-9/11 novel emphasizes not the man on the wire himself, but the vision of it from below. This inverts the common conceptualization of the Burkean sublime. It reorders the universe and turns the masses of spectators into the very witnesses of delight and terror at once. Yet, it is not felt with regard to their immediate experience of personal doom; their terror is for someone else. It is displaced. It provokes a heightened vision that forces both spectator and reader toward transcendent awe, beyond the self. August of 1974 is not, of course, September of 2011. As one critic reminds us, "the rhetoric of political violence from St. Just [Louis-Antoine-Léon de Saint-Just, a Jacobin leader of the French Revolution who promoted the Reign of Terror] to the present is constructed of models of sublimity" (Brett 29). Political violence is associated with the sublime from the period of the French Revolution, just as the word terror itself becomes common usage for a form of political violence after the Revolution's Reign of Terror. McCann's depiction of the Towers relates not only to the sublime but its undergirding structures of political and historical violence in the period before 9/11. Yet, the first image of displaced sublimity recalls not just of the now-absent towers that the walker is on, but the dramatic destruction of them *and* the workers who are witnessing the man on the wire. One of the most heart-wrenching and terrifying aspects of that morning of so many years ago was the entrapment of people on floors who had the choice of incineration by fire or escape by flight. Those who jumped, perhaps in suicide, nonetheless inspire a panicked hope of personal escape and a transcendent survival. Yet, McCann's vision of the towers relates both to September 2001 and to earlier events both the legacies of twentieth-century conflicts in general and the tightrope walker of 1974 in particular. A sublimity of excess is suggestive of 9/11 due to the events "exceed[ing] the bounds of ...representation" (Rampley 258). McCann uses the challenges and perhaps even impossibility of representation to capture the response of the viewers on the street. They gaze not at the towers on the morning of 2001 but at the sublime transcendent awe of 1974. There is a conflict in appreciation for the figure hanging in the sky. He is encouraged to take to the air, walk out into nothingness, or venture beyond the limit by one group at the same time as he is discouraged from doing so by another set of viewers. When they "want him to stay, to hold the line, to become the brink, but no farther" (7), they betray a personal fear that he will erase the boundary and defy their fears of the precipice and the unknown. One critic finds that "the 9/11 novel employs the trope of suicide to scrutinize American complicity, to underscore the slippages between art and terror, and paradoxically to query the status of postmodernism in the wake of what might be deemed the quintessential postmodern event" (Anker 464). The "falling man" or fallen men of the towers are drawn in relief against the transcendence of the wire and yet, the spectacle of the sublime destruction of those events also relate to a broader tension within American society. The scene continues: "And then they saw it. The watchers stood, silent. Even Those who had wanted the man to jump felt the air knocked out. They drew back and moaned. A body was hanging in the middle of the air. He was gone. The body twirled and caught and flipped, thrown around by the wind" (7). The passage of the fear/delight of the falling body operates as a kind of tease in the post-9/11 text. It notes, "it was falling, falling, falling, yes" (7), but it then undercuts the expectation created by giving further information of "a sweatshirt, fluttering, and then... high above the man had unfolded upward from his crouch, and a new hush settled over the cops above and the watchers below, a rush of emotion rippling among them, because the man had arisen" (7). Resurrection is at hand, on foot, on the wire. Anker finds that "what is unusual about the allegories of falling that abound within the 9/11 novel is the extent to which those figured suicides—along with their necessary corollary, the scene of terror—operate as spectacles that demand analysis vis-à-vis the aesthetics of the sublime" (470). The terror of the fall, however, indicates in an unexpected gesture a desire for flight and transcendence. It becomes a reversal of expectation that provides a sense of release (Anker 472).

The foreboding end of the towers remains clear even in this scene set twenty-seven years earlier. McCann describes a riveting perspective of the walker from the street level, "his gaze was fixed on the far tower, still wrapped in scaffolding, like a wounded thing waiting..." (7). The coming end, the collapse or the falling, is not, in fact, that of Philippe Petit, but of the thousands who died that September morning three decades later. The collapse of the towers is unrepresented, and perhaps unrepresentable, for the writers under discussion. Their fall is too close to see clearly. Anker writes:

> the specter of falling ... taps into ambivalent intensities best deciphered as sublime ... the sublime resides in pain and danger

"analogous to terror" and accrues its power by defying and hence overwhelming reason. ...Notably tied by Burke to the Jacobin terror of the French Revolution, the analytic of the sublime also furnishes a generative prism for disarticulating the implications of post-9/11 ... While the World Trade Center suicides may index that day's raw terror, their appropriation to magnify the trauma of 9/11 risks transforming that injury into an exhilarating spectacle.

(472)

The falling man of the World Trade Center image has been censored in the media, widely considered too upsetting for viewers, though the image and the original photograph are now held in a private collection. The aftermath of the trauma endures with each potential new viewing of the spectacle of horror.

McCann's primitive sublime and its othering of dislocation and death often relies on the technological developments of the late twentieth century, which include not only the construction of the World Trade Center, but also the development of computer technology. McCann incorporates narrative detailing the early network coding of ARPANET, Advanced Research Projects Agency Network, with the horrors of death, finding that the development of this US Defense Department network that becomes a precursor to the internet, is used to count the bodies of dead US service people in Vietnam. A son who will himself become one of the dead, writes to his mother, Claire, the Park Avenue housewife, of his work in Vietnam:

> Everything they did centered around their machines, he said. They divided, linked, nested, chained, deleted. Reroutes switches. Cracked passwords. Changed memory boards. It was a sort of *black magic*. They knew the inner mysteries of each and every computer. They stayed inside all day. Working with hunches, failures, intangibles... The Death Hack was his core project.
>
> (87–88, emphasis added)

A crashing helicopter in Vietnam prefigures the explosive flights into the Twin Towers. The "horror and engrossment" of McCann's technological sublime then juxtaposes the crash of the helicopter in Vietnam against the crash of the planes into the Towers. The "black magic" of the development of computer technology to count the dead suggests "Marconi's voodoo" of Friel's *Dancing at Lughnasa* and presages the Caribbean intrigues in Joseph O'Neill's *Netherland* (2).[4]

The aspects of the technological sublime in McCann's novel, often associated with US Government projects, also gesture toward New Orleans, a city flooded due to the failures of levees designed and constructed by the

US Army Core of Engineers. The prologue set in 1974 ends with an image of collective identification and individual achievement that links the French tightrope walker with a uniquely American art form, jazz. McCann explains, "the watchers below pulled in the breath all at once. The air felt suddenly shared. The man above was a *word* they seemed to know, though they had not heard it before. Out he went" (7, emphasis added). The sharp intakes of breath, the oxygen suddenly pulled out of the air, at once suggests the collective fear and delight experienced by the watchers. Perhaps the most profound vision that reaches back to the formations of human understanding is the sublime experience of transcendence. McCann captures the buzz on the ground and the vision in the sky in a description that underlines a sense of innovation and awe. The *word*, however, is one that they will have heard before though not one associated with visions of an artist flying in the sky but is suggestive of musicians on the ground: jazz. The jazz form, where nothing repeats exactly as before and where improvisation is the method and delight is the result. The unexpected and improvisational tension that creates the delight of jazz portends the importance of the persona of Jazzlyn, a sex worker who dies alongside the Irishman, John A. Corrigan, two central figures in the novel.[5]

The funeral scene of Jazzlyn highlights historical injustice and the potential transcendence of it. When speaking on Jazzlyn's life, the preacher links great difficulty with a modest degree of beauty. The "way" to the promised land in the afterlife is alluded to in the funeral oration. Just as salvation and eternal emancipation from the sale of her flesh is the right way, the wrong way was alleviated by her time with Corrigan on earth. The preacher explains that "slavery may be over and gone... but it was still apparent" (145). He continues: "You will follow the path and it will be good. Not easy, but good. *Full of terror* and difficulty maybe, but the window will open to the sky and your heart will be purifies and *you will take wing*" (146, emphasis added). Jazzlyn becomes transcendent in death, if not in life. McCann's incorporation of Jazzlyn, a complex figure of hybridized African American identity, reaches back to the appearance of African figures in Joyce's *Portrait of the artist as a Young Man*, *Ulysses*, and *Finnegans Wake*, from the Hottentot Venus to Josephine Baker. Jazzlyn's potential promise of a primitive sublime relies on an early death in the context of the sale of her body; the sex worker descended from enslaved peoples, achieves flight.

New Orleans serves as a recurring geographic touchstone in the novel because of its association with the innovations of jazz. New Orleans as a city does not overtly appear in the novel until the final section. Yet, its great creation, jazz, is not only the name of a central character, a maternal figure, Jazzlyn, of troubled fecundity who dies too soon, but it is also frequently used in verb form: "jazzed" (7). McCann writes in what initially seems a peculiar word choice in the opening of the novel as people look toward the tightrope walker above: "They were *jazzed* now./Pumped./The lines were drawn" (7, emphasis added). Within the looming terror of a description of the end of the event of August 1974 that clearly portends the fall of the towers, McCann inserts the great American art form, jazz, born in bayous surrounding the Crescent City, which has been as well so perilously close to oblivion and alarm for centuries. New Orleans remembers the selling of human beings in its main square and has continuously faced a long history of hurricanes, wars, and epidemics. The old New Orleans seems a metropolis that occupies a peculiar contrast to a more contemporary New York. If New York's 9/11 suggests the technological sublime, New Orleans seems to revert from the technological "sublime of human construction to nature" and back again (Rampley 252–53). Yet McCann's insertion of New Orleans jazz into New York is a means through which he suggests that even New York resides within a long legacy of cultural syncretism. In this way, McCann's truly primitive sublime city comes into the consciousness, not of Jazzlyn, the sex worker in New York, but Jaslyn, the daughter who worked in social services after Hurricane Katrina.

Jazzlyn's daughter returns to New York, after some work travel, but this return to one wounded city conjures another in her memory, New Orleans. New York and New Orleans both become urban locations whose destruction and wounds allow for the eruption of the primitive sublime. New Orleans is a city unlike any other due to its unique cultural geography: Caribbean writers such as Mary Seacole and Alejo Carpentier claim the city as part of Latin America or the Caribbean, while authors of the American South (William Faulkner, Kate Chopin, Eudora Welty) insist upon its centrality there. In this way, it is a city beyond easy identification or categorization, remaining beyond any facile means of measure or definition—a city that delights in shadows and drowns in water. New Orleans defies expectations and mocks any efforts of facile definition. This is, in part, due to its transnational historical incorporation into the US: leaders of the Haitian Revolution (Toussaint L'Ouverture, Jean-Jacques Dessalines, and Henri Christophe) and the rebellious enslaved African subjects of Saint Domingue bled Napoleon's treasury to such an extent that he sold *La territoire Louisiane* to Thomas Jefferson in 1807 for a pittance.

Jaslyn serves as a syncretic figure both geographically and culturally. The daughter of a prostitute, her paternity unclear though often associated with the legacy of one of the Corrigan brothers, she has been raised as an adopted daughter by Claire, the Park Avenue mother who lost her son in Vietnam. She changes her name from that of her mother to a more socially advantageous spelling "to better fit into her Yale life" (325). She connects the New York of her upbringing with the New Orleans of her adult life. Jaslyn thinks of the fluidity of perspective and fixity of geography: "one of the beauties of New York is that you can be from anywhere and within moments of landing it is yours" (325). She is called back to New York and a sense of her belonging and rightful ownership of the place. Finding a photograph of the Philippe Petit tightrope walk between the towers, she fixates on the transcendence much like the watchers of the early August day in 1974. McCann describes the image, "up there in his haunted silhouette, a dark thing against the sky, a small stick figure in the vast expanse. The plane on a horizon. The tiny spread of rope between the edges of the buildings. The bar in his hands the great spread of space" (325). Jaslyn brings this photo with her throughout her life, from room to room, dorm to dorm, place to place. The man on wire is now cast as a dark shadow, and the plane in the background now seems a grotesque image of coming doom, presaging collapse and death. McCann continues,

> The photo was taken on the same day her mother died—it was one of the reasons she was attracted to it in the first place: the sheer fact that such beauty had occurred at the same time... One small scrap of history meeting a larger one. As if the walking man were somehow anticipating what would come later. The intrusion of time and history. The collision point of stories. We wait for the explosion but it never occurs. The plane passes, the tightrope walker gets to the end of the wire. *Things don't fall apart.*
>
> (325, emphasis added).

The anticipation of the event does seem to foretell the end. Yet, it is the juxtaposition of great, beautiful sublime transcendence with terror of death that endures for Jaslyn (and for the reader). McCann, of course, invokes W. B. Yeats's "The Second Coming" and Chinua Achebe's novel of colonial subjugation, *Things Fall Apart.* in the final line of that paragraph: "things don't fall apart" (325). Yet, is it a reversal entirely? The tension between terror and delight remain for Jaslyn and, McCann suggests, for America; while the fall may never come—things never *do* fall apart—its potential haunts the characters of the novel. The new terror for Jaslyn is Hurricane Katrina when McCann lists: "Sabine Pass and Johnson's Bayou, Beauregard and Vermilion, Acadia and New Iberia, Merryville and DeRidder, Thibodaux and Port Bolivar, Napoleonville and Slaughter, Point Cadet and Casino Row, Moss Point and Pass Christian, Escambia and Walton, Diamondhead and Jones Mill, Americus, America." These "names in her mind, flooding" (332), record a litany of New Orleans, of streets flooded and houses painted in postmodern hieroglyphs designating searches made and bodies discovered, that becomes not simply a list of local streets but a list of return, of points in the American geography, but also points on return to the past linguistically. "Americus" implies

Latinate origin, the root of so many languages that therefore traces a history of so much belief that has been shattered, drowned. The collective self-deception of any form of American exceptionalism is revealed to be as shallow as Bayou St. John and as bloated as a sack of unopened mail from the Ninth Ward.

In a later moment in the novel, the Petit figure of a white man above in apparent flight is reshaped into a mailman figure, into a black man dead, aloft in a tree, in a profoundly disturbing moment that evokes a lynching:

> My boy was the mailman, the [old New Orleans] woman said. Right there in the Ninth. He was a good boy. Twenty-two years old. Used to work late if he had to. And he worked, I ain't lying. People loved getting his letters. They waited for him. They like him coming knockin on the door. You listenin'?... And then the storm blowed in. And he didn't come back. I was waiting. I had his dinner ready. I was living on the third floor then. Waiting. Except nothing happened. So I waited and waited. I went out after two days looking for him, went downstairs. All those helicopters were flying over, ignoring us. I waded out into the street, I was up to my neck, near drowning. I couldn't find no sign, nothing, 'til I was down there by the check-cashing store and I found the sack of mail floating... I was sure he'd come floating around the next corner, alive. I looked and looked. But I never did see my boy. I wish I woulda drowned right there and then. I found out two weeks later he was caught up high in a treetop just rotting in the heat. In his mailman uniform. Imagine that caught in a tree.
> 
> (337–38)

The mailman figure at the end of the novel replaces the Petit figure. Yet, instead of being lauded by crowds in New York and inspiring transcendent aerial awe, the man in New Orleans remains upward, but alone, ensnared in the wreckage. The primitive sublime is displaced geographically and culturally onto an/"other," a body trapped in an enduring horror. Fredric Jameson notes that "the representation of space itself has come to be felt as incompatible with the representation of the body" (34), yet, for McCann they seem to intersect. The space of New Orleans after Katrina holds the bodies of the dead just as the World Trade Center's fiery implosion into an ash-covered city scatters the ashes of human remains. McCann's body and space nexus are displacements, not absences or incompatibilities. The bodies and the houses of New Orleans remain in McCann's vision as a reminder that the sublime terror endures even as its object of ideology, the body of an African-American man, decays in the rotting sun, aloft in a tree.

McCann's novel features two brothers: the elder, John A. Corrigan, a monk, and Ciaran Corrigan. The Corrigan brothers share a troubled legacy of an absent father and a mother who died too young. While both men return to Ireland after their New York journeys, the monk, the figure of salvation who offers accommodation and sustenance to the streetwalkers of New York, returns only in death, as ash. This ashen bequest of the Corrigan family relies upon a fictional legacy associated with their name. Corrigan is the name of a character in Joyce's *Portrait of the Artist as Young Man* who is contrasted with the other Clongowes boys as Stephen stands up for his sense of justice against authority in the first chapter. Stephen remembers, "how big Corrigan looked in the bath. He had skin the same colour as the turfcoloured bogwater in the shallow end of the bath" (54). For Joyce, Corrigan's body is notably dark. This symbolic darkness relates to the characterization not only of the Corrigan who is united with Jazzlyn in death, but also to a symbolic location, associated with darkness and Caribbean culture, in the New York of Joseph O'Neill's *Netherland*.

In *Netherland*, Joseph O'Neill positions his central character, Hans, a white Dutchman, as a foil to a Trinidadian character, Chuck Ramkissoon, in New York. Chuck dreams of a cricket stadium in the old airfield now in extreme disrepair and held by the U.S. National Park Service, Floyd Bennett Field. O'Neill explains Chuck's idea:

> His first thought had been to call the field Corrigan Field. After "Wrong Way" Corrigan, Chuck said happily. Corrigan, Chuck related, was the "legendary aviator" who in 1938 flew out of this very airfield to Ireland in an airplane of his own construction. He'd been flatly denied permission to make the crossing but went ahead anyway, afterwards explaining that, confused by a fog and a misreading of his compass, he'd erroneously believed himself to be en route to California.
> (79)

Chuck's tale, however, is not entirely truthful, as the aviator merely equipped his plane with larger than normal fuel tanks rather than constructing the entire vessel. Corrigan's flight lasted for over a full day, but he landed with his plane intact outside of Dublin. The historic aviator feigned shock that he was in Ireland and not in California, faulting fog and his instrument panel. He became so well-known for this shocking deed of ostensibly faulty navigation that he portrays himself in *The Flying Irishman*, a 1939 film put out by RKO Pictures. O'Neill thus fashions a Trinidadian character who sees this Irish-American aviator as a model to find his own way home through a transatlantic fog to Ireland when authorities have denied him permission. O'Neill's references to Corrigan link the historic Flying Irishman and Joyce's fictional rendition of an Irish child, a boy, drawn and described in the legacy of island darkness and a union of text, territory, body, and bog.

Images of the primitive sublime repeat throughout Joseph O'Neill's *Netherland*.[6] *Netherland* is the only one of our three novels that actually takes place within the immediate aftermath of 9/11 (and published in 2008, a year ahead of McCann's and Tóibín's works). *Netherland* is the old Dutch term for New York, which is described in the novel as a community of "men supposedly driven by unfeigned *primitive* cravings, men hungering for a true taste of homeland" (50). O'Neill joins this primitivism in the novel with encounters of the sublime as he writes "the bald eagle represents the spirit of freedom, living as it does in the *boundless void* of the sky" (72, emphasis added). The juxtaposition of fear and wonder, of those "cravings" of men and "boundless" movement of the nation's avian symbol, encapsulates the primitive sublime in New York in the wake of September 11th.

The central foil in the novel, Chuck Ramkissoon, utters the latter phrase about the eagle unconsciously, thus appearing to be a true believer in the mythos of New York and the promise of the American dream. He is countered in the text by Hans, a Dutch banker living in New York who is estranged from his wife and son. O'Neill describes Hans' connections to local ethnic and cultural history in Chuck's eyes as "everything for miles and miles around, all of it was Dutch farmland. Until just two hundred years ago. Your people" (149). Hans reports that "the word 'Yankee' itself… came from that simplest of Dutch names—Jan" (149). Chuck's unsubtle reminder to Hans of New York's first colonial settlers who subjugated the indigenous peoples is a marker of identity and ownership in the "New World." Chuck has been escorting Hans around New York in his Cadillac so that Hans can practice for his US driver's license. As Hans ventures upstate for his test, he thinks,

> Set against these Dutch places, in my mind, were the likes of Mohegan, Chappaqua, Ossining, Mohansic, for as I drove north through thickly wooded hills I superimposed on the landscape regressive images of Netherlanders and Indians, images arising not from mature historical reflection but from a child's irresponsibly cinematic sense of things… redskins pushing through ferns, and little graveyards filled with Dutch names, and wolves and deer and bears in the forest, and skaters on a natural rink, and slaves singing in Dutch.
>
> (231)

The colonial legacies at the heart of New York *as* Netherland seem clear.[7] Hans' perceptions reinforce Chuck's acknowledgment of the Dutch bequest that remains in New York. This passage recalls both the geographic litany of New Orleans street names in *Let The Great World Spin* and the "cinematic" childlike sense of young Stephen Dedalus in *A Portrait of the Artist as a Young Man,* who while at Clongowes imagines his geographic location from the local to the universal as if in cinematic parlance he goes wide and moves from a close up to a long shot.

*Netherland* features the traditional sublime as a form of transcendent aerial awe in the flight of the troubled young man at the Chelsea Hotel, wearing angel wings, who tempts gravity and fate with a desire for flight. This figure is identified as Turkish, from a wealthy family, who pursues art and studies in New York courtesy of an indulgent and generous father.[8] O'Neill invokes the sublime using the Turkish other overtly with Hans's vision of the man. He writes, "Taspinar, wearing only his angel's outfit and bare-footed apart from his slippers headed off elsewhere with small skipping steps. He began calling for his cat in Turkish. I advanced in the direction of a tree dotted with fairy lights and found a spot out of the wind. The lighted Empire State Building loomed ashen and *sublime*" (33, emphasis added). The presence of the angel, a son without a nearby father, and his quest to connect with Hans, a father without a nearby son, despite or perhaps because of his family situation, is drawn in relief against the portrait of the technological sublime of the Empire State Building. New York's Empire State Building was the tallest in the world when it was built, just as the World Trade Center twin towers were the tallest in the world when they were constructed a half-century later. O'Neill draws attention to the vision of debris that covers the city particularly the Empire State Building. This landmark Art Deco building represents the desire for human flight and transcendence, to reach the skies and touch the heavens. Yet, once covered in the ashen remnants of death, imploding fire, ultimate collapse that coated most of Manhattan and parts of Brooklyn for many months, the sublime symbol is tarnished.

For O'Neill, the tensions of invisibility and frustration over the lack of identity acceptance reach back to the earliest incarnations of racial "difference" in the US. Hans utters, at one point, that "Americans are savages" (204), a label disputed by Chuck. Chuck envisions the height of "civilization" as an effect to be brought about by cricket (203). However, as a central character, Chuck's performance of identity is held suspect: "He is in memory, weighty. But what is the meaning of this weight? What am I supposed to do with it" (128). Chuck is not only the weight, the pressure of his memory, but he is the unexpected and troubling primitive sublime encounter, a difficult and tense affiliation of identity that works throughout the entire text.[9] Yet, despite his amusing and seductive force of humor, his death and descent into the Gowanus Canal becomes a representation of the core of unknowing, suggestive of Jameson's incompatibility somehow of body and space, of the primitive sublime encounter in a post-9/11 world (34). It remains unclear if Chuck dies before or due to his being in the Gowanus Canal.

McCann's suggestive "black magic" in *Let The Great World Spin*, becomes, in O'Neill's work, explicitly named as voodoo/voodou. Possession, which is a culturally hybridized form of spiritual practice that incorporates both European and African elements, operates as a key element in O'Neill's text. Chuck warns Hans about voodoo/voodou as he explains his complex Trinidadian family and their shared past. After the traumatic death of a son, Chuck's brother, Roos, Chuck notes that his father "'was angry my mother was falling for this black people's voodoo'" (234). The African Caribbean's spiritual practice is available to the family even if they practice Christianity or Asian Hinduism, both possibilities given the family's South Asian heritage. Chuck describes his mother's response to the loss of her son, his brother:

> My mother wanted to take part in a Baptist ceremony for my brother. You know who the Baptists are? You know about Shango? Self-answering as usual, he said, "The Baptist church is this Trinidad brew of Christian and African traditions—you'll see them in Brooklyn on a Sunday, wearing white and ringing bells and trumpeting the spirits. They believe spirits take *possession* of you. Sometimes one of them will catch the power on the street, shaking and trembling and falling to the ground and speaking in tongues. It's a *spectacle*.
> (234, emphasis added)

The clear representation of possession as a mixture of both Christian and African elements relies on both the witnessing and performance of possession and is noted as clearly incorporating multiple religious systems. Chuck explains the practice through a memory of his upbringing in Trinidad and notes its continued practice in his present-day New York City. As Chuck and Hans wander around Manhattan on Thanksgiving day, Chuck disappears during what Hans describes as a carnivalesque scene: "Bandsman with huge drums wandered round, as did a pack of elves. I said sorry to a *mermaid* for stepping on her tail... I instinctively grew closer to the *spectacle*" (226, emphasis added). The aftermath of the celebratory performance, the witnessing of a spectacle, of Thanksgiving in midtown Manhattan portends the coming end of Chuck. The mermaid vision evokes the Caribbean goddess, *Lasiren*, figured as a siren and mermaid who is the last vision of those doomed to perish in water. And while Chuck does reappear in the text, his fate is already established.

Chuck's death and the sense of doom saturate the text. Yet, Han's enchantment with Chuck becomes crystalized as the narrative begins to close and reveal Chuck's cultural syncretism. Near the end of *Netherland,* Chuck recounts a trek through the jungles of Trinidad, when he was trapping songbirds, attempting to capture art and aerial transcendence at once, and has to outrun some marijuana growers whose illegal stash he has stumbled upon. This leads Chuck to describe the Trinidadian islandscape. As Edward Said avers, "imaginative geography and history help the mind to intensify its own sense of itself by dramatizing the distance and the difference between what is close to it and what is far away" (55). Chuck's memories of this foundational experience in Trinidad seem to intensify in dramatic detail even as he notes the geographic distances. He remembers and reimagines at once when he recounts, "In those mountains are remote and wild valleys, and one of these, the Maracas Valley, is the site of the famous maracas Waterfall… it's quite something: the stream flows to the edge of the mountainside and drops three hundred feet" (234). He continues:

> The moment you stepped inside the forest… you were under a thick, almost unbroken canopy. Where a tree had fallen down, the sunlight came through: everywhere else was dark. So you have these brilliant columns of sunlight in between the trees. That's where you'll find the undergrowth. Otherwise the ground is almost bare. People think of virgin forests as jungles, but they're nothing like that, not these mountain forests. I could run freely; I had to grab on to saplings to slow me down, stop me from falling down the hill.
> 
> (236)

Chuck's memories delineate the danger of the "fall" in the wilderness which is highly suggestive of the Christian undercurrent of the Garden of Eden and the "fall" of humankind in the Christian tradition. Chuck, however, is not a believer in a traditional kind of Christianity, especially given his maternal legacy. Like his Mother's, Chuck's is one of Caribbean syncretism and even reversal. Chuck needs to grab onto the young trees to stop his "fall" (236). Though the island landscape is described in terms of a getaway, the danger within them comes not only from the marijuana-growers who pursue him, but also from the danger lurking beneath him: "the snakes….boy, if one of them bites you, it's certain death. They're night animals, but it's easy to disturb them… I was… terrified by the snakes" (237). The primitive sublime encounter of the Maracas waterfall, and the knowledge of local snakes, suggests not only Shiva, the Hindu god who is often represented with a snake to figure past, present, and future, and would be well-known in Trinidad's South Asian community from which Chuck Ramkissoon's paternal legacy hails, but also and more significantly *Damballa,* the African derived-Caribbean god, who is often represented as Saint Patrick. Damballa is the African-Caribbean snake god that lives near woods and streams. The patriarchal figure of devotion, he is the progenitor of the lesser *loas* or gods. A well-known depiction of Damballa on a prayer flag, or *Drapo sèvis*, is a figure of the snake god as Saint Patrick.

The representation of Saint Patrick is drawn from a common chromolithograph of the mythic Patrick.[10] In this iconic representation of Patrick, holding a staff with a circular pattern at its apex and walking the shore of Ireland, he directs the snakes at his feet toward the water and off the land that is clearly marked as Christian with the church in the background to the left. The jagged cliffs and landscape emphasize the Irish landscape as well. Yet, in his representation as Damballa on the flag, he is placed without a surrounding landscape: there is no island here. However, the snakes at his feet, the church in the background, and the staff remain. He directs the snakes with his right hand as in the original, but the influence of his power goes well beyond a mere island boundary. He is placed on a field of colorful sequins next to the love goddess, Ezili Freda, who is figured as the Virgin Mary. Strikingly, the color scheme remains true to the chromograph. He wears green vestments, as he is a master of the snakes, amid the sequined-filled blackness of the universe. One critic elaborates on this dress: "Ritual flags (drapo Vodou), the most celebrated genre of Vodou's sacred arts, clearly reflect the creative impulse of Vodou and the intense process of cultural synthesis from which the religion emerges" (Polk 7). This image reflects the syncretic cultural mixture(s) that emerge so profoundly in *Netherland* through the figure of Chuck Ramkissoon. Chuck is at once familiar with and a reflection of multiple identities and geographies. His character is not a simplistic figure but rather a subversion of any facile understanding of personal and cultural subjectivity.

In certain Caribbean religious practice(s), African-Caribbean gods are frequently represented as European Saints, not as gestures of cultural hybridity, but as subversive appropriations of the more socially acceptable iconography of European religion. The intent of such representations is to disrupt the very belief system they might initially appear to celebrate. Chuck is afraid for his life over something that he encounters within the jungle that he is unable to see. With the representation of this fear of snakes, Chuck manifests the syncretic tension within the representation of Damballa as St. Patrick. This encounter of the primitive sublime is beyond representation, as he himself becomes the disruption in the narrative of which Hans, the European man, is often afraid. As Maniquis avers that in "Burke's description of the stages of the sublime… we imagine our annihilation and then overcome it" (387). Chuck Ramkissoon is the disruption. His syncretic being defies easy understanding. Chuck's body represents the obliteration form in which the protagonist, Hans, ultimately flees.

Chuck recounts his escape from his pursuers in great detail. He notes of the wound—"I was broken" (238)—resulting from the pursuit, but he is nonetheless able to elude both capture and death in Trinidad. This, it would seem, is a survival ensured by repeatedly invoking and feeling a terror of snakes. He concludes his tale with another snake story:

> A man who rode his bike from Sangre Grande to San Juan with a pet snake wrapped round his neck—a boa constrictor. Dumb idea. The snake started to choke him and he fell off his bike, totally blue. Lucky for him somebody came by and pulled the snake off... Then I rode down to the shore in the back of a pickup truck carrying a load of coffee And that was it. End of story... Or beginning of story."
> (239–40)

The implication is that the wounds that Chuck suffers in the rainforests of Trinidad function as a catalyst for his move to New York. Yet, his wounds venture with him. He wears the mantle of Western Christian myth and perhaps the most ancient or, I suggest, primitive of all our myths: that of the snake as a harbinger of the fall, ultimate death, and ejection from the garden of paradise. Chuck does not recover, though he does seem momentarily to advance. Ultimately, however, O'Neill writes that "Chuck's 'remains' have been found in the Gowanus Canal. There were handcuffs around his wrists and... he was the victim of a murder" (3). Chuck's wounds, first suffered in Trinidad, finally catch up with him in the notoriously polluted waterway of New York City.

This catalog of the primitive sublime in post-9/11 Irish writing rests upon the Irish immigrant experience in New York, in fact, *In America*, that shapes its encounters with an "other." Sheridan's film operates as a bridge between the late twentieth-century resurgence of the primitive sublime in the living dead, especially as it is framed within an intimate family setting. The three novels central to this discussion, *Brooklyn*, *Let The Great World Spin*, and *Netherland*, move in a retrospective arrangement of the primitive sublime and a core of unknowing related to terror and trauma. The striking tensions in each of these novels between the pleasure and beauty of the sublime—a girl's dream of the Irish landscape, the man on wire between the Towers, and the idea of a transcendent flight of an angel at the Chelsea Hotel—with the primitive depravity that seems tied somehow ineluctably to those moments—the wreckage of humanity after the Second World War, the body of a mailman discovered after Katrina, and the handcuffed Caribbean figure associated with the avatar of Damballa as St. Patrick after the Towers' collapse—suggest that we struggle still to fully examine what in the late nineteenth-century William Wilde termed "the vestiges" of primitive humanity's footprints "still attaching to his modern representatives." (245). In fact, what I suggest here is that these vestiges are not merely attached to but are a central part of our capacity to experience the wretched awe that is the primitive sublime, projected onto another but intimately reflecting the Irish self.

## Postscript

Doireann Ní Ghríofa's recent work, *A Ghost in the Throat*, that is a mixture of poetry, memoir, and translation, examines the missing aspects of the life of the eighteenth-century Irish language poet, Eibhlín Dubh Ní Chonaill, as she laments her murdered husband in a famous poetic mourning.[11] Her *"Caoineadh Airt Uí Laoghaire"* or "Lament for Art O'Leary" is a keening in verse incorporating loss and enduring memory. Eibhlín Dubh Ní Chonaill's family did not approve of the marriage due to the reputation of O'Leary, despite their similar aristocratic backgrounds. When O'Leary is murdered, Dubh Ní Chonaill remains estranged from her family, who have not forgiven her, and lives as an outcast, increasingly frantic for the economic security that reconciliation would seem to provide. Ní Ghríofa's dual language text, where the contemporary poet translates the original, reimagines the journey of loss for a husband with the enduring wake of cultural loss of language and autonomy. Ní Ghríofa, in both Irish and English, places her own journey of maternity against the long history of impossible sanctuary and fractured potential for generation that Dubh Ní Chonaill incorporates as she drinks the blood of her dead husband upon discovering his body. This work is both shockingly original and moving, just as it disturbs the contemporary reader with the bloody gestation and ingestion of another form both literally and symbolically.

Ní Ghríofa's work responds to not only the original Lament, but also suggests the keening rituals immortalized in the Revival plays, such as Yeats's and Gregory's *Cathleen Ni Houlihan* and Synge's *Riders to the Sea*. The import of the keen, for Ní Ghríofa, in verse is that it endures. This creation of a poetic legacy seems to compensate for the inability of the dead to wake in her text. Ní Ghríofa's poetic personae/narrator is unable to locate the missing grave of her poetic forebear. Even the date of Dubh Ní Chonaill's death is unknown, the dead poet's brothers seemingly ensure that she is written out of their family story. Her own grave cannot even be located. Thus for contemporary readers, she remains elusive in Ní Ghríofa's version. In *A Ghost in the Throat*, unlike the bodies of the dead who rise again in the poetry of Heaney and Boland in the late twentieth century, the husband's corpse is not reanimated. While Ní Chonaill famously describes drinking the blood of her murdered husband in her text, perhaps attempting to regenerate his being through ingestion, it fails. While the husband's murder at the core of the "Lament" is individual, it operates as a part of a broad colonial context of subjugation in Ireland. The body of the dead and the island of Ireland are both contested during the eighteenth century in a way that powerfully resonates in the twenty-first century. As Robert M. Maniquis explains, "mass violence will contrive to deliver up the primordial ideal of fear as a moral force. Surely terror, which has a much older history than the sublime has a very long life ahead" (405). The terror at the core of Ní Ghríofa's text has endured, even as the body of the poet has not. In an interview with Rhian Sasseen in *The Paris Review*, the author explains that "to spend such long periods facing the texts of the past can be dizzying, and it is not always a voyage of reason; the longer one pursues the past, the more unusual the coincidences one observes." In some ways, the 9/11 novels presage the concerns and anxieties about a lost inheritance and missing embodiment that Ní Ghríofa's work imagines. While her work does not lend itself to a discussion of the 9/11 novels per se, it does suggest a new vision of how the primitive sublime might operate further in Irish writing of the twenty-first century.

## Notes

1 Paul Gilroy finds, in *Postcolonial Melancholia*, that "multicultural society seems to have been abandoned at birth. Judged unviable and left to fend for itself, its death by neglect is being loudly proclaimed on all sides" (1).
2 Irish writers have always found ways to work New York into their narratives. Even James Joyce refers to a tragic event in New York, the Slocum disaster, in *Ulysses*. The Slocum was the ship that sank in the East River carrying hundreds of immigrants to their watery ends on June 15th, 1904 and made the Dublin papers the following day, Bloomsday, the 16th, of June.
3 Note the censorship concerns in Kate O'Brien's *Pray for the Wanderer* in the chapter on "Mid-Century Malaise and Desublimation."
4 The writers in this and the previous chapter all use the now defunct spelling of voodoo. I have incorporated the new critical/scholarly spelling of vodou as a marker of the change in language but have retained the original spelling in all textual quotations.
5 Much like the link between Mateo and the Irish child in Jim Sheridan's *In America*, the link of the Irishman and the prostitute becomes absolute in death.
6 Joseph O'Neill himself is the product of a globalized Ireland. Born in Cork to an Irish father and Turkish mother, he has lived on four continents. His family memoir, *Blood-Dark Track*, tries to uncover the meaning of his two grandfathers: the Irish grandfather was an IRA man who was captured and interred, and the Turkish grandfather was accused of being a spy by the British and imprisoned in Palestine.
7 Elizabeth Anker notes that "O'Neill's *Netherland* (2008)… purports to evaluate race only to minimize it. O'Neill's post-9/11 New York City depicts US race relations and immigration policy as something of a multicultural success story, or a testament to the mythology of America as ethnic melting pot. This elision of racial struggle largely emerges from a romanticization of the sport of cricket, which O'Neill amnesiacally uncouples from the cartography of the

British Empire. Cleansed of its imperial legacies, cricket is instead heralded to vindicate O'Neill's vision of cosmopolitanism... O'Neill's treatment of race occurs in a historical vacuum, Netherland rehearses a predictably colonialist 'moral redemption of the white man' narrative, in which the real terms of postcolonial dispossession are occluded while yet providing a vital backdrop for Hans's edification" (468-69).
8 O'Neill himself is of Turkish descent on his mother's side and moved to New York as an adult.
9 According to one critic, he is "a charismatic Trinidadian entrepreneur and storyteller, who comes across as a combination of Jay Gatsby and one of Philip Roth's long-winded, comic cranks" (Kakutani 2).
10 Due to production restrictions on images, I am sadly unable to reproduce these images here. See Patrick Arthur Polk's *Haitian Voodoo Flags* for the image of the flag and for the chromolithograph of St. Patrick (48, 54). The Drapo sèvis for Danbala/Erzili, about which Polk writes, is in the collection of the Fowler Museum of Cultural History at the University of California Los Angeles.
11 I am indebted to the reader of this manuscript for calling my attention to this work as it relates to the fiction discussed in this chapter.

## References

Anker, Elizabeth S. "Allegories of Falling and the 9/11 Novel." *American Literary History*, vol. 23, no. 3, 2011, pp. 463–82, https://doi.org/10.1093/alh/ajr017.

Barton, Ruth. *Irish National Cinema*. Routledge, 2004.

Brett, David. "Heritage: Celto-Kitsch & the Sublime." *Circa*, no. 7, 1994, pp. 26–31, https://doi.org/10.2307/25562734.

*The Flying Irishman*. Directed by Leigh Jason, RKO Radio Pictures, Inc., 1939.

Gibbons, Luke. *Edmund Burke and Ireland: Aesthetics, Politics, and the Colonial Sublime*. Cambridge UP, 2003.

Gilroy, Paul. *Postcolonial Melancholia*. Columbia UP, 2004.

*In America*. Directed by Jim Sheridan, Fox Searchlight Pictures, 2002.

Jameson, Frederic. *Postmodernism or, the Cultural Logic of Late Capitalism*. Duke UP, 1991.

Joyce, James. *A Portrait of the Artist as a Young Man*. Viking Penguin, 1964.

———. *Ulysses: The Corrected Text*, edited by Hans Walter Gabler with Wolfhard Steppe and Claus Melchior, Random House, 1986.

Kakutani, Michiko. "Post 9/11, a New York of Gatsby-Size Dreams and Loss." *The New York Times*, 16 May 2008.

Maniquis, Robert M. "Filling up and Emptying Out the Sublime: Terror in British Radical Culture." *Huntington Library Quarterly*, vol. 63, no. 3, 2000, pp. 369–405, https://doi.org/10.2307/3817749.

McCann, Colum. *Let The Great World Spin*. Random House, 2009.

Mellor, Anne. *Romanticism and Gender*. Routledge, 1993.

Ní Ghríofa, Doireann. *A Ghost in the Throat*. Tramp Press, 2020.

———. "History Is the Throbbing Pulse: An Interview With Doireann Ní Ghríofa." *The Paris Review*, By Sassen, Rhian, 2 June 2021, www.theparisreview.org/blog/2021/06/02/history-is-the-throbbing-pulse-an-interview-with-doireann-ni-ghriofa/.

O'Neill, Joseph. *Blood-Dark Track: A Family History*. Vintage, 2010.
———. *Netherland*. Harper Perennial, 2008.
Polk, Patrick Arthur. *Haitian Voodoo Flags*. U of Mississippi P, 1997.
Rampley, Matthew. "The Ethnographic Sublime." *RES: Anthropology and Aesthetics*, vol. 47, 2005, pp. 251–63, https://doi.org/10.1086/RESv47n1ms20167669.
Said, Edward. *Orientalism*. Pantheon Books, 1978.
Said, Edward. *Orientalism*. Vintage, 1979.
Sheridan, Jim, Naomi Sheridan, and Kristen Sheridan. *In America: A Portrait of the Film*. Newmarket Press, 2003.
Suleri, Sara. *The Rhetoric of English India*. The U of Chicago P, 1992.
Tóibín, Colm. *Brooklyn*. Scribner, 2009.
Wilde, William. "The Early Races of Mankind in Ireland," *The Irish Builder*, September 1, 1874, pp. 245–246.
Wills, Claire. "The Aesthetics of Irish Neutrality During the Second World War." *Boundary 2*, vol. 31, no. 1, 2004, pp. 119–45, https://doi.org/10.1215/01903659-31-1-119.

# Index

*Note*: Page numbers followed by "n" refer to end notes.

Abbey Theater 13, 17, 39n20, 67, 71
Achebe, Chinua 140
*adrenaline of terror* 129
Aengus/Angus 18
*Africa Speaks* (Hoefler) 59, 61–62
Anderson, Nathalie F. 103
Anglo-Irish War 16
animalistic brutality 17, 47
Anker, Elizabeth S. 130, 150n7
*Aran Islands, The* (Synge) 6, 13, 28–29, 36–37, 40n30
archaic tribe 98
*Aristotle's Bellows* 25, 39n20
*At Swim-Two-Birds* (O'Brien) 9, 67, 77, 120; bird imagery 73; as carnivalesque rebellion 72; central reality, destabilization of 72; desublimation 74; disappointments of independence 74; domestic realities 71; figures of myth 74; mockery, Irish Literature 72–73; plagiarism 92n2; terror as subject of ridicule 73
avian language 31–34

Baartman, Saartje 54
Beckett, Samuel 9, 48, 67–71, 74, 77, 79, 87, 89, 92
Benítez-Rojo, Antonio 114
*Beowulf* 103
*Best Are Leaving, The* (Wills) 68
Bhabha, Homi 6
Black Diaries 62n3
blarney 11n4
blood sacrifice and suffering 13, 22, 25

*Bog People, The* (Glob) 99
*Bog Queen* (Heaney) 100–101
Boheeman-Saaf, van Christine 43, 48, 61
Boland, Eavan 10; *23 Poems* 105; Atlantic imaginary 114; "Atlantic Ocean" 107–108; birds, vision of 111, 113; *Cynic at Kilmainham Gaol, A* 106; "I Colony" 113; language of displacement 97; "Mise Éire" poem 107–108; past, the 109; past and history, nuances between 110; patriarchy, poetry 105; personal subjectivity 108; primitive sublime 111, 113–114; rising dead 113–114; *In a Time of Violence* 110, 112; transnational affiliation, Gulf Stream 108; Viking past of Ireland 110; watery incursion, Ireland 106; women, exclusion of 110
Brayfield, Celia 94n17
Brett, David 2, 5
British Imperialism 13
*Brooklyn* (Tóibín) 10–11, 128, 130; commonality of brutality 132; Holocaust, horror of 132–133; primitive sublime 133; recognition of horror 132; transcendent aerial sublime pleasure 131
*Buile Suibhne* 71
Burke, Edmund 4–5
Burris, Sidney 105

Carpentier, Alejo 139
Carroll, Jerome 3
Carville, Conor 16
Carville, Justin 31
Casement, Roger 8, 43, 46–47, 59, 61; sexuality 59–60, 62n3
Castle, Gregory 33
*Cathleen Ni Houlihan* (Yeats and Gregory) 13, 22–25, 37, 75, 83, 85
Catholicism 20
Cave, Richard Allen 119
Caws, Mary Ann 69
Celtic Antiquarian 20
Celtic Ireland 14
Celtic primitivism 69
Celtic Revival period 8, 13, 19, 67, 72, 77
Celto-Kitsch 4
centrality of language 7
Cheallaigh, Máirín Ní 14
Christian dichotomy of salvation 19
Christianity 18
civilized and savage, relational dichotomy of 75, 99
Civil War 16
Clark, Heather 6
Clissmann, Anne 71, 77, 92n3
Collins, Lucy 106, 113
colonial rule 68
Congo Reform Movement 45–46, 60
*Congo Report* (1904, Casement) 43, 45–46, 59
Conrad, Joseph 21–22, 46–47
*Cook's Traveller's Handbook to Paris, 1931* (Elston) 57
*Countess Cathleen, The* (Yeats) 9, 13, 19–20, 25, 43, 67, 71; self-sacrifice 13, 25
*Country Girls Trilogy* 10
*County Girls, The* (O'Brien) 68, 88
*Critical Writings* (Joyce) 48
cross-cultural misunderstanding 74
cruelty 17; *see also* animalistic brutality
Culleton, Claire A. 2, 11n2
cultural appreciation 13
cultural homecomings 13
cultural knowledge 15
cultural memory and identity 17
cultural nationalism 67, 73

cultural "otherness" 74
cultural performance 7
cultural recuperations 13–14
cultural syncretism 139
*Cure at Troy, The* (Heaney) 103–104

Dalsimer, Adele 81, 83, 86
*Dancing at Lughnasa* (Friel) 10, 115–122, 137
Deleuze, Gilles 3
desublimation in Irish writing 9
de Valera, Taoiseach Éamon 68, 72, 77–81, 85–86, 92, 133
Diehl, Joanne Feit 114
*Doctor's Dilemma, The* 8, 17
Donoghue, Denis 18, 22
Donoghue, Emma 93n9
Dowling, Conor 71–72
Dunn, Kevin 45

Eagleton, Terry 7, 11n4–11n5, 48, 91
*Easter 1916* (Yeats) 19–23, 38n9, 73, 87, 106
Easter Rising 46
*Edmund Burke and Ireland* (Gibbons) 131
Ellmann, Richard 43
Eolus 26

Fadlān, Ibn 99–100
Fanon, Frantz 36
*Faustus Kelley* 9
*Faustus Kelly* (O'Brien) 67–68, 71, 74; "civilized" *vs.* "savage" as relational dichotomy 75–76; dichotomous terminology 75–76; life in Irish politics 75, 77; political deviousness 76
fear of indistinction 68
feminine sacrifice 100
feminine sublime 63n9
feminist orientalism 94n16
*Finnegans Wake* (1939, Joyce) 7–9, 43, 48, 51, 57–59, 67, 74, 83, 94n12, 110, 123, 138
*Fragments of the Feminine Sublime* 61
French Revolution 3
Friedrich, Casper David 38n8
Friel, Brian 1–2, 10, 97; concepts of Irishness 115; *Dancing at Lughnasa* 115–122; globalized

British colonialism, resisting 117; historical past 115; Ireland and globalized other, relation 115–116; primitive sublime 115; technological sublime 119

Gaelic League 13, 38n2
Garrigan Mattar, Sinéad 2
German bombing campaigns 9
*Ghost in the Throat, A* (Ní Ghríofa) 11, 128, 149
Ghriofa, Doireann Ni 11
Gibbons, Luke 3, 131
Gillespie, Alana 73–74, 93n4
Gilmartin, Elizabeth 40n27
*Girls in Their Married Bliss* (O'Brien) 88, 94n17; cultural fear 90; intersection of cultures 89; Irish migrants, post-war British society 89–90; primitive *vs.* the civilized 91; racial intersection, fear of 90–91
Glob, P.V. 99
*Golden Bough, The* 40n25
Good Friday/Belfast Agreement 7, 11n6, 103, 128
Green, Alice Stopford 62n4
Green, Carlanda 98
Gregory, Augusta Lady 8, 13, 15, 23–25, 39n18
Grene, Nicholas 15, 22, 40n27, 40n31

*Hamlet* (Shakespeare) 83
Harpies 19
Heaney, Seamus 10, 20–21, 71, 97, 110–111; archaic tribe 98; bog poems 99–100, 102–103; *Bog Queen* 100–101; defining poetry 98; elemental syncretism 101; feminine sacrifice 100, 102; historical memory and contemporary witnessing 102–103; metaphors 105; poetic consciousness, tribalism of 102; primitive elements, Northern European history 99; primitivist trope, writing 103; ritual sacrifices 99–100; seminal experience 98–99; "song and suffering," Ireland 97; sublime 103, 105; temporal dislocations, Irish landscape 98; *Tollund Man, The* 103–104; unconscious preoccupations 99; Viking Age, cruelty and violence of 101–102; "Viking Dublin: Trial Pieces" 104
*Heart of Darkness* (Conrad) 46
Hillan, Sophia 92
Hoefler, Paul 57–59
Holocaust 11, 131–134
Honsou, Djimon 129
Hottentot Venus 51, 54
*Hurakán* 34

*Ideology of the Aesthetic* (Eagleton) 48
imaginative geography 31–32
immortalization 7
*In America* film 128, 148
*In a Time of Violence* (Boland) 110, 112
indigenous Irish primitivisms 1
indistinction 61
*Inhuman, The* (Lyotard) 62
*Inventing Ireland* 36
Irish Famine 7
Irish indigeneity 7
Irish modernity 3
Irish primitivism 2
Irish radical memory 15
Irish "self" 68
Irish writing of revival 15

*James Joyce* 88
Jameson, Fredric 3
Johnston, Dillon 103
Joyce, James 7, 43, 48, 55–56, 63n6, 67, 74, 76, 79, 82–83, 88, 97, 104, 110; *Critical Writings* 48; Cyclops 13, 43–47, 58, 76; *Finnegans Wake* (1939) 7–9, 43, 48, 51, 57–59; Irish primitivism 43, 48; *Portrait of the Artist as a Young Man, A* 43, 47; primitive sublime 43, 58; *Ulysses* 7–9, 43, 48, 74, 76, 82–83, 138; *Waking Women* 48
*Joyce and the Subject of History* (Valente) 49

Kant, Immanuel 3–5, 49, 63n7
Kant's Aesthetics 3

Kavanaugh, Patrick 74–75, 93n5
keening tradition 25
Keogh, Shawn 36
Kiberd, Declan 36, 40n30
Kristeva, Julia 3

*L'Afrique vous parle (Africa Speaks)* 61
*Let the Great World Spin* (McCann) 10–11, 128, 130, 144–145, 148; fear/delight, falling body 136; funeral scene 138; language denoting sublime 134–135; legacy of trauma 134; political violence 135; primitive sublime 134, 137–139; resurrection 136; sublime experience of transcendence 138; technological sublime 137, 139; tension, terror and delight 140; trope of suicide 136; vision of the towers 135; word choices 139
literary arts 7
Livia, Anna 51–53, 63n10
Lloyd, David 101
*Lonely Girl, The* (O'Brien) 88
Longinus's conception of sublime 3–4
*Lost Land, The* (Boland) 113
lynchpin of Romanticism 5
Lyotard, Jean-François 3, 62

Mahomet 17
Mahon, Christy 36
*make the present past* 36
marriage consecration 22
*Mary Lavelle* (O'Brien) 77–78, 93n8
Mathews, P.J. 38n2
Mattar, Sínead Garrigan 56
Matthews, Kelly 68
McAllister, Elizabeth 114
McCann, Colum 1–2, 10–11, 128, 130, 133–143, 145
McDiarmid, Lucy 19, 21, 24
McGarrity, Maria 11n2
*Meadowgate* 39n18
Meehan, Paula 111–112
Mentxaka, Aintzane Legarreta 78–80, 82
Meyer, Carolyn 125n9
mid-century malaise and desublimation: Beckett's work 67–71, 74, 77, 79, 87, 89, 92; O'Brien, Edna's work 68, 88, 92; O'Brien, Flann's work 67–68, 71–77; O'Brien, Kate's work 67–68, 77–85, 94n13
"Mise Éire" poem 107–108
mockery, Irish Literature 72–73
monotheism 14
Morash, Christopher 11n5
Morrígan, The 22
*Murphy* (Beckett) 9, 67–68, 74, 77, 79; common everyman interpretation 69; confinement and illusory freedom 69; degradation 69; humorous finale 70; literary labyrinth 69; mid-century desublimation 71; mid-century movement, primitive sublime 68; remains of protagonist 70–71; self-created and imposed prison 70

native Irish folklore 7
*Netherland* (O'Neill) 10–11, 128, 130, 134, 137, 142–149; *Damballa* 146–147; possession 145; primitive sublime 146, 148; primitivism 143; Saint Patrick, representation of 147
neutrality 68
Ní Ghríofa, Doireann 128, 149–150
Nolan, Emer 88
Norris, Margot 49
*North* (Heaney) 104
notion of permeability 16

O'Brien, Edna 9–10, 68, 88, 92
O'Brien, Flann 9, 67–68, 71–77, 120, 125n13
O'Brien, Kate 9–10, 67–68, 77–85, 94n13
O'Neill, Joseph 10–11, 128, 130, 133–134, 137, 142–145, 148, 150n6
O'Nolan, Brian 71–77
oppression 68, 114
orientalist 17
Ó Síocháin, Séamus 45
O'Sullivan, Michael 45
*Outcast of the Islands* 21

Paris Colonial Exposition of 1931 43, 54–56
Pearson, Nels 38n12
Pelletier, Martine 115–116
*Pillow Talk* (Meehan) 110
*Playboy* (Synge) 13, 36–38
*Player Queen, The* 38n14
Pocock, Stephanie J. 33
political violence 135
*Portrait of the Artist as a Young Man, A* (Joyce) 43, 47, 72, 82, 104, 111, 138, 144
*Pray for the Wanderer* (O'Brien) 9, 67, 93n9, 125n16; censorship in Ireland 77–78, 81; creative repression 81; entrapment 79; free thinker 77, 79; non-traditional sexual and personal relationships 79; portrait of Irish society 81; pronounced desublimation 79; protestant and Catholic morality 79; rejection of matrimony 80; small-minded hypocrisie 77; social control, state 78–79; social taboos, intimate relationships 83; struggle, artist and society 78
primitive sublime 1–6, 67; archaeology 15; invocation of 20; medieval texts 15
primitivisms 11n3; construct 2; indigenous Irish 1; in Irish art 1–2; in Irish writing 2; romantic 2; and terror 16
*Princesse Tam Tam* (1935) 54
promulgation 13

Rabaté, Jean-Michel 56
radical memory 15–16, 27, 74
Rafroidi, Patrick 69
Rampley, Matthew 4
reanimations 97
*Red Rubber* 45, 63n12
Reform Movement 59
resurgence of primitive sublime: Boland's work 105–114; Friel's work 115–123; Heaney's work 98–105; reanimations 97
*Riders to the Sea* (Synge) 36, 43
Rising, The 20–21
romantic primitivism 2, 56

Saddlemyer, Ann 25
Sailing to Byzantium 20
Scheible, Ellen 5–6
Seacole, Mary 139
Second World War 67–68, 117, 134
self-aggrandizement 74
sexual consummation of marriage 40n31
sexual expression 22
*Shadow of a Glen, The* 39n21
*Shadowy Waters, The* 38n6
Shakespeare, W. 83
Shaw, George Bernard 8, 16–17, 19
Sheridan, Jim 1–2, 10, 128–129
*Shoelace, The* 39n18
*Siren of the Tropics* (1927) 54
social conservatism 85
social criticism 81
song of sacrifice (Cathleen) 24
spiritualism 18
Spurr, David 51
Stallworthy, Jon 20
Steinberg, S.C. 69
Suleri, Sara 4, 131
*Sweeney Astray* (Heaney) 71
Symons, Arthur 6
Synge, John Millington 8, 13, 15, 28–32, 35, 39n22, 40n23, 43

technological sublime 30
*terrible beauty* 21–22
terror, primitive sublime: McCann's work 133–142; O'Neill's work 142–149; post-9/11 Irish novels 128, 130; Tóibín's work 130–133
*Things Fall Apart* (Achebe) 140
Tóibín, Colm 10, 128, 130–134, 143
*Tollund Man, The* (Heaney) 103
Torgovnick, Marianna 11n1
*Trauma of History* (van Boheeman-Saaf) 48, 61
Troubles, the 7
*23 Poems* (Boland) 105

*Ulysses* (Joyce) 7–9, 43, 48, 74, 76, 82–83, 138; Cyclops 13, 43–47, 58, 76

Valente, Joe 49
*Various Legends and Lyrics* 20

158  *Index*

Verstraete, Ginette 48, 50, 63n7, 63n9
Viking cultures and rituals 99
"Viking Dublin: Trial Pieces" 104
violence of entrapment and sacrifice 18

*Waking Women* (Joyce) 48
Walshe, Eibhear 78
*War Horse, The* (Boland) 107
Wayne, John 129
Weaver, Harriet Shaw 56
Weekes, Ann Owens 82, 93n10

Whelan, Kevin 15
*Wild Colonial Girl* 92
Wilde, William 1, 29
Williams, Mark 14, 18
Wills, Claire 68, 88–90, 133
World War II 77, 90

Yeats, W.B. 6–8, 13, 15, 17–20, 22–24, 38n5, 40n23, 73–75, 83, 106, 108, 140

Žižek, Slavoj 123

Printed in the United States
by Baker & Taylor Publisher Services